Postcolonial Indian English Fiction

Postcolonial Indian English Fiction

Decentering the Nation

Editors
M. RAJAGOPALACHARY
K. DAMODAR RAO

RAWAT PUBLICATIONS
Jaipur • New Delhi • Bangalore • Guwahati • Kolkata

ISBN 978-81-316-0758-9

Published by
Prem Rawat for **Rawat Publications**
Satyam Apartments, Sector 3, Jawahar Nagar, Jaipur 302 004 (India)
Phone: 0141 265 1748 / 7006 Fax: 0141 265 1748
E-mail: info@rawatbooks.com
Website: www.rawatbooks.com

New Delhi Office
4858/24, Ansari Road, Daryaganj, New Delhi 110 002
Phone: 011 2326 3290

Also at *Bangalore, Guwahati* and *Kolkata*

Typeset by Rawat Computers, Jaipur
Printed at Nice Printing Press, New Delhi

Contents

Contributors

A. S. Dasan, Professor of English (Retd), Mysore University, Mysore.

Mohan Ramanan, Professor of English (Retd), University of Hyderabad, Hyderabad.

H. Kalpana, Associate Professor of English, Silver Jubilee Campus, Pondicherry University, Puducherry.

Jagdish Batra, Associate Professor & Head, P.G. Department of English, Hindu College, Sonepat, Haryana.

Rajeshwar Mittapalli, Professor of English, Kakatiya University, Warangal.

P. Shailaja, Professor of English, Kakatiya University, Warangal.

M. Sridhar, Research Scholar, Department of English, Kakatiya University, Warangal.

M. Madhusudhana Rao, Professor of English, Acharya Nagarjuna University, Guntur.

M. Prabhakar, Assistant Professor of English, UPGC, Nirmal, Kakatiya University, Warangal.

Mujeebuddin Syed, Professor of English, University of Hyderabad, Hyderabad.

M. Narendra, Professor of English, S.V. University, Tirupathi.

V. Nagarani, Research Scholar, Sri Venkateshwara University, Tirupathi.

K. Purushotham, Professor of English, Kakatiya University, Warangal.

M. Rajagopalachary, Professor of English (Retd), and Emeritus Fellow, Kakatiya University, Warangal.

K. Yadagiri, Assistant Registrar (Retd), Kakatiya University, Warangal.

G. Sujatha, now a freelance content-cum-copy writer based in New Jersey, USA.

T. Viswanadha Rao, Professor of English (Retd), M.S.N. P.G. Centre, Andhra University, Kakinada.

B. Krishnaiah, Assistant Professor of English, Osmania University, Hyderabad.

K. Damodar Rao, Head, Department of English, Kakatiya University, Warangal.

P. Mallikarjuna Rao, Professor of English (Retd), Kakatiya University, Warangal.

Tenneti Shyama Krishna, Research Scholar, Department of English, Kakatiya University & Junior Lecturer (Retd), Govt. Junior College, Janagaon, Warangal Dist.

S. Latha, Professor of English, Kakatiya University, Warangal.

K.V. Ramana, Assistant Professor of English, Gitam University, Vizag.

J. Yellaiah, Professor of English (Retd), Kakatiya University, Warangal.

K.V. Ramana Chary, Assistant Professor of English, Telangana University, Nizamabad.

Jibu Mathew George, Assistant Professor of English, EFLU, Hyderabad.

Pramod K. Nayar, Professor of English, University of Hyderabad, Hyderabad.

T. Vinoda, Professor of English (Retd), Kakatiya University, Warangal.

Anuradha Roy, Associate Professor and Head, Department of English, Seshadripuram College, Bangalore.

N. Anil Krishna, Assistant Professor of English, Osmania University, Hyderabad.

Introduction

M. RAJAGOPALACHARY AND K. DAMODAR RAO

Examine any country's history
What is there to be proud of?
All history of human glory is
Ridden with oppression, in gory strife.

—Sri Sri ('The March of History')

Improbable, you say?
No, fellers,
All improbables are probable in India.

—G.V. Desani ('Warning!' to *All About H. Hatterr*)

Over the past sixty years or so postcolonial literatures have attracted analyses of literary works, studies of understanding the old and new texts in the light of the social-political-historical interpretations and formulating philosophical implications of the theory throughout the world. Particularly since the Second World War, there has been 'a massive intellectual, moral and imaginative overhaul and deconstruction of Western representation of the non-Western world' (Said xxi). While theory has contributed much to the expansive nature of literature, it has also dampened the literary spirit, mired in abstractions. However, the argument in favour of the literary text's analysis and appreciation without going overboard as well as criticism's intelligibility vis-à-vis other branches came to be viewed with sensitivity in recent times. For long, the African experience has provided a fertile ground for the proliferation of postcolonial debates. And the widely acknowledged intervening text in shaping postcolonial aesthetics and cultural theory was Frantz Fanon's *The Wretched of the Earth'* (Parker and Starkey 5). Postcoloniality has been recognized as a process involving a continuous engagement with and resistance to the colonizing influences in pre and post independent societies.

India is one with, yet unique from, other postcolonial societies. As Stuart Hall says, 'Not all societies are "post-colonial" in the same way .... But this does not mean they are not "postcolonial" in any way' (quoted in Innes 3). The postmodern is considered as one of the strategies to come to terms with modes of oppression, the colonial enterprise. It has been pointed out that 'apparent "postmodernisms" found in non-European literatures, colonial, postcolonial and otherwise', might have been drawn on indigenous precursor traditions (Stilz 88). An attempt is made in this section to show that Indian experience of the above two largely western constructs predates their recent theoretical formulations; that hybridity is central to its mores; its regional writers effectively captured the subtleties of its social and cultural matrix, especially the social history; that in the history-fiction interface, Indian fictionists in English initially captured the political realities whereas the post-1980s saw the novelists coming to terms with its multifarious complexities. 'Postcolonial' here is primarily used as a historical and social-political category and 'postmodern' as predominantly cultural-literary mode.

As far as post-independent disillusionment and neo-colonial manifestations are concerned, India has similarities with other former colonies but politically it consciously treaded a path that shunned coups and totalitarian tendencies which were a common feature in post-independent African and Latin American continents. But India had to grapple with other challenges such as communalism on the religious front and caste inequalities on the social front, peculiar to the soil. Going back in time, one finds that India's long history and strange phenomena of settlements from different corners of the globe, their subsequent absorption, co-existence of contraries, cultural geographies, and linguistic accommodation, all have intimations of postcolonial hybridity and postmodern irony.

'Hybridity', both as a biological term and political-cultural paradigm, negates the notions associated with homogeneity, centrality, truth, purity and unity. At the same time, as Gerhard Stilz maintains, hybridity is dialectically divided against itself. On the one hand, it contains notion of difference within its constituent parts often referred to as diversity, dislocation, polyphony and heterodoxy: 'But it holds out, on the other hand, a new integral unity, a fusion that is created from diverse origins (as expressed in the semantic field of assimilation, ... mélange, mixture, symbiosis, syncretism ... etc.)' (Stilz 85). It is this heterogeneity as well as synthesis that marks the course of Indian history reflected in its literatures including Indian novel in English. Therefore, hybridity has 'powerful implications for the evaluation and self-assertion of Indian literature in English' (Harder 351).

India's experience of colonialism and the means adopted to wrest freedom from the imperial agency offer alternative forms of resistance. In the first place, Gandhi's resistance to British colonialism was grounded on the notion of self-rule, swaraj, not based on the western concept of nationalism. It was bound with his professed ethical and moral principles. A shrewd leader who could capture the idea of India, he mobilized the consciousness of an entire nation. His blending of politics and ethics, advocacy of traditional Indian society with a reformatory programme led to his stiff opposition to capitalism. Fanon was also against capitalism but his attacks on French colonialism in Algeria were potent and vehement. Secondly, the colonial exploitation was not viewed by Gandhi in binary terms of opposition between colonizer and native Indians. In their attitude towards British colonialism, Gandhi and other leaders of the freedom movement adopted a policy not one of confrontation, but of ambivalence and passive resistance. It is also evidenced in post-independent India's proclivity in adopting the framework of colonial law and administration. Jane Hiddleston observes, 'The movement to overthrow British colonialism was a deeply fractured and ambivalent process ...' (55).

Based on the colonial experience in Algeria and other parts of Africa, Fanon advocates violence as a redeeming factor and ennobling, purgatory mechanism. The principles of satyagraha and non-violence as enunciated by Gandhi were rooted in the country's ethos of peaceful co-existence and passive resistance: 'If Fanon was a revolutionary political philosopher whose work had ethical undertones, Gandhi, with his critique of violence, conceived politics and ethics or morality as inextricably bound together' (Hiddleston 56). It is interesting to note that the Indian experiment of satyagraha and non-cooperation as viable means of anti-colonial struggle found votaries in the influential figures of Martin Luther King (Jr) in America and Nelson Mandela in South Africa.

The Indian English novel came into its own in the 1930s with the pioneering efforts of Mulk Raj Anand, R.K. Narayan and Raja Rao. It also coincided with Gandhi's political innovations. Gandhian thought and idealism permeated through the consciousness of fictionists of the thirties and, thereafter it gave rise to literary nationalism. These three novelists were cited as 'markers for a new kind of English, an Indian English prose, which was capable of moving beyond a crass mimicry of the British intelligentsia and was able to offer a uniquely Indian contribution to the cosmopolitan world of English letters' (Shingavi 357). Gandhi appeared as a character or a theme in many of the novels that dealt with themes of nationalism and freedom movement: 'And so Gandhi would become the way that these novelists were indigenized' (Shingavi 373).

One important aspect of this phase is that social history of India was not properly dealt with by Indian English novelists with the sole exception of the first few novels by Anand. Political history of India has been well captured by Indian novelists in English. Malgonkar's *The Princes* (1963), Anand's *Private Life of an Indian Prince* (1953, 1970) and Kamala Markandaya's *The Golden Honeycomb* (1977) deal with the history and predicament of the Indian princes on the verge of the fall with the Accession Act after the Independence of India. Raja Rao's *Kanthapura* (1938) deals with a phase of Indian freedom struggle from the point of view of an old rustic woman. Rejecting the British denigration of 1857 revolution as a Sepoy Revolt, Malgonkar re-writes the event as the first war of Indian Independence in *The Devil's Wind* (1972) from the Indian perspective and objectively evaluates the role of Nana Saheb in it. Khuswant Singh's *A Train to Pakistan* (1956), Malgonkar's *A Bend in the Ganges* (1964) and Chaman Nahal's *Azadi* (1975) deal with the Partition and its ghastly aftermath in different ways.

But the political spectrum in India is based on social structures. Differentiating between political history and social history and the concerns of modern historians, C. R. Das points out:

> The objective of history (political history) got entangled with the objectives of the nation-state. In a way, it was the nation-state that provided the framework for writing the history of states and nations. In brief, traditional history, especially 'classical political history,' was based on the concept of 'subject' ... the subject was a preconstituted centre and, therefore, actions were caused and fully explained by the intentions that motivated them ... social history, on the contrary, was based on the concept of society. For social historians, subjectivity and culture are not rational creations, but representations or expressions of the social context in which the causes of actions were to be found. (Das 153)

It is the social determinant that guides, shapes and empowers political, economic heavyweights and power-wielders. Privilege and power in India are determined by social status. The upper caste communities and the privileged sections garnered and exercised power for the most part in different states of India. Those at the bottom of the ladder remained on the margins for many years even after Independence. These dispossessed groups in Indian society have undergone the processes of awareness, assertion and emancipation in recent times.

The second half of twentieth century witnessed a large scale proliferation of fiction-history interface across continents and cultures. The modern novelist is especially concerned with his perception of what constitutes his identity, his community, his position in the larger matrix. As such history becomes an integral part of his fictional account: 'It was perhaps this need, variously felt in cultures throughout the world that led to the upsurge in the sixties and seventies of creativity that tried to interpret man in terms of his social historical past' (Vrinda Nabar 19). In the domain of history, the new way of looking at reality has been termed as 'New History' that adopted a radically different approach from the previous historians in eschewing the older historians' concern for politics, nation, and diplomacy. While mentioning that New History is far more inclusive of the diverse and neglected groups of people, Pushpa Bhave comments:

> Through new history's doors have entered into historical consciousness for the first time slaves, peasants, workers, women, children and numerous other groups .... They have entered conscious history, not as in the past as objects of some powerful elite, but as subjects and agents of their own history. At the same time, the concerns and questions of new history have expanded in all directions away from the older, political and diplomatic story of nation-states and their leaders to focus on exciting new areas of human activity such as

> death, sex, nutrition, disease, community, cosmologies, and most of all, human associations and human meanings. (Bhave 15)

In tune with the changing trends in history, fiction too witnessed remarkable shift in its focus, orientation and direction. Indian Fiction in English has also captured the contours of the shift in history and began to concentrate on the hitherto forgotten, neglected sections in the society. Romila Thapar says with the entry of new communities into the social mainframe, new questions came to be asked: 'Historical knowledge is not static and like all knowledge it changes with more information and new methods of analysing it. When new communities are brought into the historical frame, or new questions are asked about their inter-relationships, this changes the picture as is happening now with gender and Dalit history' (Thapar 1).

It must be pointed out that when it comes to social history, it is the regional writers of fiction who have provided vigour and a direction in creating a large corpus that could be termed as an insider's account. They interrogated social inequalities, stratified hierarchy, women's position in it, the injustices meted out to dalits and other underprivileged groups with authenticity and intensity when compared to their Indian English counterparts. Prem Chand, for instance, in a realistic mode captures rural India in his Hindi novel, *Premashram* wherein he portrays the struggle between the peasant and the landlord. Regional fiction writers like Amrita Pritam, Gurdial Singh, Kartar Singh Duggal, Chandrashekhar Kambar, Mahasveta Devi, Gopinath Mohanty, Chalam, Raavi Shastri, Vattikota Alwar Swamy, Takazhi Sivashankara Pillai, Basheer, O.V. Vijayan, besides enriching the corpus of regional literatures have also chronicled the social history of India. Two observations need to be taken into account in this respect: In a special feature on recent Indian English Fiction brought out by the news magazine, *The Week*, Meenakshi Mukherjee is quoted as saying: 'Whether we like it or not, the class composition of the Indo-English writers is rather uniform, which is not the case with writers in other Indian languages' (Mukherjee 15). In the same feature, M. Krishnan Nair observes that the hallmark of great literature is the 'spiritual dimension' and our regional language writers are better positioned in this respect (Nair 20).

The period of 1970s and 1980s witnessed a blurring of divisions of thought in a big way. Interdisciplinary studies, the Subaltern Studies Collective under the stewardship of Ranajit Guha concentrated on bringing to light the hitherto marginalized areas and people in history. New ways of looking at things, fresh perspectives marked all disciplines of knowledge. While mentioning that historians so far have not cared to document the narrative of 'what the soldiers ate when they followed Shivaji on his road to Surat', Aniket Jaaware says, 'Concepts from literary criticism of the novel and the narrative in general could now be used to understand historical narratives .... It seemed, in those days, that everything was a narrative, everything had a literary character to it, including history and philosophy. Having found a narrative, we looked for it everywhere' (57).

Theory may have multifarious explanations for re-visiting and re-presenting history, but a viable answer could be found in a Nirmal Verma statement, 'the experience of hegemony is a truth as eternal as the experience of the hegemony of truth' (2000: 22). Truth, like history, could be approached in different ways; it accommodates multiplicity in societies, traditions, plurality in perspectives. Various assumptions which held sway for long and also modernity's epistemic authority have been questioned; notions such as the individual as the maker of history, at the centre of society, the oneness of humanity, supremacy of the west, widely held belief of science as truth, the idea of rational, continual human progress, have been subjected to scrutiny which gave way to alternative belief systems and values. When the old order changes, a re-viewing of history becomes imperative. The agencies of hegemony vary from time to time depending on the historical/social context, ranging from the colonial, dictatorial, racial, religious, national, as well as local and familial. Nirmal Verma says: 'Behind all hegemonic structures is some power, be it family or religion or the state. All institutions that mediate the relation of man to man or man to environment, come within this category' (Verma 22).

A literary artist is, by nature, opposed to any kind of colonial experience or hegemony and hence, presentations and re-presentations of social and political history happen; they depend on the fact whether one is dealing with colonial oppression, or dictatorship in a postcolonial situation, or racial, religious, and caste segregation in the beautifully phrased 'first and largest' democracies. S/he feels compelled to disrupt the official formatting of history and present his version. Of all the literary forms, it is fiction that is most suited to re-present social and political history in its programme of offering resistance narratives. The hegemonic centre is, thus, sought to be challenged and de-centered so also its version of truth/history.

The postcolonial writer, while showing that there is always a dominant and a subaltern version of history attempts to rewrite history 'restoring facts that suffered erasure in public memory' (Padma Malini Sundararaghavan 1). The discourse of history-fiction interface sanctions many similarities insofar as coming to terms with reality, representation, perceived truth are concerned, but 'point of view' and 'perspective' remain central to both history and fiction. While mentioning that an artist lives both in historical time and outside of it, K. Ayyappa Paniker observes:

> Since he (the creative writer) is the link between the throbbing present and eternity, he has the long-term perspective although he is tossed about by the same anxieties as anybody else. Living both in the historical time and outside of it, he has to transform the transient into eternal, the contemporary into the perennial, the historical into the metaphysical. (33)

Drawing on similarities between the intersecting domains of history and fiction, Padma Malini Sundararaghavan says: 'Any discussion about the nature of truth, fact, interpretation and belief will lead us to epistemology, language and modes of representation .... The historian, however, cannot merely list facts. He must wrestle with the problems of language and representation, objectivity and subjectivity. He must choose facts from a chaos of data available, select them to form a narrative and by doing so, he works more like a writer of fiction (3).

This interface has, inevitably, attracted the attention of creative writers across continents. It opened up new and exciting possibilities as far as fiction is concerned. The colonizer's programme, or the neo-colonialists programme of erasure and/or distortion of social-political-cultural history is countered chiefly by the fictionists. Gabiel Garcia Marquez's portrait of a typical dictator in *The Autumn of the Patriarch* (1982), Achebe and Ngugi donning the role of educator-anthropologists in their novels, Ghosh's delineation of things past and present in his genre-defying, unclassifiable work, *In An Antique Land*, (1992), Mukul Kesavan's refurbishing the few years preceding the Indian Independence in *Looking Through Glass* (1995), offer but a few instances of the contemporary writers' preoccupation with history and its re-contextualization.

English is owned by the former colonies in such a way that they began to tell their stories, and there are many, in a very effective, culture-specific manner: 'The manipulation of language to fix and enclose the history of empire, on the one hand, and the potential of language to unfold and address the experience of the colonised, on the other, have stimulated major developments in literatures written in English throughout the 20th century' (Parker and Starkey 1). The novelists have nativised the foreign language to suit their culture specifics and narrative strategies in an uninhibited manner. It could be said that what the African novelists did to the colonial language and the way they approached their society, history and culture in relation to colonial intervention is sought to be achieved by the Indian novelists in English since the 1980s. Rukun Advani says, 'On account of its post-colonial existence, the new generation of writers had little to do with the English as a people, or as a presence, or as an oppressive race, and everything to do with the nicest legacy of colonialism—the English language' (Advani 16). They subverted English to make it their own, while drawing their inspiration from history that offered a vast repertoire. The question of identity at multiple levels, and/or multiplicity in a totality becomes prominent here.

A trend-setting new course is charted by the publication of Salman Rushdie's *Midnight's Children* in 1981 giving rise to a new mode of writing, the postcolonial-postmodern narratives. The novel marked a new direction and verve in the ways history is used and English is employed by Indian English Fictionists. It has often been cited as an example of 'hybridity as intermixture' in a postcolonial framework, of 'postcolonial literature of a (formally) postmodernist bent' (Monika Fludernik 22). Insofar as the themes of social history, politics, foregrounding the marginal, and construction of hybridity are concerned, the postcolonial mode comes to the fore. At the same time, Rushdie's experimental narrative has all the attributes of postmodern novel—pastiche and freewheeling, irreverent prose, the comic and the burlesque, multiple points of view and magic realism. The genesis of this hybrid kind of narrative, postcolonial-postmodern novel could be found in G.V. Desani's *All About H. Haterr* (1948). The novel can be read as 'an early, largely underrated (post) colonial text which makes full use of the literary strategies of postmodernism in order to come to terms with the colonial condition' (Stilz 80). The playful tone of Desani, 'I assumed the style-name of H. Hatterr ('*H*' for the nom de plume

'*Hindustaniwalla*', and '*Hatterr*', the nom de guerre inspired by Rev. the Head's too-large-for-him-hat), and, by and by (autobiographical *I*, which see), I went completely Indian to *an extent few pure non-Indian blood sahib fellers have done*' (Desani 33) coupled with Hatter's confession of his 'autobiographical' written in a 'language deliberately designed to mystify the majority, tempt 'em to start guessing, and interpreting our real drift, and allegory, what the hell we mean: pursue our meaning on their *sthula* (gross), the *sukshma* (subtle) and *para* (supreme) planes and levels, and still miss the issue and dash their heads against the crazy-paved rock of confusion' (Desani 120) testifies to the postmodern intimations. Rushdie caught up with the spirit since 1980s and as the saying goes, there was no looking back.

Indian English Fiction of the 1980s and thereafter has been preoccupied with the social-political-cultural history like Saleem Sinai of *Midnight's Children* who is described in the novel as having been 'handcuffed to history' (Rushdie 3). In the next few decades, a host of novelists like Amitav Ghosh, Upamanyu Chatterjee, Shashi Tharoor, Nina Sibal, Allan Sealy, Arundhati Roy, Amit Chaudhuri, Jhumpa Lahiri, Mukul Kesavan, Kiran Desai, Firdaus Kanga, and others have pursued this postcolonial-postmodern narrative. They have re-visioned Indian traditions, myths, culture and the social-political history of post-Independence India in a new narrative form. As Hasan Suroor remarks, the new crop of novelists are engaged in 'reworking old myths, drawing on historical characters—on turning inwards portraying private griefs and dilemmas' (xvii).

During this period, some of the writers of older generation also started looking at the Indian history and politics from a fresh point of view and started adhering to the new mode of postcolonial-postmodern narrative. Anita Desai provides a case in point: For a long time she avoided a writing that would be labelled as social document novels and rather concentrated on the psychological novels that are purely subjective and hence employed the language of the interior. But in her novel, *Baumgartners Bombay* (1988), she departs from the previous practice and follows the new Indian English novel 'in order to interrogate the relation of discourse to history, the language of the interior to that of the outer world' (Judy Newman 195).

The twenty-six articles in this volume cover a wide range of this postcolonial Indian English Fiction spectrum from varied angles and different postures: the recent Indian English novelists' fictional treatment and re-writing of history and politics, of nation, identity and narration, the shifting perspectives, the mingling of the traditional, mythical, and historical that lent uniqueness to it. Some of the essays included here were papers presented at the UGC national seminar on 'Re-Presentation of History in Recent Indian English Fiction' organised by the Department of English, Kakatiya University, Warangal, during 30–31 March 2008 and subsequently revised for the purpose of this critical anthology.

Besides, eminent scholars from different universities all over India have contributed articles to this anthology. We are thankful to all of them for enriching the content of the volume with their critical insights. We are especially thankful to Prof. Pramod K. Nayar for permitting us to include his articles published some time back in *Critical Practice* and *Haritham*. Prof. A.S. Dasan's article was published in *Littcrit*. We thank him for permitting us to use it for the purpose of present anthology. We also thank the editors of *Kakatiya Journal of English Studies* for according permission to reprint some of the articles published in earlier volumes on this theme. We hope that the anthology will add significantly to the critical scholarship on the postcolonial-postmodern narrative as well as history and fiction interface in Indian English Fiction.

References

Advani, Rukun. 'Novelists in Residence'. *Seminar* 384. Spl number on New Writing in English. (August, 1991). Print.

Bhave, Pushpa. 'History: Old and New'. *Historiography: Past and Present.* Eds Kirit K Shah and Meherjyoti Sangle. Jaipur: Rawat Publications, 2005. 12–45. Print.

Das, C.R. 'Postmodernism and History'. *Historiography: Past and Present.* Eds Kirit K Shah and Meherjyoti Sangle. Jaipur: Rawat Publications, 2005. 147–62. Print.

Desani, G.V. *All About H. Hatterr.* London: Aldor, 1948; rpt. London: Penguin, 1972. References are to the Penguin edition. Print.

Fludernik, Monika. 'The Constitution of Hybridity: Postcolonial Interventions'. *Hybridity and Postcolonialism: Twentieth Century Indian Literature.* Ed. Monika Fludernik. Jaipur: Rawat Publications, 2006. 19–54. Print.

Harder, Hans. 'Indian Literature in English and the Problem of Naturalisation'. *Literature and Nationalist Ideology.* New Delhi: Social Science Press, 2010. 323–52. Print.

Hiddleston, Jane. *Understanding Postcolonialism.* Durham: Acumen Publishing Ltd, 2009; rpt. Jaipur: Rawat, 2012. Print.

Innes, C. L. 'Introduction'. *The Cambridge Introduction to Postcolonial Literatures in English.* Cambridge: Cambridge UP, 2007. Print.

Jaaware, Aniket. 'Relevance of Recording the Past'. *Historiography: Past and Present.* Eds Kirit K. Shah and Meherjyoti Sangle. Jaipur: Rawat Publications, 2005. 46–61. Print.

Mukherjee, Meenakshi. Quoted in 'An Area of Brightness'. *The Week.* (July 28, 1996). Print.

Nabar, Vrinda. 'The Tale and the Teller'. *Seminar.* Spl issue on New Writing in English. 384 (August, 1991) 19–22. Print.

Nair, M. Krishnan. Quoted in 'An Area of Brightness'. *The Week.* (July 28, 1996). Print.

Newman, Judy. 'History and Letters: Anita Desai's *Baumgartner's Bombay*'. *Postcolonial Literatures: Achebe, Ngugi, Desai, Walcott.* Eds. Michael Parker and Roger Starkey. London: Macmillan, 1995. Rpt 2007. 195–208. Print.

Paniker, K. Ayyappa. 'Self-Reflexivism in Cultural Evolution: A Note on the Breakdown of the Value System'. *Contemporary Indian Literature: Positions and Expositions.* Ed. Santosh Gupta. Jaipur: Rawat Publications, 2000. 32–38. Print.

Parker, Michael and Roger Starkey. Eds. *Postcolonial Literatures: Achebe, Ngugi, Desai, Walcott.* London: Macmillan, 1995. Rpt 2007. Print.

Rushdie, Salman. *Midnight's Children.* UK: Jonathan Cape, 1980. Print.

Said, Edward. *Culture and Imperialism* London: 1993, xxi. Print.

Shingavi, Snehal. 'The Mahatma as Proof: The Nationalist Origins of the Historiography of Indian Writing in English'. *Literature and Nationalist Ideology.* New Delhi: Social Science Press, 2010. 353–75. Print.

Stilz, Gerhard. 'Truth? Hell, You will Get Contrast, and no Mistake!' Sanitizing the intercultural polylemma in G.V. Desani's *All About H. Hatterr'. Hybridity and Postcolonialism: Twentieth Century Indian Literature.* Ed. Monika Fludernik. Jaipur: Rawat Publications, 2006. 79–102. Print.

Sundararaghavan, Padma Malini. *Fictionalising Myth and History.* Hyderabad: Orient Blackswan, 2013. Print.

Suroor, Hasan. 'Race for the Booker'. Rev. of *Beethoven Among the Cows* by Rukun Advani. *The Hindu* (1 October 1995) xvii. Print.

Thapar, Romila. 'Ideas of History'. In interview with Praveen Swami, *The Hindu,* Sunday Magazine, (6 April 2014). 1. Print.

Verma, Nirmal. 'A Tryst with Humanity'. *Contemporary Indian Literature.* Ed. Santosh Gupta. Jaipur: Rawat Publications, 2000. 22–31. Print.

1

Questing for Truth: History-Fiction Interface in the Recent Indian English Fiction

A.S. DASAN

Life is so large, vast and variegated that all its implications and impacts cannot be contained in its entirety by history-fiction interface alone. While writing about the ramifications of violence in the twentieth century China, David Der-wei Wang, in his book, *The Monster That is History: History, Violence, and Fictional Writing in Twentieth-Century China* (2004), implies that 'neither history nor fiction could contain fully the human monstrosity life is'. Yet, the range and quality of inward looking into literary and historical representations of pain and suffering could be so deep, insightful and thought-provoking that the truth revealed or connoted by a writer may be viewed as truth stranger than fiction. It is well said that in history, nothing is true except names, and in literature, everything is true except names. This gives us a clue to how the novelist's use of history can serve as epiphany of art that conveys man's poetic awareness of his location in time.

An awareness of the contributions of Allesandro Manzoni (mid-nineteenth century), Georg Lukacs (1930s), Avrom Fleishman, F.J. Tickner, and Joseph Turner, to name a few, to the novelist's use of history may help us grasp the assumptions underlying the nature and scope of history-fiction interface, discern the theoretical, ideological, and methodical base for the interaction between the historical spirit and the great genres of literature, and derive the aesthetics of assimilating 'the totality of history'. In his book, *History-Fiction Interface in Indian English Novel* (1999), T.N. Dhar makes ample references to these contributions while making a study of the Indian English novelist's involvement with history. His analyses of the novels of Mulk Raj Anand, Nayantara Sahgal, Salman Rushdie, Shashi Tharoor, and O.V. Vijayan illustrate the variety, focus on the social, political, and cultural dimensions of historical events, and inform the reader on the novelists' ways of subjecting history to critical examination and on their choices of fictional narratives and modes of characterization and style.

II

In the Indic tradition, mimesis is a way of seeking truth, the *apurva* and the *arputha*, and it is such truth that is the ultimate altar of wisdom all of us aspire to genuflect. And this truth inspires and facilitates the *rasika* to experience *sahrdayata*, an empathetic communion with the author, and embrace and exude a compassionate worldview against monstrosity of life. This explains why Indian poetics views art as the language of the soul and why Indian aesthetics is inclined to promote literature as emotional memory. Via emotional memory, imaginative interpretation of history serves as a poetic way of questing for truth and identity. This is how figural realism sublimates narratology and obliterates all that is oppressively hegemonic, constricting and dehumanizing in the temporal arena.

Among the early literary pioneers using modernism, via history-fiction interface, in shaping the indigenous image of India, the contributions of Bankim Chandra Chatterjee and Mulk Raj Anand may be mentioned here. Bankim's *Anandamath* (1882), translated as 'The Sacred Brotherhood', and Anand's *Untouchable* (1935), one of the early Indian English novels, could serve as foundational texts for the understanding of Indian nationalism or the nation's identity. Bankim's imagining the nation as 'mother' was a trend-setter in interrogating the British imperialism and in defining nationalist 'self-identification'. His 'Vande Mataram' inspired freedom fighters of India to re-define Indian political history as an indigenous cultural act.

Anand stands apart as a beacon light via his manifold writings. His imaginative fictional output, despite clumsy characterization and overdose of didacticism, collectively represents a vibrant re-reading of the historiography of contemporary India with its deep contradictions. In his narration, the fate of the individual is warped within, and evolves through the historical narrative. His historical sense is similar to that of Georg Lukacs to whom history as narrative is an 'unfolding in the socially mediated narrative of individual fate', which is reflected in 'the typicality of character' within the narrative (1971). To Anand, history as narrative was not merely an imaginative portrayal of the epistemological knowledge and the empirical realities of India vis-à-vis nation, narration and identity. More importantly, it was also a way of dissenting against all forms of oppression and marginalization of the common man. His focusing on human centrality with an abiding love for the poor and the oppressed sensitized and shaped him as 'a dissenting pilgrim artist' (Dasan 2004) who resolutely used sociological imagination as a means of critical realism and ceaselessly pursued the cause of compassionate humanism, via articulating the angst of the subalterns, which evoked in the reader compunctious 'visitings of nature'.

Representation of history in the recent Indian English Fiction may be viewed as myriad re-presentations of the 'inner history', to use the expression of Malena Kuss, of human lives that provide an entry into the aesthetic, moral and spiritual perceptions and conceptions of the world, particularly the world of cultural identities rather than national/nationalist identity under the impact of globalization, migration, and multiculturalism. It may be viewed as a way of questing for truth, truth free from hegemonic angularities and truth that foregrounds viewpoints, marginalized and ignored hitherto. Engagement with history in fiction involves interpretation of the history of lives and relationships—national, institutional, family, gender and personal. It implies acknowledging the presence of many voices in search of 'the hidden layers of meaning', which, when put together, as Jasbir Jain visualizes, may yield 'a new meaning' or meanings (2002). What artistically and ultimately matters in narrative patterns within history-fiction interface is the poetic intensity of 'figural realism', to use the phrase of Hayden White, in terms of questing for inner dimensions of truth which historians may not be able to capture.

Re-presentation of history in the Indian English Fiction today has come to mean accommodativeness—accommodating different perspectives which include review of received meanings and aesthetics, deconstruction of 'legitimized' knowledge structures and problematization of national and personal identity. 'Why problematization?', one may tend to ask, and the answer is because monosyllabic centrality or essentialism, as if it were the only truth, is suspected. Conflict, fragmentation, dislocation, and search for missing links and turning points are part of the global, local and day-to-day experiences which cry for solutions. In his novel, *A Fine Balance* (1995), Rohinton Mistry says: 'Living each day is to face one emergency or another' (571).

Against the backdrop of 'the celebrity status' Salman Rushdie enjoys in the West, particularly North America, and the media-hyped privileging of the recent Indian migrant/diasporic fiction in English, one could ask, 'whose history' or 'which version of history' does the Indian English novel represent or re-present today? The Indian reader is in a state of 'to be or not to be' vis-à-vis the Western epistemological tendency to drift into postmodernist or meta-fictional modes of narration and interpretation as well in the name of culture studies or autonomy of the text. In the context of 'literature-centeredness' being ignored, writing in order to 'kill the author' or language as a means of 'impoverishing the subject or striping it of being and meaning' is seen to be a way of celebrating indeterminacy of semantics *ad infinitum*. This is how postmodernism posits itself as an irritant to modernism challenging and questioning the validity of the judicious use of reason towards enlightenment and progress.

This trend needs to be arrested if human centrality were to remain as the major focus of literature-centeredness. Viewing history-fiction interface as a social act can be one way of doing this. Within the aesthetics of fiction-writing and the historiography of the novel as a social act, fictional representation not only re-presents facts of history but also mythifies history, transfigures reality and transcends time and elevates the paradigms of history into poetic verities. Transcending facts with poetic presence of mind is a perennial recurrence in great fiction writing, including good historical novels. The Indic way of storytelling has been part of this tradition. The therapeutic value of poetry as pity and act of writing as an epiphany of eclectic and compassionate humanism is one of the seminal Indian contributions to the novel as a social act through the elegance and the resonance of language. The richness of this contribution is best understood by comparative studies. The tapestries of both the Indian novel and the Indian English novel offer a rich variety in this regard. And towards this end, the Indian novel in general transcends linguistic boundaries.

Today, the question of identity is defined and understood in the light of 'cosmopolitan identity' paradigms, courtesy migrant diasporic writings. And Nyla Ali Khan, author of the book, *The Fiction of Nationality in an Era of Transnationalism* (2005), observes that no single theory could adequately frame or incorporate the multiple inheritances of the current diasporic subjectivities. Whether these cosmopolitan identity paradigms are free from the impact of Western influence is a moot point. The strong presence of the migrant/diasporic intellectual in the age of globalization has come to mean, as Karim H. Karim writes, 'the end of cultural hegemony' and 'imagining transnational citizenship' (67). In the diasporic imagination of Rushdie, the past is seen as a 'foreign country'. He is of the view that 'literature has little or nothing to do with home address'. Rushdie states: 'The past is a country from which we all have migrated ...; its loss is part of our common humanity' (1991). To the Indian diaspora, conscious of their twice-born identity, yesterday is a fabled history, today a world of anxiety, and tomorrow a fantasy of hope and uncertainty. This awareness has its effects in their constructions of identity, space, time and narrative form. Their migrant imagination hovers around nonlinear dynamics. To them, fixity of identity is a thing of the past, and identity as a fluid experience within the terrain of mobility is an inevitable, if not indispensable, quest. In the process, the anxiety to retain Indianness as part of authentic Indian English writing has been problematized resulting in two fronts—one, 'the homegrown front' that tends to see Indian diasporic writers as 'cultural outsiders', and the other, 'the Indian diasporic front' that is complacent enough to think of the homegrown front as outdated 'cultic worshippers of cultural insiderism'.

The postcolonial articulations of the Other against experiences of hegemony, colonialism, notions of essentialist, totalizing and male-centered worldviews have all contributed not only to re-presenting the mental 'cartography' of history and notions of nationhood but also foregrounding heterogeneity and hybridity of thought, grasp and narration in which both poetics and politics consort and nestle together, and in which eclecticism is privileged as a natural corollary of postcolonial approaches to comprehend reality. Magic realism that blends the fantastic and the real, as Salman Rushdie and Arundhati Roy do, satire that combines the humorous and the serious, as Upamanyu Chatterjee does, and the use of English language that accommodates Hinglish as part of narrative have been used as techniques in foregrounding heterogeneity of perspectives within the narrative patterns of history-fiction interface. Though the postcolonial writer tends to view the projection of national identity as a colonial legacy and intends to make ruptures in the colonial perception of history, his/her approach to narrative is spiral rather than linear—connecting different ideas to the personality of the author rather than to any prefigured logocentric views.

Against this backdrop, re-presenting history implies both an interdisciplinary, multicultural and multi-prorogued strategy to deconstruct so as to 'decolonize the mind' in terms of de-learning and re-learning, and to give identity to 'plurisignifying voices' as representations against homogeneity concerning the grasp of nation and identity. It provides a scope for looking at the older texts with fresh understanding, and for appreciating 'silenced perspectives' from the point of view of the subaltern and the marginalized. All said and done, for the East to meet as equal partner with the West, is a perennial challenge. Moreover, the axis of neocolonialism—both economic and intellectual, and modes of 'depersonalization' that curtail critical consciousness under the impact of Western culture and Western ways of thinking still continues to haunt the Indian postcolonial reader and critic.

In terms of individual identity and cosmopolitan personality, common to both the Indian English novels of the 1980s and the 1990s is 'their assertiveness' against subjugation and passivity on the one hand, and against the original centre of location or received truths on the other. From an Indian feminine perspective, as Syed Mujeebuddin notes with reference to his reading of Anita Desai's novel, *Clear Light of Day* (1980), the articulation of 'other knowledge, different from Brahminical knowledge or Vedic wisdom' located in the Indian feminine psyche and born of her inner strength to break through society's prison, is a valuable ingredient of postcolonial approach to defining identity (2003).

The era of economic globalization, information technology, 'software activism' and consequent migrations of people across the globe have also impacted upon the writers' psyches. The rise of the middle class surging forward in India today and migrations effecting cross-cultural fertilization of ideas and causing mutations and alterations in cultural, literary and aesthetic sensibilities are significant factors associated with dialogical re-presentation of history which also projects 'semiotic democracy', to quote a phrase of Elizabeth Stark, as a value. One result of re-presentation is that the question of identity has become more cerebral than concrete or geographical, more transnational and transcultural than national and cultural, more dialogical/pluralistic than hegemonic and 'monological', and more intellectual than humanistic. The trend, with a few exceptions of course, is more and more towards 'the expression of the private voice' with an ambivalent emphasis upon social responsibility or moral visions of compassionate humanism.

One wonders if such a trend is one of the outcomes of the Stephanian or the Doon school elitism to which a considerable number of the post-Rushdie generation of writers belong. Nowadays, elitism of different sorts—Indian metropolis and diasporic—within the literary circle has a tendency to bypass reflections on the fate of the poor, as if 'the poor had no right to be born'. If such a trend persists, the casualty could be humanitarian focus in artistic re-presentation and representations of reality which was a foundational canon in the writings of the early architects of Indian Fiction and Indian English Fiction starting from Bankim Chandra, Premchand, Tagore, Mulk Raj Anand, R.K. Narayan, Raja Rao and others.

In this context, foregrounding the real struggle of the people, who are oppressed, within the scope of history-fiction interface, may be christened as 'the interventionist strategy' in examining the relationship between history, narration and representation. And as Sukalpa Bhattacharjee, observes, 'telling a 'tale' could perform an ideological function of competing with the agenda of other narratives that constitute the field of opposition and negotiation'. Whether the writings of the present-day Indian diasporic writers, with a few exceptions, are attempts in presenting the Otherness 'palatable to the West', or exercises considered as 'intellectual pastime' with possibilities for 'hefty advances', or whether these writers, as part of postcolonial diaspora, have become a minority role model in colonizing the internet or print media space for articulating their angst in redefining their ethnic identity or 'disrupting the fossilization of Indianness within their diasporic communities' need to be debated and discussed at length in different fora so that certain clarity emerges to erase misgivings and distortions.

III

The allegorical presentation of Salman Rushdie's own perception of India's post-independent national history in *Midnight's Children* (1981) gives him an opportunity to problematize Indian historiography, deconstruct Indian political realities and critique the Nehru-Indira Gandhi dynasty with his penchant for cynical satire, high-class black humour and narrative brilliance. In tune with his worldview, Rushdie discusses the complexities involved in the cross-cultural migrations of modern society taking place in the midst of globalization across the world in two of his other novels, *The Ground Beneath Her Feet* (1999) and *Fury* (2001). Rushdie is a firm believer in his own principle that 'no aesthetics can be constant', as he states in *Imaginary Homelands* (1992), and therefore, it is open to corruption and mutation. His novel, *The Moor's Last* Sigh (1995), as Nicholas Palffy points out, is a reflection of 'the aesthetics of disfiguration and the politics of transfiguration' (1996). In the novel, 'nothing is kept whole, normal. People, places, ideas, language and moral principles are being turned upside-down, inverted or disfigured' (Palffy 1996).

Rushdie's influence can be noticed in other Indian English novelists' writings such as Anita Desai's *In Custody* (1986) and *Baumgartener's Bombay* (1988), Amitav Ghosh's *The Circle of Reason* (1986) and *The Shadow Lines* (1988), Mukul Kesavan's *Looking Through Glass* (1995), Upamanyu Chatterjee's *English August* (1988) and Arundhati Roy's *The God of Small Things* (1997). The Rushdie influence has gone even beyond India. M.G. Vassanji's *The Gunny Sack* (1989) has been reviewed as Africa's answer to *Midnight's Children* for its presentation of history mixing the personal and the colonial in the backdrop of East African life interconnected with four generations of Asian immigration.

Amitav Ghosh offers vivid glimpses of intertwined histories with a subversive or subaltern dimension packed with anecdotes, symbolic meaning and extraordinary range of characters in almost all his novels. In *The Circle of Reason, The Shadow Lines, In an Antique Land* (1992), and *The Glass Palace* (2000), Ghosh readers will have little difficulty in visualizing the range of Amitav's cross-cultural sweep and his imaginative capacity to encompass and engage with the cultural heritage of the world. Ethics of multicultural representation and heterogeneity defining and characterizing the whole are the guiding lights of his narratology. The effortless passage of some of his characters through Asia, Europe and America is a metaphor for 'connecting people' emotionally. Silenced subaltern voices get recuperated and recognized because they represent the people at the grassroots and they are believed to be truer than official versions. Ghosh implies that truths revealed by his characters are truer than the truths of individuals narrated in history books. A thriller-like multi-generic style pervades his narratives and his presentation of episodes and characters. His reconstruction of history explores the psychological dilemmas experienced by individuals whose quest for personal identity is a predominant theme. His readings of the history of fascism, colonialism, and communalism serve as contexts to juxtapose defeats and frustrations of people with reasonable grounds for survival and hope.

Rohinton Mistry's novels are poignant portrayals of modern India seen through a deft weaving of conflicting situations and redemptive moments. His narratives are a fine blend of Persian, South Asian and European conventions of storytelling. His own Parsi Zoroastrian background helps him to give an insider view of the Parsi experience of inheriting hybrid culture. His affinities with the Parsi community traditions are different from those of Bapsi Sidhwa's as indicated in her debut novel, *The Crow Eaters* (1983). Mistry does not have a tendency to caricature or to have a satirical gaze at Parsi traditions. The delineation of Parsi experience that Mistry does with reference to history and modernity has wider social connotations.

Mumbai, 'the city by the sea' is an oft-used metaphor for his diasporic and minority-perspective discourses. Overcrowded apartment living is another metaphor for his realistic presentation of individual catastrophe and family conflicts intermingled with social canvases and political events. The spirit of compassionate 'verism' Mistry believes in, by juxtaposing politicians playing with human lives for the sake of votes and power, and promotes vis-*à*-vis his presentation of the lives of the urban poor of Mumbai's apartments, is a sign of his rootedness in Indian aesthetics.

Social issues such as poverty, corruption and injustice intertwined with humour and tragic beauty in his novels, *A Fine Balance* (1995) and *Family Matters* (2002), convey to the reader the novelist's postcolonial perception of the life of the urban poor. The ire and indignation of the writer is subtle when he hints at the indifference of the local ruling elite against the brutalities of modern life. His grasp of the broken dreams of his characters, of the tragedies in their lives, and of the hardships they face in the midst of economic misfortunes and lack of opportunities tacitly point to the arrogation of power in the hands of a few and the resultant political mismanagement. His novel, *Such a Long Journey* (1991) may be read as an allegorical presentation of an alternative reading of history. The context is India's war against Pakistan and the subsequent birth of Bangladesh. Set in Bombay, the novel represents multiple narrative voices challenging the rigidity of historiography and monological mode of apprehending the objectivity of truth and converging towards dialogical re-presentation of the historical discourse. In *A Fine Balance*, the reader could notice traces of Mistry's 'neorealism' (Takhar, Web.) with which he attacks what he sees as 'Indira Gandhi's fascism' and revises 'institutional history which has for far too long shamelessly neglected the lives of the common man'.

Using hybrid contexts mediated through migrations and diasporic locations Vikram Seth's novel, *A Suitable Boy* (1993) figures out different realities that constitute India after Independence. In his reconstructed narrative of the Indian nation, Seth, unlike Rushdie in *Midnight's Children*, eschews magic realism and adopts an integrated approach within a given and accepted notion of India, India as a secular State with traditions of multiculturalism and tolerance towards other religions. As Neelam Srivastava analyses and comments, 'in *A Suitable Boy,* the nation is an all-inclusive concept that moves from the individual, to the locality, to the regional state, and arrives to embrace the entire nation. Seth invents a state, Purva Pradesh, whose regional, specifically North Indian dimension, is stretched to make it representative of India in its totality' (2003).

Though essentially a love story dealing with Lata's quest for a husband, the novel gives an insight into the life of the upper middle-class of the mid-twentieth century India. 'Seth's concern is society' but satire becomes necessary because Seth is aware of self-serving pursuits of different forces manipulating and controlling the social and the political concerns of the people of India. Religious fundamentalism is shown to be self-serving and Indian politics empty of ethical values. Even families become the butt of Seth's satire. The successful suitor is, in fact, a 'self-made man' and has little family connection. Seth seems to indicate that 'happiness is a private affair'. The poet in the novelist overwhelms his preoccupation with satirical modes and inspires him to be 'an unacknowledged legislator' of India as he suggests that decency and dignity, instead of corruption and jockeying for power, should guide Indian politics.

Shashi Tharoor is a writer who believes in narrative structures which focus on multiple perspectives. His novels, *The Great Indian Novel* (1989) and *Show Business* (1992) reveal that interpretation of history cannot afford to have single/univocal ownership. He facilitates the reader to cultivate a fine sense of 'eclectic tolerance', to use his own phrase. Using *the Mahabharata* epic to strike a contemporary resonance in his retelling the story of modern India, he conveys colourful and complex versions of Indian realities with an eye for details and with what they mean to the future in terms of India's kaleidoscopic culture. His portrayals of India's struggle for Independence, secularism of Nehru, spirituality of Gandhi and the scourges of terrible poverty and communal sectarianism in India's history, and his use of Indian Bollywood/cinema as a metaphor for modern Indian society reflect and reveal the depths of his soul in reconstructing India's contemporary history with any subjective or private agenda. The way he handles *the Mahabharata* myth has certain comparable traces with T.S. Eliot's 'mythical method' which to him, as Joyce Wexler elaborates, was 'a way of controlling, of ordering, of giving a shape and significance to the immense panorama of futility and anarchy which is contemporary history' (1999: 60–73).

In his novel, *Riot* (2000), Shashi Tharoor goes deep into the subtleties of power politics in contemporary India in the backdrop of the Hindu nationalists' version of cultural revivalism, the rise of Hindu militancy and the demolition of the sixteenth century-mosque in Ayodhya. Writers like Kushwant Singh had long ago looked at the reality of religious communal tension with a straight-forward narrative. Rukun Advani did it so in a little humorous way in his novel, *Beethoven Among the Cows* (1994). Kiran Nagarkar's *Ravan and Eddie* (1995) and Salman Rushdie's *The Moor's Last Sigh* (1995) contain ingredients of satire on the abettors and accomplices of communal tension. But, Tharoor's *Riot* is, as Tripathi wrote in *The Asian Wall Street Journal* in 2001, is a reflection of a deft handling of the complicated problem presented with 'an accurate picture of the thinking of the various forces that are competing for supremacy in contemporary India'.

In his presentation of the cultural divide vis-à-vis the Sikh militancy, Partap Sharma experiments with alternative modes of creative writing which has certain resonance with the modes of presentation in the film, 'Shakespeare Wallah' (1965) directed by James Ivory. The 'candour' with which Sharma deals with reality of day-to-day world is 'ruthless'. His novel, *Days of the Turban* (1986) is one imaginative articulation of juxtapositions—two contrasting domains, the domain of 'the hegemonic project' of building up India as a modern State and the domain of 'the fragmentary consciousness' that shows resistance to the official hegemonic project.

The historical context in the novel is the military action—known as 'the 1984 Operation Bluestar', taken against Sikh militants led by Bhindranwale in Amritsar. Foregrounding the male metaphor of the turban as 'a structural device', Sharma delves into the cultural divide caused by hegemonic imposition of modern States—a divide that forces individuals and groups conscious of their identity with reference to their religious faith and traditions. The cultural divide can also be understood as a conflict between the material schemes and the religious/spiritual aspirations, the elite agenda and the subaltern perspectives, and the State-regimented bureaucracy and the populist movements. One implication of his juxtaposed narrative is that the elite may help to attain political freedom but they cannot make a nation or build up a society that ensures 'so many freedoms' and yet safeguards and nurtures the roots of cultural identity of the people.

Upamanyu Chatterjee who joined Indian Administrative Service (IAS) in 1983, does a fine and funny language-mix with usage of English and Hinglish in his first novel, *English, August: An Indian Story* (1988). His presentation of modern India influenced by American culture and his view of Indian bureaucracy are witty and satirical. *The Mammaries of the Welfare State* (2000), which won the Sahitya Akademi Award, may be viewed as a sequel to his first novel, *English, August.* Characters evolve as 'types' reflecting real life situations of Indian polity and its eccentric bureaucracy. Varied moments of caricatures embellished by black humour and gibes abound in the story. The way he de-centres modern India has more to do with humour and entertainment than with scatology. As a hilarious satire, the novel focuses on the fate of the common man who is either a victim or a mute spectator in the backdrop of the nexus between politicians and bureaucrats. By implication, the reader is given to understand the predicament the citizenry are put in while facing the plight of the nation. The protagonist's disillusionment is a pointer towards the failure of India's Enlightenment project.

This novel reminds me of another novel, *Bunker 13* (2003) by Aniruddha Bahal, co-founder and former CEO of Tehelka.com, which shakes our sense of cocooned existence as all of us are involved in corruption in one way or the other, as agents or victims. With his ability for and experience in investigative journalism, Bahal re-presents contemporary India in the context of corruption and bribery as a way of life. The 'jungles' of Kashmir conflict serve as a backdrop only to expose the bribery culture to which even a few rogue army men succumb via drugs and arms deals in connivance with smugglers. Minty Mehta, better known as MM in the novel, is aptly portrayed as 'an anti-hero' with a penchant for self-destruction even though he has been sent by a Delhi magazine to the Kashmir border to report on the Indo-Pak hostilities. Commenting on the anti-hero's crooked ways, Amitava Kumar writes:

> MM is no social meliorist. He is in it for the money. Writing is a game of high commercial stakes. The staid world of Nehruvian socialism and protected markets is gone. The Indian nation, and indeed, even a part of the world outside, is up for grabs. Everyone is suspect in the book because everyone is on the take. (2003: 3)

That India cannot dream of developing when bribery culture overwhelms decent governance and public outrage seems to be one of the authorial implications, rather than intrusions, in the novel. The novelist takes cognizance of the trends in the upward mobility of the middle-class in India today and uses the genre of fiction to imagine the history of the present and sensitize the middle-class nation against the rampant evil of corruption.

Vikram Chandra's debut novel, *Red Earth and Pouring Rain* (1995) is a brilliantly conceived work of art that entwines history, myth and fiction linking continents, centuries and contemporary India through tales told by Sanjay, the monkey-man. In the process, the author explores the impact of colonial and contemporary India and intertextuality of the lives of Indian expatriates caught between Indian and American values. With a spiral approach to history-fiction interface, his narrative strategy focuses on his idea of India which has a fine balance between modernity and tradition. A reading of the novel reinforces the truth that transculturation nullifies nothing. It modifies thought-patterns and reshapes language, celebrates multiculturalism and creates sensibilities which are coherent and holistic.

There are fictional narratives that deal with family sagas and gender relationships which capture the inner turmoil and redefine identities caught up in traditional moulds or suppressed by convention. Shashi Deshpande's *The Dark Holds No Terror* (1980) and *The Binding Vine* (1993), Nina Sibal's *Yatra* (1987), Gurucharan Das' *A Fine Family* (1990), Arundhati Roy's *The God of Small Things* (1997) and Githa Hariharan's *The Thousand Faces of Night* (1992) and *When Dreams Travel* (1998), Manju Kapur's *Difficult Daughters* (1998) and *A Married Woman* (2002), Anita Rau Badami's *Tamarind Mem* (1996) and *The Hero's Walk* (2001), Kavita Daswani's *For Matrimonial Purposes* (2003) and *The*

Village Bride of Beverely Hills (2004), Anjana Appachana's *Listening Now* (1998), and Jaishree Misra's *Ancient Promises* (2000) may be counted as part of the narratives dealing with family, conjugal and gender relationships.

IV

Indian English women novelists then and now have never failed to unveil the feminine psyche despite odds and challenges faced and indifference shown by society by and large. Writings by Indian women today unveil steadily and argue firmly that values like freedom of thought and expression, liberation from oppression and marginalization, and equality as a quest for dignity are the prime movers of their imagination and creativity.

Readers already familiar with writers like Kamala Markandaya, Nayantara Sahgal, Mirnalini Sarabhai, Anita Desai, Shashi Deshpande and others, are given new treats by the new generation of women writers residing in India and women writers of Indian diaspora. Indian women's consciousness straddling the worlds of tradition and modernity has been one of the major themes Indian women writers have been preoccupied with. As Anita Vashishta observes, women novelists' portrayal of Indian woman as 'a nodal point for change and transformation'—despite her precarious existence in a tradition-bound, patriarchy-bound and male dominated Indian society—is a very significant social act that problematizes certain culture-specific oppressive traditions, highlights and articulates the female angst and contributes to new critical awareness. It is appropriate that this random survey ends with brief comments on select imaginative output of Arundhati Roy, Gita Hariharan, and Kiran Desai.

Arundhati Roy's *The God of Small Things* (1997) deals with the private world of Ammu, Velutha, and the twins, who dare to challenge the status quo of the public world. The conflict in the novel consists of the differences between these two worlds of privileges vs. despair. The way Roy juxtaposes the theme of abiding love among the victims with the double standards of the privileged world reflects the canon set by Anand for Indian English writers. Like Kamala Markandaya's Rukmani, Roy's Ammu refuses to be cowed down by a hostile world, a world of caste, class and regional hegemony. Ammu's capacity and acts of resisting in small ways, transgressing societal restrictions, and firmly loving Velutha, the dalit-carpenter, may be viewed as significant countermoves against her inevitable awareness of women's powerlessness.

Githa Hariharan's *In times of Siege* (2003) can be read as a contesting narrative that foregrounds 'historiography as a site of conflict' with contemporary relevance. Told with elegance, indirection and implied meanings, the progression of the plot in the novel revolves around the ideological position of Professor Shiv who espouses the cause of egalitarianism resonating the twelfth century poet, Basavanna's tradition and the ghetto fundamentalist position of Arya who along with his goons opposes and attacks Shiv in order to maintain status quo via caste hierarchies. An intelligent reader cannot miss to notice the similarities between Arya's ideological association with Itihas Suraksha Manch (History Protection Society) and the present day Hindutva fundamentalism. The point implied is that humanity cannot be defrauded by age-old historiography of caste hegemony, and preserving culture and civilization cannot be left into the hands of zealots who behave like fanatics and thugs in the name of religion, morality and caste hegemony. The writer's re-presentation of historiography in the novel challenges hegemonic notions that mean discrimination and subjugation. The way the writer transfigures and disfigures history is an indication of her empathy with the stance of Shiv.

Kiran Desai's *The Inheritance of Loss* (2006) may be viewed as an astute social commentary on modern dichotomies observed in the lives of people who migrated and returned as in the case of Jemubhai Patel, a retired judge, who endures a profound sense of spiritual loss with memories of the past and the predicament of the present. The mingling of the family saga (the judge's personal and household history) and the political history (unrest and campaign for independent Ghurkaland) within the plot-structure is juxtaposed with the sense of alienation every character in the novel experiences. The novelist's sense of human warmth which she believes is 'innate in Indians' guides her perception of 'what it means to live between East and West and what it means to be an immigrant'. In a dissenting note, questioning the writer's 'exotic and Orientalist representation' of the entire community of Nepalis of Kalimpong and Darjeeling in the novel, Namrata Chaturvedi has criticized the 2006 Man Booker Prize award to the author on the ground that the novelist 'inherits the mode of trivializing marginal communities, in this case the Nepalis of the Darjeeling hills' with a condescending look at the community (2007).

V

In conclusion, the Indian English novel, particularly the diasporic Indian novel today, is an entity in which the abstract and the concrete merge together via concerns of cultural identities, rather than national/nationalist identity. With memories from their home country, diasporic Indian writers have been focusing on the personal and the social implications of living in the midst of transnational and multicultural identities. In the process, they have contributed not only to the transformation of the positions of postcoloniality but also to the transformation of the Indian English novel. The younger generation of writers have shown a higher level of maturity in handling the effects of migration and dislocation vis-à-vis the question of identity. Their arguments in favour of emerging trends of cultural identities are complex but lively, nuanced but evocative, and transcultural and yet contextual. They have better knowledge and awareness of what kind of fiction is successfully marketed and consumed. Media hype is a powerful agent today that determines the salability of what is written.

Reading and interpreting the Indian English novel today is an intertextual act that accommodates centrifugal and centripetal dimensions. Interdisciplinary, and therefore comparative in nature, it is a multilingual and multicultural act with pulrisignifying possibilities in terms of semiotics and semantics. When the text is open to hermeneutics, meaning becomes a construct of the reader. It is great to feel that the Indian English novelist has the imagination to create variegated images of postcoloniality, celebrate difference, contest hegemonic and homogeneous identities and social/standardized constructions of reality, and use the English language as an instrument of creativity and liberation.

In the course of re-presenting history in fiction in today's context, various approaches to narratology do make sense in an ambience of semiotic and semantic democracy. Re-presentation paves way for fresh intellectual and multidisciplinary openings in terms of cultural studies, postcolonial readings, disrupting boundaries, and giving value-recognition to paradigmatic status of marginalized, ignored cultures, ideological views, and diasporic and transnational and transcultural positions. Variety maps and privileges a wealth of vibrant forms and modes of representation, continuity of research and traditions of scholarship. It reflects the divergent ways of creative writing by which literary imagination impacts human life and shapes cultural history and identity.

While assuming that readings and meanings can be plural, the Indian English novelist and the critic as well could still be schooled in Indian poetics and aesthetics which would equip him/her with a sense of spiral approach to narratology. Indian poetics is eclectic enough to accommodate 'cultural holism' as a means of characterizing the current modes of cross-cultural and transcultural inquiries. Influenced by Betty Jean Craige's idea of cultural holism, I would say that the Indian English novelist could imagine and write like an ecologist. Ecologists, as Betty notes, are intimately aware of the reciprocal patterns of interconnectivity among diverse parts of ecosystems.

It is tenable that telling a tale and interpreting the tale can have an ideological function. It is only a means, a strategy. But, the greatness of a storyteller lies in his capacity to transcend the binaries within re-presentations. What ultimately sustains the greatness of a novel is the human warmth, compassionate worldview, ingrained in between the lines of the narrative. It is the rhythm of human warmth that liberates humanity from the brutality of existence. Indian poetics helps the writer and the reader as well to analyse the relation between knowledge and literary fiction in a critical but humane way. A browsing of an article by T.N. Snitko (Pyatigorsk), titled 'Cognition vs. Understanding' vis-à-vis Japanese culture, ignites my mind to state that unlike the 'cognition culture' of Western epistemology, ours is an 'understanding culture' (1999). Understanding culture seeks a fusion between reason and emotion, and between man and the world while Western cognition culture aims at reducing everything into an epistemological abstraction. Indian aesthetics is inclined to promote literature as emotional memory. The burden of optimism against all odds is the power of Indian aesthetics.

And finally, art distils and unifies. The great poetic soul of Kalidasa (320–455 A.D.) has taught us that the art of writing lies in communicating the unity of the artist's innermost experience. Indeed, art is the language of the soul. This is why an artist is a seer in the Indian literary tradition. He not only sees but also 'sees' what others ordinarily cannot. Narratives of history-fiction interface provide us an opportunity to discern this unity. It is this discernment that helps us quest for truth in and through these narratives.

Works Cited

Chaturvedi, Namrata. 'The Inheritance of Stereotype.' *Himal Southasian* 20.3 (March 2007). <http://www.himalmag.com/index.php> Web.

Dasan, A.S. 'Mulk Raj Anand: A Dissenting Pilgrim Artist.' First Anand Memorial Lecture. New Delhi: Lokayata, 2004. Print.

Jain, Jasbir. 'Towards the 21st Century: The Writing of the 1990s.' *Indian Writing in English: The Last Decade*. Ed. Rajul Bhargava. Jaipur: Rawat Publications, 2002, 11–25. Print.

Karim, Karim H. 'Diaspora and Citizenship.' *Re-Public* (an Online Journal). <http://www.republic.gr/en/?p=67> Web.

Kumar, Amitava. 'A History of the Present as a Whodunit.' *The Hindu*, Sunday (3 August 2003). p. 3. Print.

Lukacs, Georg. *The Theory of the Novel*. 1920. Cambridge, MA: The MIT Press, 1971. .

Mistry, Rohinton. *A Fine Balance*. New York: Vintage Books, 1995. .

Mujeebuddin, Syed. 'Past and Present in Anita Desai's *Clear Light of Day*'. *Postcolonial Theory and Literature*. Eds P. Mallikarjuna Rao, Rajeshwar Mittapalli and K. Damodar Rao. New Delhi: Atlantic, 2003. pp. 107-18. Print.

Palffy, Nicholas. 'The Aesthetics of Disfiguration and the Politics of Transfiguration in Salman Rushdie's *Moor's Last Sigh*.' *Paradigme Communication* (1996). <http://www.paradigme.ch/pages/rushdie. html> Web.

Rushdie, Salman. *Imaginary Homelands: Essays and Criticism 1981–1991*. New York: Granta Books/Viking, 1991. .

Snitko, T.N. (Pyatigorsk). 'Cognition vs Understanding as Ultimate Understanding Operator in Japanese.' *Hermeneutics in Russia* 3.1 (1999). .

Srivastava, Neelam. 'The Invention of India in Vikram Seth's *A Suitable Boy*.' *Research South Asia—IIAS Newsletter* 32 (November 2003). .

Takhar, Jennifer. 'Rohinton Mistry's Indian Neorealism: The Voice of the People.' <takharjennifer@hotmail.com> Web.

Tripathi. 'Review of Shashi Tharoor's *Riot*.' *Asian Wall Street Journal* (14 December 2001). <http://64.227.213.236/reviews/riot/asianwsj. html> Web.

Wexlar, Joyce. 'Realism and Modernists Bad Reputation'. Studies in the Novel. 31.1 (1999): pp. 60–73.

2

History and Literature: A Note

MOHAN RAMANAN

The manner in which history intersects with narrative is the burden of this note. My illustrations will be from the tradition of Indian writing in English. When Sir Philip Sidney attempted a defence of literature he spoke of the competing disciplines—philosophy and history and showed that literature was in a profound way more philosophical than philosophy and more historical than history. His contention was that philosophy dealt with abstractions and history with concrete particulars. Poetry or imaginative literature which was inventive could marry the abstract with the concrete. It not only generalized about life but it also showed these generalizations as admitting of particular instances. Thus love is an abstraction but if a poet whom Sidney did not know but who wrote years later says: 'My love is like a Red, Red, Rose'—there we have an abstraction beautifully concretized. Love is passion and colour. Therefore, it is reasonable to say that literature has within it a modicum of history and all narrative is both fiction and history. These days we say that there is both the fictionality of fact and the facticity of fiction. An event which occurs today is reported in the newspapers tomorrow by two rival journalists belonging to two rival publications. One speaks of the event—a student has been run over by a lorry—as an accident. The student did not watch where she was going and the lorry could not stop in time because it was driven by a drunken driver. The other journalist says that the student was depressed after a dressing down she received from her teacher and deliberately came in the way of the lorry which means that she committed suicide. So in one narrative the event is a killing because of drunken driving, in the other it is a suicide. History is after all narrative, and events which happened centuries ago have a way of accruing a significance which may have little to do with the actual event, but then we don't know what the actual event was. The impossibility of trying to reproduce fact is a given in this context.

Fiction and literature assume this. As Sidney put it—the world is brazen but literature produces a golden world.

It was the Belgian thinker Georg Lukacs who showed the intimate link between history and the novel. The Realist novel is his focus. In this, history becomes a character. A good example of this is Walter Scott's *Heart of Midlothian* (1818). It is a perfect example of the historical novel. Jeannie Deans and Effie Deans are sisters. Efiie under English law which is imposed on the Scottish people is condemned to death for the killing of her illegitimate child. It is a harsh punishment and the Scottish people are in any case unhappy with English hegemony. The Porteus riots described in the novel are an example of this resentment. Jeannie travels the length of the British Isles from Scotland to London to meet the Queen and to convey to her the injustice of the law which punishes her sister. The Queen persuades the king to repeal the law. It is done. Jeannie returns triumphant to Scotland and Effie is free. The novel is able to show the processes of history and the manner in which it becomes a character in the novel. It interpenetrates the lives of the characters. The public becomes informed by the private and the private is in its turn impacted by history. When this symbiotic relationship takes place we may say that we have a historical novel. But there are many fictions which use history not as a profound presence but as a cardboard background. In Scott himself we see this happening. In *Ivanhoe* (1820) we have all the trappings of the Middle Ages, the Crusades, the Robin Hood legend, the Norman tyranny and the Saxon resistance. The Jew, a figure of ridicule, in Catholic Christendom is also there in the persona of Isaac. But the history is only superficial and the real interest in the story is the lovely love triangle of Ivanhoe, Rebecca and Rowenna. That is a staple of literature and film and if we understand that this could have been dramatized in any historical period, the medieval flavour of Scott's novel becomes extraneous. This is not to suggest that history does not exist here, only to point to its being an add-on. *Ivanhoe* is a historical romance while *Heart of Midlothian* is a historical novel.

This kind of use of history is what I want to touch on with respect to some Indian Fiction in English mainly. 1980 is the high watermark of this tradition. It was the year when Salman Rushdie published *Midnight's Children.* It is the tale of Saleem Sinai, a child of the midnight hour when India awoke to freedom. Saleem is irrevocably yoked to Indian history by being born that night. He is India and Rushdie shows how in many ways India becomes Saleem. This is a variation of the manner in which public and private, the personal and the political, the historical and the individual blend. It is a classic historical novel in the Lukacsian sense. It is further complicated by the magic realism of Rushdie. This is basically a question of blurring time and space distinctions. We are never quite sure when an event begins and when it ends or when another event begins. This derangement of time and space adds a postmodern dimension to the historical novel. Rushdie's procedure initiated a tradition of family saga fiction in India. Allan Sealy, Boman Desai and many others attempted a Rushdie in their own work. Boman Desai in *The Memory of Elephants* (1988) does what Rushdie does for Saleem. Three generations of a Parsi family and their complex relation with India is the burden of the novel. In Allan Sealy it is seven generations of the Anglo Indian Trotters who are linked with India. This is the new nationalist fiction if you like. It is a nationalism of the minority consciousness.

In *The Moor's Last Sigh* (1995) Rushdie does the unimaginable. He marries a Cochin Jew to a Syrian Catholic from Kerala. In life this is impossible but in fiction it is possible and Rushdie's child by this unlikely marriage is Moraes Zogoiby. He is a Church of One. He is as much an Indian and has a claim to India as any Muslim, Jew or Hindu or Catholic might. It is this radical revision of the idea of India which makes history such a potent presence in this kind of fiction. Then Mukul Kesavan wrote *Looking Through Glass* (1995) using history in a radical way. He makes his protagonist travel on the Gomti Express. He is going to Varanasi to immerse the ashes of his dead grandmother. On the way, being an inveterate photographer, he leans out of the stationary train which has halted over the Gomti Bridge and falls into the water. When he is fished out it is no longer the Nineties. It is 1942. This as we all know is a momentous year in India's history. It is Quit India time. It is the beginnings of Pakistan. It is telling Cripps to go home. Kesavan makes his protagonist present at crucial political conclaves and overhear the musings of India's leaders. The implication seems to be that if these leaders, whom the protagonist overhears and whose secret is with him, had acted differently perhaps India's history would have been different. The book is, therefore, very engaging.

Finally, I shall turn to the way history and myth are employed in fiction. Every nation has a foundational myth and these myths have a powerful impact on the way the people of a nation conduct themselves. American Exceptionalism, for example, is still very much in evidence when a President can speak of an axis of evil and see America as *us* and the evil nations as *them.* This very Puritan idea which gave Americans a sense of identity is no longer the potent unifier of a nation which is fast becoming a multicultural cauldron but it does play a role because it is an abiding belief with Americans. Novels, as scholars have pointed out, very often reflect these national myths. In India the idea of nationhood is problematic in the extreme and there is no governing national myth especially since India as a modern nation-state is very recent in its origins. But the nation as a cultural entity, as having a cultural unity, one believes, was a governing principle for most of India's history. That is why we have those great epics which show a Rama traversing the length and breadth of the geographical space we now call India. That is why Sankara's perigrinations are so important and that is why an early Telugu text like Veeraswami's Journal *Kasiyatra Charitra* is part of this imagining of a modern nation-state. It uses an old trope to project a modern instance.

It is in this context of history in its mythic dimensions that I wish to consider a few works of Indian literature both in English and in English translation. Shashi Tharoor's *The Great Indian Novel* (1989) is a retelling of the Mahabharata story. The use Tharoor makes of the myths and the heroic characters to comment on modern India is astounding and it is a very entertaining piece of writing. The novel ends with Yudhishtira claiming that there is no such thing as the Truth but that there are truths. This realization of the plurality of voices and the plurality of the country makes the novel truly a reflection of the reality of India, not so much as a nation-state but as a civil society. We must not forget that the novel is sometimes the Other of the Nation, this last in its more unpleasant manifestations. The novel often talks of the lived life of the people and their identities which are often fragments of the nation and not the nation as a monolith. The novel, therefore, is a vital way of representing those aspects of a nation which the official version marginalizes. I shall conclude by saying something about the Kannada novelist Bhyrappa's retelling of the *Mahabharata.*

Bhyrappa is easily one of modern India's greatest writers. His *Parva* (1979) is a wonderful recreation of the Mahabharata story. In this massive retelling we are allowed to assume that we know the myth and the tale of our great heroes. Bhyrappa is interested in motives and unconscious drives. Much of his narrative is psychological exploration of the inner workings, desires, motives and purposes of Bhisma, Dhritarashtra. Arjuna, Bhima, Kunti, Gandhari, Karna and Vidura. He does not hesitate to lead us to the personal lives of the great characters and to present them in all their nakedness, warts and all. Scenes of unreason and cowardice and mixed motives bring alive episodes from the myth which put a completely different interpretation and meaning on well-known moments of our national history. Bhyrappa repeatedly refers to bodily functions, to defecation and urination. Even Bhisma urinated! It is a grim narration. But finally it is about the complex nature of Dharma which after all the scriptural texts and our epics are also about. The difference is that we see these questions in their starkness and in their unromantic state. Krishna is presented as a wise one which, of course, he is but he is no divinity here, only a more evolved person. It is a fitting way of showing how the history of India, informed as it has been by the Dharmic questions of the Mahabharata story, continue to have its modern resonances. Here History and Literature meet and illuminate each other. That is a consummation devoutly to be wished.

3

History and Nationalism at the Crossroads: Review of Indian Writing in English

H. KALPANA

The formation of the colonial subject, from a postcolonial perspective has no doubt undergone a number of determinants—social, economic and political. Therefore, a postcolonial rewriting of the past is dependent on this multiplicity, which to some extent gets tackled in subjects like history and politics. However, literary discourses address this issue in a minor way. The concern of the writers has, by and large, been an attempt to re-invoke cultural values thereby allowing the readers to accommodate men and women automatically into a postcolonial valency. This is reiterated when Raja Rao in his foreword to *Kanthapura* mentions: 'The tempo of Indian life must be infused into our English expression, even as the tempo of American or Irish life has gone into the making of theirs' (1989: v). This reading, one hopes, would lead to a comprehension of the fact that the nation in Indian Writing in English becomes as Bhabha points outs, a 'system of cultural signification and a representation of social life' (1990: 1–2). In order to probe this question of an Indian identity set within a homogenous historical footing the present analysis has been attempted. The article endeavours to explain briefly the milieu of postcolonialism and nationalism to contextualize the texts and follows it with an analysis of how the writers writing in the English language have failed to accommodate fictional lives and have repeatedly circumscribed their characters into the mainstream lifestyles thereby limiting the characters' choices to seek for secular, democratic identities.

In the past two to three decades the Anglo American literary circles have continued to focus largely on issues of postcolonialism. The seminal work of Edward Said and Bill Ashcroft et al. became an important point in Anglo American academia to think that the colonized-colonizer conflict needs to be studied closely and analytically. Later incursions by various critics such as Gayatri Chakravorty Spivak, Homi Bhabha and others made this a lucrative business for literary scholars and critics. Postcolonial studies also helped to chart a burgeoning interest in the colonized region because it now became evident that imperialism and colonialism are very much part of the contemporary world and it is difficult to escape the same. Colonial discourses stress the interrelationship of a number of text and practices that belong to the colonial and postcolonial period. It, however, brings in the political dimension of this dynamics that exists in terms of relationship of power between the colonizer and the colonized. In a way, ignoring the dynamics of power in relationship to history has led the critical work, *The Empire Writes Back* (1992), to be rather redundant in the reading of contemporary texts. The authors, Bill Ashcroft, Helen Tiffin, and Gareth Griffiths argue that all English literary works produced by societies affected by colonialism can be read as postcolonial is rather naïve and over a period of time a number of writers have criticized this aspect. What, however, is heartening to note is that postcolonial studies have focused on the issue of colonialism and its attitude of dominance giving rise to critical and theoretical language that employs its own jargon. Yet postcolonial studies have failed to accommodate the idea that the fiction, especially, emerging from the Indian sub-continent has focused repeatedly on the temporality of culture and social existence. The fictions produced by writers do have a large part to play in understanding issues such as identity, culture, religion, tradition and so on. As Bhabha states, 'To study the nation through its narrative address does not merely draw attention to its language and rhetoric; it also attempts to alter the conceptual object itself. If the problematic 'closure' of textuality questions the totalization of national culture, then its positive value lies in displaying the wide dissemination through which we construct the field of meanings and symbols associated with national life' (1990: 3).

Postcolonial theory has attempted to create a binary opposition of self-other, metropolis-colony, centre-periphery, etc. In these binaries one of them is also the reference to time passed and post-time. Drawing on the words of Anne, McClintonk states:

> The postcolonial scene occurs in an entranced suspension of history as if the definitive historical events have preceded us and are now in the making. If the theory promises a de-centering of history in hybridity, syncretism, multidimensional time and so forth the singularity of the term effects a re-centering of global history around the single rubric of European time. Colonization returns at the moment of its disappearance (2003: 255).

In this kind of reading the issues of multiplicity, plurality itself takes a back seat. It also ignores the political dimensions existing in the present moment as it takes into consideration only a view of history being at all times a single, unified structure. The work *The Empire Writes Back* had put in motion the idea that postcolonial writing is usually an act of resistance trying to set right the center-margin axis and hinted at a 'more liberated and positive future' (1992: 24). Thus, it was believed that writers such as Raja Rao, Anand and others were, through their writings, displaying the center-margin axis. If one of the problems had been the reading of literature through a postcolonial framework another issue of concern had been the mere fact of nationalism.

II

The Indian nationalism in 1940s had given rise to euphoria on account of a sense of liberation but this soon paved the way for a feeling of disappointment and frustration, due to the emergence of neo-colonialism. This happened because as Fanon pointed out the national ideology had been formed either by a bourgeois nationalism or a liberal anti-imperialist nationalist perspective. The bourgeois nationalism was a representation of the elite indigenous classes that aim at capturing the colonial state while the second category promoted a more radical liberal nationalism. As Fanon states, the 'mission' of the national elites has nothing to do with transforming the nation it unites, rather grapples with a capitalism, rampant though camouflaged, 'which today puts on the mask of neo-colonialism' (1965: 152). Of course to some extent Spivak does claim a place for the subaltern and yet even she is unable to transgress the attitude of the neo-colonial. Neil Lazarus substantiates this when he mentions 'In her own work, however, the deconstructive interrogation of subalternity is typically given precedence over the radical historiographical account of native agency' (1999: 206).

Historically, it is pointed out that the natives from the margins could not contest the sites of power. As Ranajit Guha mentions with reference to how insufficient the subaltern politics was within the nationalist struggle:

> The initiatives which originated from the domain of subaltern politics were not, on their part, powerful enough to develop the nationalist moment into a full-fledged struggle for national liberation. The working class was still not sufficiently mature in the objective conditions of the social being and its consciousness as a class-for-itself, nor was it firmly allied yet with the peasantry. As a result, it could do nothing to take over and complete the mission which the bourgeois had failed to realize. The outcome of it all was that the numerous peasant uprisings of the period, some of them massive in scope and rich in anticolonialist consciousness waited in vain for a leadership to raise them above localism and generalize them into a nation wide anti-imperialist campaign (1994: 6).

Yet this was not going to happen even at a later stage for as Fanon states even after years of Independence the leader is incapable of urging on the people to a concrete task. He is unable to open the future to them or show them the path of national reconstruction. The leader most often, according to Fanon, reassesses the history of Independence and recalls the sacred unity of the struggle for liberation. Although at the time of the struggle for liberation the leader might have awakened the people and promised them a forward march, at the present moment 'he uses every means to put them to sleep, and three or four times a year asks them to remember the colonial period and to look back on the long way they have come since then' (1965: 168–69). Therefore, the spirit of nationalism is defeated and it is interesting to note how the Indian writers writing in English view the same.

III

Edward Said in his reading of W.B. Yeats, 'Yeats and Decolonization' (1990), narrates that in the decade long struggle to achieve decolonization and independence from British control, literature has played a crucial role in the re-establishment of a national cultural heritage, in the reinstatement of native idioms, in the re-imagining and re-configuring of local histories, geographies, communities. As such then, literature not only mobilized active resistance to incursions from the outside, but also contributed massively as the sharper, creative aspect of illumination within the realm of the colonized. If this was the scenario in the Irish nationalism then the Indian nationalism took a different turn. Most writers writing in English depicted either a passive nationalist struggle or moved into token form of spiritualism or revealed anguished lives or propagated weak solutions for their marginalized characters or stuck to a return to culture and tradition.

The period from 1930s to 1960s was a period when novels were mapped out to construct a nation that seemed to have one identity, namely the liberation of the nation. These novels—Raja Rao's *Kanthapura* (1938) and *The Serpent and the Rope* (1960); R.K. Narayan's *The Guide* (1958); Mulk Raj Anand's *Untouchable* (1935), Kamala Markandaya's *Nectar in a Sieve* (1955)—have been read variedly as novels that had used the master's tongue beautifully and had by their narratives destabilized the centre's dominance and yet a re-reading of the novels reveal the fact that these novels once again seem to address the making of a single identity and a glorification of the past. To get a picture of this a good example would be to read Raja Rao's *Kanthapura*. The novel is set during the last stages of Indian national movement in India and depicts the protagonist, Moorthy's struggle to unite his village by invoking the spirit of nationalism. In the very first section of the novel, Kanthapura is depicted as an Indian village that has been split up on casteism: 'Till now I've spoken of the Brahmin quarter. Our village had a pariah quarter too, a Potters quarter, a Weavers quarter and a Sudra quarter' (11). The novel through the activities of Moorthy and Rangamma attempts to unify the village. It is, however, an arduous task and Moorthy realizes this when he asks the village women to spin yarn:

> 'I ask you, will you spin a 100 yards of yarn per day?' But Madanna's wife says, 'I'm going to have a child', and Satanna's wife says, 'I'm going for my brother's marriage', and her sister says, 'I'll spin if it will bring money .... And Moorthy feels this is awful, and nothing could be done with these women .... (78)

The novel ends by revealing a much accepted truth which Moorthy narrates: 'And I have come to realize bit by bit, when I was in prison that as long as there will be iron gates and barbed wires round the Skeffington Coffee House, and city cars that roll up the Babbar Mound, and gas lights and coolie cars, there will always be pariahs and poverty' (183).

In a way *Kanthapura* has been time and again praised for its masterful and skilful narrative technique and its utilization of the Harikatha form to narrate the story. Yet what is not realized is the novel still unequivocally narrates the story of a Hindu nation. The other who also forms the national identity is hardly given space to breathe. It seems that Rao deliberately, in his resurrection of Gandhian ideology, is also rooting for an Indian past that was the glorious period of spirituality. This is substantiated in his later work, *The Serpent and the Rope*.

The second phase of Indian writing in English was the period from 1960s to 1980s which saw a swing from external reality to an interiorization of the mind. This was essential as the nation was making itself; and in its trial to rebuild the nation, it was also witnessing technological and scientific growth. As a result of the process of alienation, writers such as Anita Desai, Arun Joshi, and Shashi Deshpande sought to depict the selfhoods of their protagonists. If Arun Joshi's *The Strange Case of Billy Biswas* (1971) revealed Billy's escape into tribal society, Desai's women were wrought with hyper sensitivity and underwent mental estrangement, isolation and alienation. The theme of the period seemed to be a quest for a spiritual peace that was almost non-existent. On the other hand, Deshpande's protagonists were caught within marital webs and were continuously straining to get out of the patterns of their existence. Interestingly enough, Deshpande's women are also stigmatized by issues such as rape and feel that they have been caught in the throes of victimhood. In her short story, 'Intrusion', the protagonist feels she is caught in a loveless marriage wherein her body is possessed by her husband. The issue of the sexual assault in 'It was Dark' becomes the major idea in *Roots and Shadows* (1983). In *The Binding Vine* (2002) it goes a bit further with a real rape contrasted with a narrativised or manuscripted rape account. Deshpande, in one of her interviews explains that *The Binding Vine* has 'three strands, the stories of three women: Kalpana, who is unconscious throughout; Mira, a poet who is now dead, and Urmila, who discovers Mira's poems and also learns about Kalpana' (1998: 233). The main character in the novel contrasts the politics of so called normal heterosexual relationships and wonders at the relationships of Vaana-Harish, Inni-Papa, Mira and her husband. She also critically examines her own relationship with her husband, Kishore. Similarly Desai too expects her women to be independent but at a certain point she does not allow them total freedom. The women such as Jaya in *That Long Silence* (1989), Anita Desai's Monisha in *Voices in the City* (1965), Maya in *Cry the Peacock* (1963), Nanda Kaul in *Fire on the Mountain* (1977), Sita in *Where Shall We Go This Summer* (1975) and Bim in *Clear Light of Day* (1980) are continuously trying to remake themselves. Although Desai's women are educated and intelligent they all end up being 'good' wives. The only exception is possibly Bim in *Clear Light of Day* who assumes to a certain extent the representation of the nation as symbolic. Her iconisation leads one to understand that within the Indian nation there is the question of assimilating women. Thus, once again these narratives reveal a quest for the spiritual past and also depict women succumbing to social and cultural values of being 'good' women who play their roles well.

The modern period constitutes works written from 1980s to the new millennium. These novels were greatly influenced by Rushdie's *Midnight's Children*. The story of Saleem Sinai triggers off questions of the Indian nation, the historical roots, modern angst and critiques the neo-colonial attitudes of the nation. Illustrations of such novels are the works of Amitav Ghosh, Vikram Seth,

Anita Nair and Shashi Tharoor. If Ghosh subverts colonial constructs in novels such as *The Glass Palace* and *The Shadow Lines* (1988) to derive a postcolonial space, Vikram Seth uses the social reality in *A Suitable Boy* (1989) to ridicule marital arrangements in India. Shashi Tharoor's *The Great Indian Novel* is an interrogation of the political history of the Indian nation through an imaginative re-reading of the great epic of India, the *Mahabharata*. The novel debates upon the political and other aspects and explains modern India as a place fraught with political instability. In fact, the history and the making of the nation had to be objective but Tharoor uses a subjective stance and the narrator, Ved Vyas's point of view many a time is that of Tharoor. The novel instead of narrating history through myth depicts a conflicted history. Gangaji in the novel is a spoof of Gandhiji and takes up Gandhian issues such as cleanliness, celibacy and so on. Just as in *Kanthapura*, the Gandhi ideology is spread out only later to lead Tharoor to comment in the course of his novel, '... we were not led by a saint with his head in the clouds, but by a master tactician with his feet on the ground' (1989: 122).

Similarly, Ghosh in his work, *The Glass Palace* (2000) uses the period of a colonized Burma, to trace the evolution of the novel's protagonists, Rajkumar and Dolly. He sets the tone of his work in Burma, Malaysia and India and extensively uses a spirit of patriotism through multiple set of voices. The novel brings alive Gandhi, Nehru, Bikaji Cama and others in its depiction of the historical contexts. Once again all these novels and writers are carried away by an intensely patriotic homogenous nation's struggle forgetting that their fiction was unable to locate and forge a new identity for the nation. Yet another novelist in this period is Arundhati Roy whose *The God of Small Things* (1997) raises the spectre of casteism, commnunalism, and political ideology. The novel is a fictional commentary on the class structures in society and is also a story of deprivation of rights. In fact, this realistic questioning of the Indian nation led to the next stage of writing, that of Bhagat and Adiga. The contemporary period belongs to novelists such as Chetan Bhagat and Aravind Adiga. Chetan Bhagat, in *The Three Mistakes of My Life* (2008) and *Five Point Someone* (2004), and Aravind Adiga, in *The White Tiger* (2008), raise the issue of a meaningless Indian society that only thrives on a quest for money. Aravind Adiga attempts to depict the relationship between nationalistic identity and other related aspects of the subject such as class, gender and sexuality in *White Tiger*. Utilizing certain socio-cultural and socio-political concepts in the formulation of an Indian identity, the novel tries to reveal how the tropes of marginality work in the Indian nation. The author's attempt to satirize the Indian class structure and the overall theme of national belonging possibly could just be a masquerade. *The White Tiger* at a certain level is thought to be a realistic portrayal of the new India, a negative aspect of the glorious nation. The story depicts a dissonance in the notion of Indianness—India as imagined and India as experienced. The opposition in the novel is between the protagonist, Balram's desires and wishes, and the firmly held beliefs and faiths of the other, in this case, the employers, Mr Ashok and Pinky.

It is, thus, clear to a certain extent that the Indian writers in English may capture an India fraught with all its problems but are quite perturbed by the notions of democracy and secularism. For some reason the Indian novelist writing in English cannot give space for the minorities and seem to make a plea for the existence of the majority population. Thus, fiction to a certain extent seems to have formulated a dubious idea of an Indian identity. Therefore, Indian Writing in English needs to go beyond its myths, its past and chalk out innovative paths by which it can explain the notion of Indian nationalism. In conclusion maybe one can accede with Paranjape when he states, 'When it comes to IE literature a related fallacy of the autonomy and self-sufficiency is also fostered. The idea is that IE literature not only stands on its own, by itself, but is more than adequate to understand India. Thus, willy-nilly, the very multi-lingual and multicultural context of the production or appreciation of this literature is undermined ... . We need more and more to see IE literature in comparison and dialogue with its other Indian languages' (2000: 123).

Works Cited

Ashcroft, Bill, Helen Tiffin, Gareth Griffiths. *The Empire Writes Back*. London: Verso, 1992. Print.

Bhabha, Homi (ed.). *Nation and Narration*. London and New York: Routledge, 1990. Print.

Deshpande, Shashi. Interview by Geetha Gangadharan. 'Denying the Otherness.' *The Fictions of Shashi Deshpande*. Ed. R.S. Pathak. New Delhi: Creative Books, 1998. Print.

Fanon, Frantz. *The Wretched of the Earth*. USA: Grove Press, 1965. Print.

Guha, Ranajit. 'On Some Aspects of Historiography of Colonial India'. *Subaltern Studies* Vol. 8. Delhi: Oxford UP, 1994. 1–8. Print.

Lazarus, Neil (ed.). *Nationalism and Cultural Practice in the Postcolonical Literary Studies*. Cambridge: Cambridge UP, 1999. Print.

Loomba, Ania, Suvir Kaul, Antoinette Burton. *Postcolonial Studies and Beyond*. NC: Duke UP, 2005. Print.

Paranjape, Makarand. *Towards a Poetics of the Indian English Novel*. Shimla: Indian Institute of Advanced Study, 2000. Print.

Rao, Raja. *Kanthapura*. Delhi: Oxford UP, 1989. Print.

Tharoor, Shashi. *The Great Indian Novel*. New Delhi: Penguin India, 1989. Print.

4

Emerging Trends in the 21st Century Indian English Novel

JAGDISH BATRA

The onward march of the genre of Indian Writing in English continues unabated, much to the amazement and, at times, envy of some western litterateurs and critics. Since 1981, when Salman Rushdie won the Booker Prize, writers of Indian origin, whether staying in India or abroad, have been much sought after by the publishers. An idea of the profusion that has taken place can be had from the fact that since the time we stepped into the new millennium, around 300 novels belonging to the 'Indian English Novel' category have appeared. We have people belonging to different vocations—teachers, journalists, doctors, computer professionals and management executives—writing novels. We cannot claim such a growth for other areas like Indian English Poetry. The Indian English Drama is, by far, lagging behind, but the growth in the field of fiction is certainly beyond expectations and it has proved wrong the pessimistic description by some of this genre as a 'hothouse plant' or the forecast of the year 2000 as the 'dirge date' of Indian English literature (Pathak 2001).

At times, the very nomenclature 'Indian Writing in English' or, for that matter, 'Indian English Literature' has given birth to controversies. Does it mean the literature written by Indians only? If yes, whether to include those migrating to other countries or not? What if the writer happens to be from the second or third generation of those who originally emigrated from this country—V.S. Naipaul for instance—who made it big, bagging the Nobel? What would be the status of the Anglo-Indian writers? While Ruskin Bond has lived like any other Indian permanently at Dehradun, poet Dom Moraes and lately, novelist Allan Sealy have preferred to stay out of the country. Again, should Anita Desai's latest novel *The Zigzag Way* (2004) not be included in the gamut of Indian English Novel because she now stays in America and the novel deals with

Mexican locale and characters? The question is not that simple considering the other dimension which is that the writers from E.M. Forster to Gregory Roberts (the writer of *Shantaram*, 2003) have written novels based on Indian life and characters. There is also the dilemma regarding which category to put a writer in, as for example, a writer might belong to the categories of woman writer, diasporic writer, social novelist—all at the same time.

For my purpose, I have tried to skim through with workable parameters which are: novels originally written in English by Indians, whether living in India or abroad; and the later generation diasporic writers if their work has Indian locale, characters or ethos. This study of the Indian English Novel is based upon subjective evaluation which has been sought to be balanced by the comments of established reviewers, fan-following on the Net, awards won and past work of the writer. It may be cynical to take into account the amount of advance royalty paid by a publishing house to an author but even that can make sense, at least, in the commerce-driven world of the popular novel.

Salman Rushdie set the trend with his *Midnight's Children* which eventually won the coveted 'Booker of Bookers' prize in 2008. In this, he beat the other Booker-winning novelists of the past forty years—including Nadine Gordimer and J.M. Coetzee of South Africa, Iris Murdoch of Ireland, Kingsley Amis and William Golding of the UK, Ben Okri of Nigeria, Margaret Atwood and Yann Martel of Canada. It can easily be taken as a clear sign of international recognition for the Indian literary talent. Through this voluminous novel, Rushdie resuscitated the art of mixing miracle with reality that is known as magic(al) realism. One may like it or not, but it was certainly a turn-around from the purely realistic novel.

Some of the socio-economic factors which have gone into shaping the content of this fiction in the twenty-first century revolve around increasing globalization. As skylines of Indian metropolises and the not-so-big cities change, so do the lifestyle and the general outlook of the people. The underlying sentiment is of hope for future which provides a fertile ground for literary activity. Besides, the popular variety of fiction seems to have gained respectability. An indication to this effect is provided by the choice of Aravind Adiga's maiden novel *The White Tiger* (2008) for the Man Booker Prize.

Social/Political Novels

Of the different themes taken up by the novelists in this twenty-first century, the novels with social perspectives outweigh all others. In the postmodern age in which man is considered a socio-cultural product of the times, it seems quite natural that the colossal changes taking place at the social plane should, most of all, draw the attention of the novelists. Within this broad category, the writers have chosen themes like crime, terror, corruption, poverty, etc.

Arvind Adiga upset quite a few veterans when he bagged the Man Booker Prize 2008 for his maiden novel *The White Tiger*. By all accounts, the novel seemed a pale shadow of what had been considered canonical so far, and therefore, makes one wonder whether the award is an attempt to re-write the canon or a simple appreciation of India-bashing, the favourite pastime of the West. Balram Halwai, the protagonist of this novel, hails from a poor family of a backward Indian village. His parents died when he was quite young. Hard times mould him into a worldly-wise, flattering and shrewd chauffeur who is jealous of the rich people. His employer is a typical corrupt businessman who, under pressure of his cunning elder brother, even thinks of foisting the blame for a road accident on the chauffeur. Eventually, Balram murders his master for money. Not only does he steal his money but his identity also, so that he now becomes Ashok and starts a taxi business in Bangalore. In e-mails addressed to the Prime Minister of China, Wen Jiabao, he offers to enlighten him about Indian entrepreneurship citing his own case as an example. The novel also focusses on problems like poverty, violence, injustice and indiscipline in public life, in a language real enough for a semi-literate chauffeur and, therefore, devoid of literary grace. However, the writer fails to convince the reader of the cause of the murder of an otherwise kind master.

V.S. Naipaul's *Magic Seeds* (2004), sequel to his last novel *Half a Life* (2001), appeared at a time when he had declared the 'demise' of novel as a form of literature. Naipaul's passion is to understand the forces of social change. Willie Chandran, the main character, is a listless wanderer in search of meaning in life which eludes him. His domineering sister Sarojini makes him join an underground movement in India that is aimed at liberating the lower castes. Here, he is paired individually with each Maoist insurgent who, in turn, tells him how he joined the movement. However, after seven years he is disillusioned and turns himself in to the police. In jail, he learns more about the caste-ridden society. Finally, he flees back to London, where another failure awaits him in yet another kind of revolutionary activity. The writer wishes to bring home the message that there are actually no magic seeds, no short cuts in life to success. There is a surprise in store for the readers in the form of praise for Gandhi's autobiography.

The widespread corruption in the Indian polity can best be diagnosed by an insider. Upmanyu Chatterjee's Sahitya Akademi Award winning novel *The Mammaries of the Welfare State* (2000) is based upon the personal experiences of the author, a former bureaucrat. The story revolves around a family which has eaten away the country's wealth like termites. It is a powerful satire on the system. Anurag Mathur is another novelist adept at studying the bureaucratic system. While one of his earlier novels focusses on corruption, in *Scenes from an Executive Life* (2000), he takes up the life of a marketing executive in a private company and talks about the travails of this competitive age.

Vikram Chandra, who teaches at the University of California, came out with his third novel *Sacred Games* (2006). Like his earlier novels, this voluminous 900-page novel is also set in Mumbai with its underbelly given wide exposure, what with actresses selling their bodies to get to the top or gangsters influencing politics. The 'sacred game' refers to the execution of the rival don which, according to the killer, is already destined. It has too much of known reality and too little of romance.

By her own admission, Githa Hariharan's main concern has been the study of power politics. Her novel *In Times of Siege* (2003) revolves around the life of a professor of history. A part from focussing on the process of recording of history, she also rakes up contemporary issues like religious fundamentalism, freedom of speech, etc. Her *Fugitive Histories* (2009) is woven around the Godhra carnage and has political overtones. The narrative relies on memory rather than history. In that sense, the approach may be called postmodern. Nayantara Sehgal published her *Lesser Breeds* (2003) which surprisingly talks of non-violence and politics rather than race, gender and sex which formed the themes of her earlier works.

Kiran Nagarkar's *God's Little Soldier* (2006) touches the contemporary issue of growing fundamentalism but in taking up the psychological study of a newly-turned fanatic, disputes its stereotype. Here is a young student Zia who converts to Christianity and becomes Luceus but terrorism is his second nature, religious affiliation notwithstanding. This novel compares well with Mohsin Hamid's *The Reluctant Fundamentalist* (2008), which apart from stylistic elegance offers a ride through aspects of the war against terror.

The changes wrought in society as a result of the globalization have attracted the novelists but mostly the genre of popular novel has been the gainer. However, Usha K.R.'s third novel *Monkey-man* (2010) is a serious work that charts the growth of Bangalore or Bengaluru, as they call it now, from the city of pensioners to its present status as the Silicon Valley of India.

A growing number of novels are being turned into films. Not long ago, Vikas Swarup's debut novel *Q and A* (2005) was turned into the film *Slumdog Millionaire.* While Swarup's first novel has clear linkage with a popular TV show, the second novel *Six Suspects* (2010) is based upon Salman Khan's shooting of black buck and the infamous killing of the bar-girl in Delhi. Another novel, *The Last Flamingoes of Bombay* (2009) written by Siddharth Dhanvant Sanghvi is also based on the Jessica Lal murder case.

The Bhopal Gas tragedy, which shook the conscience of the world forms the subject of Indra Sinha's *Animal's People* (2008). It is a powerful voice raised in favour of the victims though the element of grotesque puts off the reader. Some of the other notable novels covering social themes and published in the year 2010 are: *Blood Ties* by Amita Rathore, *Saraswati Park* by Anjali Joseph, *Come Before Evening Falls* by Manjul Bajaj, and *Lanterns on their Horns* by Radhika Jha.

Family and Feminism

Although family has deservedly been taken up for the study of feminist issues, it is by no means the only domain for such study, nor is woman the centre of every family-based novel. A number of novelists have taken up the workplace of the twenty-first century Indian woman, who is depicted as politically conscious, professionally qualified and raring to prove her worth in man's world.

Most of the writers dealing with the family as background happen to be women. Veteran feminist Shashi Deshpande came out with *Moving On* (2004) which dwells on societal expectations from women even as they play out their various roles assigned to them by society itself. They are expected to show fortitude and grit combined with a moral uprightness. There is just no scope for exercising individual choice here. Deshpande's characters do exhibit such courage but act along axes which might raise eyebrows. In almost all her novels, women's sexuality—within and outside marriage bonds—has been taken up. In this work also, Manjari has extra-marital relations with Rajan and she has the guts to reveal all this to her children.

It is not only the women writers but male writers also can deal with the theme of family quite well. Rohinton Mistry, an Indian Parsi settled in Canada, whose novel *Such a Long Journey* (1991) was recently proscribed by the Maharashtra government under political pressure, came out with his third novel *Family Matters* (2002), which was shortlisted for the Booker Prize. In this novel, Mistry takes up the cause of the aged but he cannot resist his penchant for linking private life to public events which invariably play havoc with ordinary individuals. Despite his nose for nauseating details of dirt and squalor, Mistry's is essentially a compassionate realism. This becomes evident when he deals with the life of a retired professor of English, Nariman Vakeel, who meets with an accident and is confined to bed. The financial problems of his step-children, coupled with low commitment to values, impel them to send the father to his daughter whose husband Yezad does not really like the idea but somehow keeps quiet. The story takes a turn when Yezad wishes to capitalize on the prevailing atmosphere of political blackmailing but does not have the good luck of Balram Halwai of *The White Tiger*, with the result that the rest of his life becomes a saga of repentance.

Individual identity is central to almost all of feminist fiction. A feminist to the core, Manju Kapur is known for challenging the traditional family values in her writings. In 1998, she published her debut novel *Difficult Daughters*. This was followed by *A Married Woman* (2002). The novel examines history and ideologies against the backdrop of Babri demolition. In her third novel *Home*, (2006), Kapur depicts an extended business family based in a suburb of Delhi. She covers a wide canvas and goes into the details of parents and grandparents of the protagonist.

Anita Nair in *Ladies Coupe* (2001) calls upon women to recognize their inherent powers and lead an authentic life. Among other promising novelists is Ruchir Joshi who came out with his *The Last Jet Engine Laugh* (2001), which deals with three generations of a Gujarati family who trace their Indian history back to 1930s. The conflict of generations is brought to the centre stage.

In Upmanyu Chatterjee's *Way to Go* (2010), sequel to *The Last Burden* (1997), eighty-five year old, seriously-ailing, Shyamanand goes missing. His sons Jamun and Burfi reconnect in their old home and in their search for their father find a path out of desolation. In his usual powerful prose peppered with black humour, Chatterjee conducts a moving examination of family ties and the redemptive power of love.

Amit Chaudhuri's *The Immortals* (2009) is the story of two families, one neck-deep in corporate culture and the other hooked on music. Chaudhuri's portrayal of the attractive-but-often-empty life of corporate executives in pre-boom India is masterly. The narrative depends upon petty events from which the writer derives layers of meaning. The disappearance of a South Indian café evokes the end of the old world and ride on a suburban train turns into an odyssey before the novel ends abruptly.

Anita Jain's *Marrying Anita* (2008) and Advaita Kala's *Almost Single* (2007) deal with search for the right guy by female protagonists. Reema Moudgil's *Perfect Eight* (2010) provides a fine peep into woman's heart. Abha Dawesar's *Family Values* (2009) is a vain search for values in contemporary world. Namita Devidayal's *Aftertaste* (2010) is a long narrative of a business family that is naturally obsessed with money only. Manpreet Sodhi Someshwar's *The Long Walk Home* (2009) recounts the life story of an old person with comments on changes in society over a long period. Khushwant Singh too came up with his *The Sunset Club* (2010) which centres round the life of three senior citizens giving voice to their fancies and foibles, their family life and their physical problems.

Individuals/Relationships

In novels focussing mainly on individuals, the issues of identity, love and ambition find focus. Kiran Desai created literary history, when she won the Man Booker Prize 2006 for her novel *The Inheritance of Loss*. At 35, she was the youngest woman to win this coveted prize. The press release marking the occasion described her book as 'a radiant, funny, moving family saga' (Sudarshan 2010: 2). The novel seems inspired by Anita Desai's *Fire on the Mountain* (1978) which narrated the story of an embittered old woman who broke all bonds with the world out of frustration and retired to an old house at Kasauli till such time as her great-grand daughter arrived and took her out of the self-imposed cocooned existence. In Kiran's novel, it is an old judge who retires to a home at Kalimpong in the company of his pet dog and a cook. The mantle for extricating him from this retirement falls on his grand daughter Sai. The story moves from India to the US, recording racism as suffered by the Asian immigrants and the global conflicts of religion, race and nationalism. Style-wise, it may be pointed out here that whereas Anita focuses with single-minded devotion on the psychic study of her characters, Kiran's sweep is wider and her idiom richer.

Ardashir Vakil's *One Day* (2009) focusses on adultery in a narrative of rich interior monologue mode. Another Indian expatriate Hari Kunzru published three novels in the new millennium. *The Impressionist* (2002) is a hero-centric novel in which the protagonist changes places as well as identities. His novel *My Revolutions* (2007) studies identity against the background of a foreign milieu. The Commonwealth Award winner Anita Rau Badami celebrates, in *The Hero's Walk* (2002), the hero in ordinary life—the one who survives odds in class and caste-ridden society.

The novel *Tiger Hills* (2010) by Sarita Mandanna would make anyone sit up when told that this debut novel got an advance of ₹ 35 lakhs from Penguin India. The novel is high on passion but the tempo requires a commensurate insight to sustain itself. Set against the picturesque Coorg, it depicts a love triangle in which the orphan Devanna loves Devi who would rather have Machaiah, the single-handed slayer of a tiger. Machaiah seems to be from hoary past, what with his 12-year 'no-marriage' vow! However, circumstances compel

Devi to marry Devanna and the focus shifts to the next generation of the protagonists. The botanical details delimit the appeal of the plot.

Manu Joseph's debut novel, *Serious Men* (2010), winner of *The Hindu* Best Fiction Award 2010, is also set in suburban Mumbai. It is a funny satire on the money-making people. Love and revenge provide the motive for action which is handled in a very psychological manner. Ayyan Mani, a dalit, has a boring job as P.A. to Arvind Acharya, a scientist. Moved by ambition, Ayyan ropes in his ten-year-old son Adi. Acharya is attracted towards a dubious character Oparna. Meanwhile, it is revealed that the scientist fudged the data which gives a twist to the story. The writer's skill lies in portraying a conman Ayyan in a way that he wins the sympathy of the readers through his intelligence and wit. Shashi Deshpande likes the lack of gimmicks in the novel and finds that 'everything is subordinated to the telling of the story' (Web. 2011).

Anita Nair's latest offering, *Lessons in Forgetting* (2010), shows a woman novelist shouldering the responsibility of running her family. As chance would have it, she gets the companionship of a cyclone expert, who has to look after his nineteen-year-old comatose daughter. The struggle brings them together in an interesting story full of twists and turns.

Anjum Hasan's debut novel, *Lunatic in My Head* (2007) set in Shillong, could be called a regional novel in which the small town life is followed through three characters. Hasan came up with its sequel in *Neti, Neti* (2009). It brings out the loneliness of individual in contemporary familial and social set-up. *Johnny Gone Down,* (2010) the second novel by Karan Bajaj, is a hero-centric novel. This hero is an ordinary man with uncommon approach towards life.

Travel/Adventure

Unlike V.S. Naipaul, who used his travels to study problems of different countries, Pico Iyer, in his novel *Abandon* (2003), has made a foray into the world of Sufism against the backdrop of a world riven by conflicts. An English student Johan Macmillan is studying Sufism in California. While in Damascus, he hears rumours about certain secret manuscripts taken away to Iran. A secretive Camilla Jensen, who is also a neurotic, is connected to the manuscripts. Then suddenly, the manuscripts appear and Camilla disappears. Pico is a pastmaster in creating ambience that comes in handy in describing his travels to various Indian locations. Besides, he leads the reader to mystical spiritual abstractions and to the hidden self.

Irwin Allan Sealy's latest offering, *The Brainfever Bird* (2003) deviates from his usual backdrop of nature and instead places his characters in overcrowded Delhi as also in far off Moscow. It is the story of a spy falling in love with a liberated woman and it runs along the lines of a thriller.

A surprise entry was from the renowned poet Keki N. Daruwalla who also has several stories to his credit. His debut novel *For Pepper and Christ* (2010) projects him as an explorer. The novel recounts Vasco de Gama's expeditions to India as part of the medieval colonial enterprise. Daruwalla has an unquestioned gift of words.

Time and Space

The format of historical novel, though a rarity these days, was taken up by Basavaraj Naikar. His *The Sun behind the Cloud* (2001) deals with the rise and fall of Bhaskararao, the nineteenth century king of Naragunda. His revolt against the British is the high point of the novel as it throws light on the not so-well-known chapter of the first Indian War of Independence. A.K. Srikumar's *The Begum's Secret* (2010) is a novel based upon the history of eighteenth century Awadh. It is a tale of betrayal and greed as also of love and pride. The Nawab is shown starting a food-for-work programme as a famine hits the state. The title refers to the intelligent Bahu Begam's quest for a successor to the throne since her son the Nawab Asaf-ud-Daula is issueless. The novel seems well-researched and life of the period is effectively presented. Jaishree Misra, who is known for her popular romantic novels, published *Rani* (2004) based on the life of Manikarnika, aka Rani of Jhansi.

The diasporic writer Tabish Khair's *The Thing about Thugs* (2010) is a period piece that links India with Victorian England in a mélange of literary styles in the true postmodern sense even though Khair is loath to affixing to himself any literary label. Another diasporic psychoanalyst Sudhir Kakar's *The Crimson Throne* (2010) is based upon the history of succession to Emperor Shah Jehan. His two sons—the spiritually inclined Dara Shikoh and the fanatic Aurangzeb. The writer has thrown in two foreign narrators for whose first person account distinguishes his work. The narrative couched in dry, functional language underlines the truism that sweeping events issue from personal whims also.

A votary of locale-centric narratives, Amitav Ghosh had set his *The Glass Palace* (2000) in Burma. After that *The Hungry Tide* appeared in 2006 and was acclaimed as the most significant book written by an Indian author that year. This novel deals with the experiences of a scientist Piyali, who has come from America to study dolphins in the Sundarbans region of West Bengal. She meets Kanai, who acts as her interpreter. Both of them, along with Fokir, a local fisherman who knows the area too well, go looking for the elusive dolphin. Ghosh explores their complex relationships against the picturesque Sundarbans which has an overbearing influence on the humans, but the scientific and historical details and a meandering pace are the weak points of the novel.

Multiculturalism

The second coming of the twice-born fiction happened with the help of the diasporic community led by Salman Rushdie. It goes to the credit of this community that it continues to nurture the genre of Indian English Fiction in a commendable way. The diasporic novelists are constantly in search of answers to questions of identity, pulled apart as they are between their country of origin and the country of adoption. Even though the angst of the pre-Independence days diaspora of the bonded labour is no longer shared by the young professionals voluntarily migrating in search of greenbucks, the traditionally strong family links still pull them homeward and the casual sense of insecurity due to occasional manifestations of host country's jealousy accentuates longing for home. They, then, remember their past through memory, fantasy and myth and also write about their immigrant experience. Bharathi Mukherjee, even as she refuses to be called an Indian diasporic writer, deals with the predicament faced by the Indian immigrants to the West, in her novel *Desirable Daughters* (2002). Tara Chatterjee, the protagonist, comes from the Bengali *bhadralok* family steeped in conservatism. Married to an Indian expatriate in the US, she is stung by the American cultural bug and goes in for a makeover, divorces her conservative husband, takes on an American lover, winks at the gay proclivities of her son but after sometime when she meets her ex-husband, the deep-rooted Indian sensibility asserts itself hinting at the incompleteness of the cultural metamorphosis.

Jhumpa Lahiri in her debut novel *The Namesake* (2003) weaves a story covering three decades of the Ganguli household in the USA and displays a fine-tuned sensibility that combines realism—both psychological and social with an economy of description that does not miss out on effect. The Ganguli couple's immigrant experience is contrasted with the acculturation of their America-born children. The naming of their son as Gogol and later as Nikhil represents a conflict between different identities. Through her masterly art, Jhumpa underlines the efforts required to mediate between people and situations as also between cultures and social practices.

Anita Desai has stayed in America for a long time now and her latest novel *The Zigzag Way* (2004) ushers in a pleasant change in that the setting and characters are non-Indian. Eric is an American who locates his roots in Mexico. Desai brings into play the Indian humanist sensibility while describing the travails of Eric's grandparents who were miners destined to die toiling in pits.

Chitra Banerjee Divakaruni's *One Amazing Thing* (2010) tells the story of nine persons gathered in the Indian embassy to get Visa. Suddenly, a quake demolishes the building and all of them are trapped. Without any hope of early escape, Uma suggests that they all share one amazing thing from their lives, to pass time, a la *The Canterbury Tales*. The characters are a mixed lot—Indian, Chinese, a Muslim American, English et al. and the stories have different contexts. There is reason to believe that what comes out of one with the proverbial sword of Damocles hanging over their heads would be true and authentic. However, the ending is inconclusive.

Amitabha Chatterjee's novel *Of Wooing, Woes and Wanderings* (2010) takes for its location the far-off Venezuela besides other places where the protagonist Rajarshi travels in connection with his job working at the oil-rigs. Tishani Doshi's *The Pleasure Seekers* (2010) is a novel that describes a multicultural family. Similarly, Nikita Lalwani's *Gifted* (2008) takes up the problems of the Indian immigrants to the US at the cultural level.

The first decade of the twenty-first century saw the glorious emergence of popular fiction led by Chetan Bhagat, who has been hailed as the largest selling writer of India. The genre of popular novel known by different names like Metro Reads or Quick-Reads is well-established now. It targets the young readers with little time but with plenty of penchant for reading. Other divisions of this broad popular category are—Young Women's Fiction Tech-lit, Campus-lit and

Career-lit. Major themes in this fast-emerging genre are campus and office comedies, life in a particular profession, live-in relationships, extra-marital relations, and practically anything that could be of interest to the youth—all couched in racy, colloquial language.

Chetan Bhagat's *Five Point Someone* (2004) belongs to the nascent breed of Campus Novel whose early practitioners include Prema Nandkumar, Rita Joshi et al. Bhagat makes fun of the education system which looks down upon mediocrity. Bhagat's second novel *One Night @ The Call Centre* (2005) deals with the contemporary life of the youth working at call centres. As the title indicates, within the span of a night, the youthful workers undergo experiences as varied as dancing at a disco and then listening to God's voice in a moment of crisis. The novel weaves a high romantic tale in simple language peppered with a smattering of slang. His third novel *The 3 Mistakes of My Life* (2008) cashes in on the craze for cricket in India. In between he has hitched the plot to the Gujarat earthquake, the Godhra train burning and the riots. The only lesson one can derive from it is that there is no effective reconciliatory mechanism in cases of communal riots. Unlike his previous offerings, Bhagat's *Two States: The Story of My Marriage* (2009) has not generated similar response.

Suman Hossain's *A Guy Thing* (2010) is a campus novel, in which an IITian, Sahil, shows the courage to follow his dreams. References in such novels to SMS-ing, Orkut-ing mobile-dating and online-chatting are bound to be common. Hostel life, romance and studies weave the warp and woof of the novel. Another campus novel by Daman Singh appeared under the title *Nine by Nine*. This one concerns the students of a girls college with focus on a relaxed pace of life. Anirban Bose's *Bombay Rains, Bombay Girls* (2008) celebrates success and not mediocrity. Leena Walawalkar's *You've Got To Be Kidding* (2002) is a Campus Novel but the students are not teenagers; they have left jobs to join the London School of Business. Neeraj Chhibba's *Zero Percentile* (2009) is the story of an IIT-entrance exam failed young man who goes over to Russia to study engineering.

Nothing can be as Crazy (2009), maiden novel by Ajay Mohan Jain, an IIT-ian, falls in the category of Career Novels. It focuses on love and vocational life of Suresh, a bank probationary officer. *Married but Available* (2008) by Abhijit Bhaduri, an HR professional, follows the life of friends who have passed out of B-school and embark on the journey through the corporate world. *Call me Dan* (2010)—a maiden piece by former banker Amish Trivedi is another call centre based novel. Sujita Nair, a former army officer-turned-writer has come out with her debut novel *She's a Jolly Good Fellow* (2010) which is a story of two women army officers who take on adversities, learning their lessons the hard way. There can be no two opinions about the fact that her description of life in the army should be authentic.

Quite a few fictional works have been produced by the people working with the media. One such novel is *If I could Tell you* (2009) by Soumya Bhattacharya, tells the story of an investor who is undone by the market crash. The novel is in the form of a series of confessional letters written to the narrator's daughter. In *Love from the Sidelines* (2010) by Mayank Anand, the protagonist Samira, an artist, tells her story in the first person. Ravi Subramanian's *Devil in Pinstripes* (2009) is the writer's third novel and is based upon corporate politics as played out in an MNC. Bhavna Chauhan's *Where Girls Dare* (2010) is about girl cadets at Chennai's Officers' Training Academy and Uttam Paritosh's *Drams in Prussian Blue* (2010), is about the life of a young unmarried couple. Sumit Basu's *The Simoqin Prophecies* (2006), Sagarika Ghosh's *The Gin Drinkers* (2000) and Rana Dasgupta's *Tokyo Cancelled* (2005) are some of the other popular novels which have won international readership.

In Young Woman's Fiction category Anuja Chauhan's *The Zoya Factor* (2008) is high on romance between an advertising executive and a cricket player. The story-line includes female bonding and booze parties. *Right Fit Wrong Shoe* (2009) by Varsha Dixit is a racy thriller of contemporary liberated lifestyle. Swati Kaushal's *Piece of Cake* (2004) has an Indian working girl as the central character in an interesting plot that is imbued with humour. Jaishree Misra's novels like *Secrets and Lies* (2009), *Secrets and Sins* (2010) and *Afterwards* (2004) establish her as a brilliant novelist with her deft use of male point of view.

In these postcolonial times, the marginalized groups like gays and lesbians are finding voice. However, Siddharth Sanghvi's *The Last Song of Du*sk (2004), which graphically describes lesbian ways of physical relationship, as also Tarun Tejpal's *Alchemy of Desire* (2005), which deals with characters high on sex, are a class apart. Dwelling on the human side of the queer class is one thing and dishing out 'sexcitement' and titillation for the sake of selling wares is quite another. We need perhaps to remind ourselves of what constitutes great literature—that which is as contemporaneous tomorrow as it is today.

Miscellaneous

Science fiction does not have deep roots in Indian Writing in English. Jayant Narlikar, a famous scientist himself, wrote *The Return of Vaman* in 1989 which is considered an important piece of work, particularly for the children. Amitav Ghosh supplied this genre, through his *The Calcutta Chromosome* (1996), with what was lacking in Narlikar's work, namely, a literary style. Hari Kunzru's *Transmission* (2005) is quite interesting as it tells of an Indian software expert Arjun who gets laid off in America and in a revengeful mood releases a deadly virus that shakes the entire world, reaching finally his favourite Bollywood star.

Old style murder mysteries also find occasional authors as in the case of Rajkamal Jha's *Fireproof* (2007) in which the victim's ghost has been thrown in to advantage. Vikram Seth's *Two Lives* (2005) and Ved Mehta's *The Red Letters* (2004) are biographical novels. Style-wise, Gautam Malkani has come up with his *Londonstani* (2007), which uses SMS-text abbreviations—something the youth is so much in love with today but not many find the usage easy to comprehend.

Conclusion

From this brief study, some conclusions can be drawn. One, the contemporary Indian English Novel that was rejuvenated by the Indian diaspora is still dominated by it. On the whole, we find that Indian English Novel is the monopoly of the city-bred middle class elite—the privileged public school-educated or the foreign-educated ones. Motivated by the success stories of some recent novelists, they write for the English-reading privileged classes within India or the international public outside. The role of the literary agents of the West has been found to be very significant in bringing fame and awards to upcoming writers. Clearly, this type of writing has its own preferences and limitations. The diasporic writing mostly banks upon media reports which capture reality selectively and sensationally so that what comes to light may not be the entire truth.

Further, if the diasporic of today is not able to put into print his famed sense of loss, the contemporary Indian writer also is not given to pondering seriously the Indianness that should be the hallmark of his or her novel. This class, whose 'abrogation of standard English' is considered by some as the 'sign of a certain cultural weightlessness' (Mee 2008: 361) has been responsible for selling to the West an obnoxious/exotic India. In the name of Indian reality, what we get is only a reaffirmation of the Western suspicion of our ability to govern ourselves. Is it all that is to India?

Two, despite the spurt in popular fiction, most of which falls in the category of kitsch or pulp fiction, it is a fact that the record of sale of Chetan Bhagat's books has remained unbroken. For one, it is good that this genre has been shorn of its larger-than-life image; it now occupies a niche that rightfully belongs to it. At the same time, the surge indicates widening of the readership which is a welcome sign. The trends in popular fiction are also set by publishing houses just as it happens in the case of commercial films. If a little titillation can sell, they would certainly go in for it. But there is always scope for better works. The important thing here is that the kitsch should not supplant serious literature and should be known for its actual worth.

Three, the impact of the theoretical debates raging in the Western academies is faithfully recorded in the literature produced in India. So, the concept of nation, history, subjectivity and society are sought to be problematized with abandon and without the least consideration for the context and the consequences. To my mind, deconstructing the concept of nation to underline its imaginary nature may be good theory, fit for academies, but is certainly bad in practical terms, as was the other utopian ideal of stateless society. For that matter, even the local identities, which the toast of the academics at present, are imaginary in essence. Is it possible to safeguard any local identity without providing for any overarching identity at the level of nation-state in the contemporary power-hungry world? How many countries in the world would choose to go in for their own balkanization into small Greek city states?

Four, the spirit of postmodernism seems to have moved the Indian English writer only unidirectionally. Although he is all for the alternate history and is ready to lend his ear to the narratives circulating in the public domain, yet his choice is dictated by political ideologies. What seems missing in this postmodern picture is the place that should be due to the Indian culture and thought.

Works Cited

Mee, Jon. 'After Midnight: The Novel in the 1980s and 1990s.' *A Concise History of Indian Literature in English*. Ed. Arvind Krishna Mehrotra. Ranikhet: Permanent Black, 2008. Reprint 2010. Print.

Pathak, R.S. 'Contemporary Indian Fiction in English: Some Recent Trends in Themes and Techniques.' *Points of View* 8.1 (2001). Print.

Sudarshan, Aditya. 'Indian Publishing Needs to Get Less Fun.' *The Hindu* (4 July 2010). Print.

The Hindu Fiction Award for 2010 Current Affairs. www.wikiind.com/2011/01/hindu_fiction_award_for 2010.html.web.

5

Re-presentations of Colonialism in Indian Fiction in English

RAJESHWAR MITTAPALLI

> "The past continues to speak to us."
>
> —Stuart Hall

> "… in postcolonial writing, the historical record never gets wiped clean."
>
> —Sage Wilson

> "… history does not just provide a background to the study of texts, but forms an essential part of textual meaning."
>
> —Ania Loomba

Indian history is the stuff tragedies are made of. The history of colonialism in India needs to be told and retold, not from an ideological/disciplinary stand point as is the case with the official project of writing, and then rewriting, history valorizing religious or ideological constituents, but from a politically non-partisan point of view. For thousands of years India had had no tradition of historiography.[1] History was recorded, if ever it was recorded, in the form of official chronicles and hagiographies of the rulers and does not thus serve the purpose of truth. To gain an objective idea of the past one has to depend on collective memory, folk tales, legends and formal literature. That this should happen in the case of history of the recent three centuries as well is unfortunate, but still the literary source, especially fiction, seems to be the most reliable because the novelists have no stated reason to be untrue to themselves or to their readers about history. Although their primary focus is on the characters and their vicissitudes, history often finds a concomitant articulation in their writings.

The attitude of Indian novelists in English towards the Raj has been characterized by ambivalence—articulating their ideological oppositionality on the one hand and approving of its many merits on the other. There is, except in a couple of novels, no outright condemnation of the colonial rule or open espousal of the nationalist cause, as these writers have taken a balanced view of things, giving the British credit where credit is due and faulting their own countrymen when they deserved it. This is so unlike what happens in popular Indian cinema, TV serials and to an extent in the national literatures, wherein the colonial rulers are essentialized and invariably depicted as devils. I, therefore, propose to offer an unbiased, common man's and commonsense perspective on colonialism in India as it emerges, even if somewhat patchily, in the fictional works of Indian writers in English.

At this point let us, however, ask a pertinent question: Where does the story of colonialism in India begin? What was the truth of the pre-British India? India has been home to one of the oldest civilizations. The first flowering of human mind, probably along side in Greece, occurred here. Living in congenial physical environment and enjoying complete freedom from religious impositions Indians were given to fine philosophical speculations, and to the development and refinement of arts, sciences and other mental faculties. In spite of these intellectual attainments Indians were politically not united, except for a brief three centuries during the Gupta era, nor militarily prepared, and that made the Muslim conquest and then the British conquest of India infinitely easier. But political disunity and being militarily ill-equipped were not the only reasons. There have been deep-seated psychological debilities for the repeated occurrence of colonialism in India. What I am referring to is that Indians were governed by a wrong philosophy known in this part of India as *rajyam veera bhojyam*, meaning that the crown belongs to the conqueror. Now this conqueror need not be an Indian or a Hindu. It could be a foreigner, even one so outrageously different as the British. The Hindus had a tendency to submit to the will of this conqueror and be ruled by him. Added to this unhelpful philosophy was the belief of the Indian ruling class, the *Kshatriyas,* that they should be killed in action, and not die a natural death, in order to gain sure admission into the Hindu heaven. For this reason even when there was no compelling reason for going to war with a real or perceived enemy, the men of this warrior caste used to provoke one on some flimsy emotional grounds and die in action in the hope of attaining *veer swarga*, the part of heaven reserved for the war-dead.

Given this philosophical and military background, colonialism soon made its advent in India at the turn of the previous millennium. Seven centuries of unfriendly rule that followed had laid the country waste, intellectually and economically, and robbed it of all its energy and will power. The humiliation meted out to the Indians by the British colonial rulers is insignificant when compared to the injuries inflicted on the Indian psyche by these conquerors and their descendants.

Thus, by the time the British arrived in India, Indians had already been something of veteran colonial subjects. Given the experience of terrible repression for centuries on end at the hands of various colonial rulers the British were not exactly unwelcome, for they somehow represented the lesser of the two evils. By the time the British arrived on the Indian political scene India had reached an impasse, socially and politically, with complete anarchy and lawlessness reigning all around. Indians had lost the idea of how to govern themselves. With hundreds of princely states fighting each other for power and territory, there used to be incessant and internecine wars raging across the country, quite literally bleeding it. There is, thus, perhaps something teleological about the establishment of the British colonial rule in India. India had reached a dead-end politically, Balkanised and strife-torn, and demonstrated suicidal tendencies. There was no way of keeping the Indians from committing a collective hara-kiri. One has to only read *The Sword of Tipu Sultan* (1976) by Bhagwan S. Gidwani to understand the chaos that India was before the British came.

Now, to ask the question why Indians lost out to the British should look a bit naive. Political disunity together with lack of military hardware facilitated this time the British conquest of India because the British came with their deadly war machines, and deadly designs. There was nothing in India to match their fire power or military strategy. In addition, they possessed an evil genius, sharpened and perfected by a long experience of wars overseas, which came in handy to subdue and conquer an already hopelessly fragmented India. They knew that most native rulers had scores to settle with their neighbours and therefore they strategically offered the services of their well trained and better equipped mercenary forces, consisting mainly of Indian sepoys, to one Indian ruler to defeat another in a series of wars, giving the Indian rulers the impression that they were playing the natives' game. It, however, became painfully clear in course of time that the British were playing their own game and nobody else's. But then it was too late; India was already a British colony. In his novel *Red Earth and Pouring Rain* (1995) Vikram Chandra gives us a glimpse of the British machinations and their mercenary wars by fictionalizing the lives of James 'Sikander' Skinner and Benoit de Boigne who took active part in that historical process.

Having succeeded in establishing a colonial regime in India by force and manipulative power the British realized to their surprise that they were for the first time meeting their match on the cultural, literary and religious fronts.[2] Of all their colonies, it was only in India that the British found a written literary tradition, several well-codified music and dance forms that outmatched anything the English had ever known in terms of antiquity, aesthetic appeal and finesse, and a religion which was formless and undefined, but which governed the lives of people and dated back to the prehistoric times. It was not surprising then that, to start with, they should have shown 'all signs of being ... integrated into Indian society.'[3] Then and indeed in later times, they were so attracted to India, specially its ancient learning and literature, Hinduism and its hoary traditions, that despite the professed colonial objective of economic exploitation of India, a significant number of conscientious British administrators and other functionaries felt morally compelled to contribute to its cultural, economic and even political advancement. The first in the line comes William Jones (1746–94) who made invaluable contribution to Indology by his research into Indian culture and his philological studies comparing Sanskrit with classical Greek and

Latin. C.P. Brown (1798–1884), who worked in the Madras Presidency, compiled the first Telugu dictionary and gave the Telugu language a shape, apart from translating some popular Telugu poetry into English. James Prinsep (1799–1840) worked in the Calcutta mint as assay master but he devoted all his energies and resources to the study of Indian inscriptions and numismatics. In his capacity as the secretary of the Asiatic Society and as the editor of the *Journal of the Asiatic Society of Bengal* he did much to make some sense of India's 'fluid' past. Arthur Cotton (1803–99), a British general who worked in Madras Engineers regiment, built big irrigation projects across river Godavari and river Cauveri, braving many odds, and contributed to the prosperity of the region. He is revered even today as a great benefactor by the grateful Telugu people who have put up as many as 3,000 statues of him in the Godavari and Krishna delta region alone. Verrier Elvin (1902–64) made common cause with the freedom fighters, risking the wrath of the British India Government. He started off as a Christian Missionary but eventually took such a great liking for the Hindu way of life that he converted to Hinduism and permanently settled down in India and married a Gond tribal girl. All his life he worked for the upliftment of the tribals. After Independence, the Government of India utilized his services as a consultant on tribal development and as the chief of the Anthropological Survey of India.

Nayantara Sahgal, in her novel *Plans for Departure* (1986), fashions a British character, Henry Brewster, after these Englishmen. Henry suffers from 'attacks of ruling-class consciousness' (28). He recommends 'policy changes, suggesting ... whole populations could not be treated with suspicion' (71). He is greatly perturbed by the persecution of anti-British activists such as Bal Gangadhar Tilak and Khudiram Ghose on trumped-up charges of sedition. Gen. Massy Hugh Wheeler, in Manohar Malgonkar's *The Devil's Wind* (1972), establishes warm friendship with Nana Saheb's family although this is unwarranted in the colonial context, marries an Indian woman, and even adopts Indian customs and food habits. His real life counterpart was betrayed and beheaded during the Mutiny by sepoys owing allegiance to Nana Saheb but probably without his knowledge. Bakha, the quintessential outcaste of the Hindu society in Mulk Raj Anand's novel *Untouchable* (1935) is treated far more humanely by the British soldiers and Missionaries than his own upper caste countrymen.

The received history of India has taken the view that the British rulers encouraged Christianized education, projected Europe as civilized and India as backward and semi-barbaric and attempted to denigrate Indian culture, belief systems and traditions. This may all have been attempted to legitimize the colonial rule and probably also driven by the arrogant feeling of ethnic superiority. There is absolutely no gainsaying that. But the benefits of the British rule cannot be ignored. In spite of themselves and probably to facilitate administration, the colonial rulers introduced India to modern technology, established communication lines across the country, put in place modern systems of governance, health care and education, administration of justice, rule of law and exposed creative minds to modern forms of literary expression such as the novel, which were employed in due course for subversive purposes. B.C.

Chatterjee, who was a deputy magistrate in the colonial administration and an obvious beneficiary of the English education, shapes his novel *Anandamath* (1882) as a subversive text to expose the economic exploitation of the East India Company.

After the three centuries of peace during the Gupta era, for the first time in about two thousand years the British rulers established a reign of peace that gave the Indians the first opportunity to think of their own brand of renaissance. Western rationalism, which trickled down to the Indians through educational channels, led to the abolition of outmoded traditions such as sati and reformation on the religious front leading to the founding of Arya Samaj and Brahmo Samaj by Dayanand Saraswati and Rammohun Roy, respectively. The works of the chief Indian renaissance literary figure Rabindranath Tagore, especially *Gora* (1910), critique the orthodoxies of Hinduism and underscore the need for reformation and rejuvenation in order for India to be intellectually reborn.

By bringing the whole country under a centralized administration and by checking the excesses of the native rulers, who were whimsical in matters of administration and often meted out summary justice, the British gave the Indians, again for the first time in thousands of years, the idea of their belonging to one nation. It was not because of *narration* or *metaphysics* but because of these concrete administrative measures that Indians came to see themselves as citizens of one nation. Enumerating the benefits and detriments of the British rule, Dadabhai Naoroji named in 1871 the following among the political advantages accruing to India:

> *Politically:* Peace and order. Freedom of speech and liberty of the press. Higher political knowledge and aspirations. Improvement of government in the native states. Security of life and property. Freedom from oppression caused by the caprice or greed of despotic rulers, and from devastation by war. Equal justice between man and man (sometimes vitiated by partiality to Europeans). Services of highly educated administrators, who have achieved the above-mentioned results (131-36).

And as recently as in July 2005, the then Prime Minister Manmohan Singh asserted that—

> Today, with the balance and perspective offered by the passage of time and the benefit of hindsight, it is possible for an Indian Prime Minister to assert that India's experience with Britain had its beneficial consequences too. Our notions of the rule of law, of a Constitutional government, of a free press, of a professional civil service, of modern universities and research laboratories have all been fashioned in the crucible where an age old civilization met the dominant Empire of the day.[8]

Ironically the British also gave the Indians a reason to be united as brothers in suffering by ill-treating everybody alike, calling every Indian—Brahmin or Pariah—a coolie and by heaping common humiliation upon them. One is reminded of Khushwant Singh's short story 'Karma' in which the protagonist, the English educated Sir Mohan Lal, is called a coolie and thrown out of a first-class train compartment by two British soldiers in spite of his being in possession of a valid ticket. The arrogation of superiority by the 'twice-born' castes became for a while largely irrelevant. Thus, in Raja Rao's *Kanthapura* (1938), the villagers, who are otherwise split along caste and communal lines, forget their differences in the face of a common enemy, the colonial rulers, and rise in revolt as one man.

Whatever may have been the purpose for which the British introduced English in India it gave the Indians a voice to speak for themselves and eventually to speak against the British. English facilitated communication across the vast country and helped the exchange of views among intellectuals and nationalist leaders. And above all, English proved to be a new vehicle for creative expression—Indian Writing in English, which is currently such a rage all over the world winning almost every well-known literary prize. It is the only pan-Indian literature, rising above narrow linguistic, culture/region specific considerations. The English language also acted as a great levelling force by neutralizing the superiority arrogated by certain sections of Indian society who made much of their knowledge of Sanskrit and Persian and by allowing the common man to speak the rulers' language, one that gave him an opportunity to acquire an elevated social status and offered opportunities of gainful employment. Although in later times English went on to become the language of power and power-wielders it is still the most important factor which holds India together. It is, thus, that English education in India has not been an unmitigated evil.

The first serious challenge to British colonialism, referred to variously as the Sepoy Mutiny by the British and as the First War of Independence in the nationalist historiography, occurred in 1857 and occurred for the wrong reasons. It was not an expression of resentment against a mere business company ruling a vast country, treating it as a matter of national shame, but a haphazard and desultory rebellion roused by soldiers whose religious sentiments were hurt by the purported use of certain animal extracts in the ammunition on the one hand and the company's pursuit of Doctrine of Lapse, disinheriting childless native rulers, on the other. Even Jawaharlal Nehru locates this revolt outside the nationalist agenda when he says:

> Essentially it was a feudal outburst, headed by feudal chiefs and their followers and aided by the widespread anti-foreign sentiment .... The feudal chiefs had the sympathy of the masses over large areas, but they were incapable, unorganized and with no constructive ideal or community of interest .... There was hardly any national and unifying sentiment among the leaders and mere anti-foreign feeling, coupled with a desire to maintain their feudal privileges, was a poor substitute for this (323-24).

The Mutiny was doomed to be a failure from the beginning because it started for the wrong reasons and it was ill coordinated. Its leaders had no unanimity of opinion nor could they communicate with each other. The sepoys, for example, seized the telegraph system, but had no technical knowledge to use it. Communication could not flow between Delhi, Awadh, Cawnpore and Jhansi, the centres from where the rebellion spread. The leaders—all disgruntled native rulers—were concerned more about keeping their thrones, inheritances, and pensions and continuing their line of descent than about larger national issues. Of these Bahadur Shah, the last Mughal, was not even willing to be the 'emperor' of India. He was almost literally forced to sit on the throne by the mutineers. The others, including Nana Saheb and the much eulogised Rani of Jhansi, pitted themselves against the British only after they had lost legal battles in England to keep their pensions. Once Bahdur Shah was declared the Emperor of India the first thing his supporters, as well as those of Nana Saheb in Cawnpore, did was to molest English women or keep them in captivity for sexual gratification. Khushwant Singh's *Delhi: A Novel* (1990) has devoted some space to the Mutiny, and a character candidly admits: 'It's been my heart's greatest desire to make love to a white woman .... Mirza Sahib. I have to thank you for fulfilling my ambition' (Singh 191). When the Mutiny was put down the English on their part indulged in reprisals of the worst kind—summary trials and mass executions of not just the rebels but even women and children. Thus both the parties to the conflict were immature and emotional in their reaction. The psychological fallout of the Mutiny was that the British, who were till then on friendly enough terms with the Indians at all levels, often going to the extent of taking native wives or mistresses, began to intensely distrust Indians, a distrust which finds its subtlest expression in E.M. Forster's *A Passage to India* (1924) when the British woman Adela Quested accuses the honest Dr Aziz of making indecent advances even when she is not sure.

The English novels on the Mutiny, and there are some seventy of them,[4] invariably demonize its leaders and valorise the nondescript English civil and military officers as great heroes. I am sure these novels are not taken too seriously even in England today. But the myths concerning the Mutiny leaders persist in India. In fact, many Indians did not support the Mutiny, not because they liked the British but because it would have once again brought the oppressive feudal rule back with its attendant evils. In later times, once power passed to the British Crown these same Maharajas and Nawabs settled down to an easy life of luxury and plenty. In spite of their over-sized egos, they were not averse to submitting to the authority of a central power—it was the Mughals in the past and the British now. During the 'darbar' periodically hosted by the Viceroy, they used to behave in such a servile fashion that the unorthodox Prince Rabi in Kamala Markanadaya's *The Golden Honeycomb* (1977) feels greatly ashamed of his father's cringing.

The British were clever in that they did not harm the egos of these princes: by devising the ingenious 'subsidiary alliance' system they allowed them to keep external trappings of power but actually lorded it over them. On completing the colonial conquest of India the British could have abolished the feudal economic and political order. Its abolition would have put India on the path to progress much earlier. The British did nothing of the sort. Instead, perhaps for fear of a repetition of the Mutiny and in line with the feudal traditions back home, a royal proclamation was made extending and reaffirming protection to the princely states and assuring their rulers of their privileges, rights and dignities. An opportunity thrown up by history was thus lost. Their interest was mainly economic in nature and they could achieve their economic objectives not by spending money and energy on administering a vast and quite frankly ungovernable country but by operating from behind the scenes, through the façade of the princes. It suited everyone well, except of course the common people, who were made to pay heavy taxes and subjected to many indignities.

Not surprisingly, therefore, there was uneven economic development and social advancement between the British-administered areas and the princely states. The native rulers were not interested in the economic welfare of their subjects. Having to do no fighting now, nor required to be on guard all the time, they indulged in pastimes and luxuries.[5] Some of these pastimes are rather amusing. Diwan Jeremy Das in his book *Maharaja* (1981) recounts some of them, often giving them an ironic twist: there was, for example, this Maharaja who preferred to use whisky instead of warm water in his bathtub and another of his species who played chess in his palace garden with real-life pawns. Ranga Rao's *Fowl Filcher* (1987) fictionalizes the quirks of the Maharajas when the 'Dog Raja' of the novel spends lavishly on the celebration of the wedding of his bitch with the dog of his sister, while the people he rules over undergo immense suffering. Mulk Raj Anand's *The Private Life of an Indian Prince* (1953) mounts a scathing attack on these feudal lords and their cruelty, their indifference to the suffering of the subjects and their megalomania. The eccentric protagonist of the novel, 'Victor Edward George' Ashok Kumar is the tyrannical ruler of Sham Pur. He is given to womanizing and ill-treating his subjects by levying heavy taxes, and often confiscating their property when they cannot pay these taxes. Caught in the snare of power and lust, he progressively loses his mind.

A large majority of these princes lived in the illusion that the British Raj would last for ever and that they would endlessly enjoy protection, power and privileges. They were so lost in this make-believe world that Nayantara Sahgal, in her novel *Mistaken Identity* (1988), has to get the prince, Bhushan Singh, arrested and thrown into the company of political activists in jail to get him to understand the momentous events taking place around him on the political front. But even when the princes entertained nationalist feelings and sympathised with the Gandhian cause, these feelings were either abandoned soon, as in Manohar Malgonkar's *The Princes* (1963), or were inspired by the prospect of sharing power in a future democratic order which the shrewd among them could foresee. The heir apparent to the Devapur State and son of Bawajiraj III by his mistress Mohini, prince Rabi in Markandaya's *The Golden Honeycomb* already referred to earlier, thus espouses the people's cause, with an eye on power in the future political order, although this intention is never explicitly stated. While some princesses such as Laila of Attia Hussain's *Sunlight on a Broken Column* (1961) seem to quietly mourn the demise of the feudal order together with is privileges, Jaya Singh of Gita Mehta's *Raj* (1989) cleverly prepares herself to be a feudal ruler as well as an elected representative! The princes have been the protagonists of literary works, popular legends, and folk-tales since the very beginning of civilization in India. Now, in the works of these novelists, they stand exposed, deglamourised and stripped of their glory. No tears were shed when the curtain was finally drawn on their rule.

The second challenge to the British colonial rule was posed by the nationalist movement led by the Congress, but it gathered momentum only with the advent of Mahatma Gandhi on the political scene soon after the conclusion of the First World War. Gandhi was a man of indomitable will, indefatigable spirit and sparkling personal honesty who wielded enormous moral authority. He gave an altogether new interpretation to the concept of politics. However, R.C. Majumdar and other historians have often pointed out how no serious and objective evaluation of Gandhi or the nationalist struggle has been permitted by the successive governments. It again seems to fall to the part of the novelists to challenge orthodox views about Gandhi and his ideology since they can always seek refuge in poetic licence. In several of her novels, starting with *A Time to be Happy* (1963) till *Plans for Departure* (1985) Nayantara Sahgal has brought the Gandhian thought under the critical microscope and often pointed out what is wanting in it.

Gandhi, who is seen as a messiah, deified in popular imagination and honoured with a statue put up to his memory in every village and town, pursued a policy of political dissent—peaceful non-cooperation, passive resistance and civil disobedience—that served the purpose of raising political awareness among the masses and of removing the fear of the law from amidst them in the immediate context. His intention in employing these 'weapons of peace' was certainly noble—to morally compel the British to quit India by constantly telling them that they were unwelcome and unwanted—but he could not visualize the implications of his methods to the post-Independence India. He taught the Indians how to disrupt work in order to express their political dissent, but did not regard it necessary to mentally prepare them for hard work when they would be in charge of their own destiny. His method of civil disobedience, which in essence translated in the post-Independence period as indiscipline in public life, has been since frequently misused by groups working against national interests. Tara Bannerjee in Bharati Mukherjee's *The Tiger's Daughter* (1971) and Rahel and Estha in Arundhati Roy's *The God of Small Things* (1997) thus witness how, in pursuit of their sectarian goals, such groups resort to modern versions of these methods and intimidate honest and law-abiding citizens.

Gandhi should have known that Indians developed an apathetic attitude towards work, having been required for ages to serve foreign masters, and that asking them to strike work, as an expression of dissent, would prove disastrous to the economy in the long run. After gaining Independence, Nehru, who was a workaholic, had to pathetically plead with people to work hard through his slogan *aaram haram hai* (rest is illegitimate). Further, Gandhi's message of tolerance resulted in the long run in Indians accepting with resignation the most intolerable situations such as having to offer a bribe to gain admission into a government hospital or to obtain a driving license. Freedom won by paying a price and by means of sacrifice would have been taken more seriously and threats to it by way of corruption, extremism, and communal strife would have been firmly dealt with. The one nationalist leader who made a serious enough effort to free India from the colonial yoke by military means, and who met with a tragic but heroic death in the process, namely Subhas Chandra Bose, inspires among young Indians today greater patriotism than all other leaders put together. By insisting on non-violence Gandhi was inadvertently doing what the British secretly wished—containing the underground activists who waged a violent campaign against the colonial regime.[6] The narrator in Shauna Singh Baldwin's novel *What the Body Remembers* (2000) points out how Gandhi did not protest when Bhagat Singh was executed. In return for what they saw as his 'cooperation' or 'least opposition' the British allowed him freedom of movement and speech. In any authoritarian regime he would have been extracted from the political context at the first sign of trouble and assigned to an obscure prison cell for life, but the British did not do that. He was an unconscious, and certainly unwitting, ally and he served to deflect the attention of the people by making them believe that they were fighting an epic battle of Independence and that way preventing their dissent from taking a violent turn. It is significant to note that the almost complete cessation of organized revolutionary movements in the mid-1930s coincided with the widespread prevalence of Gandhian thought in the Indian political arena. The British were insensitive to the moral pressure he imagined he was putting on them and did not take the whole campaign itself seriously enough. Finally, they left India because the Second World War drained them of their spirit and resources. They also realized that they could not command the loyalty of the Indian soldiers any longer as testified by the ease with which the Indian National Army was formed by Subhas Chandra Bose and the mutiny of the Royal Indian Navy in Bombay in February 1946. Above everything else, the administration of India was increasingly becoming unviable in economic terms. Towards the very end of the colonial rule they were so eager to quit India that Viceroy Archibald Wavell even threatened the British Government with resignation if it delayed the Indian Independence any further.

The front ranking followers of Gandhi were an enlightened lot and they had an intellectual commitment to achieving freedom and furthering national interests. But among those on the ground while there were certainly some genuinely idealistic people like Sudhir in Dina Mehta's *And Some Take a Lover* (1992) who dedicatedly works for rural upliftment and even marries an 'untouchable' girl preferring her over the heroine Roshni and Moorty in Raja Rao's *Kanthapura* (1938) who leads a village against the British without however achieving any tangible results, others were at best fascinated by the idea of being part of the political process. Two of R.K. Narayan's characters typify this latter group. Jagan of *The Vendor of Sweets* (1967) is fond of practices dear to Gandhi, such as reading the Bhagavad Gita and spinning *khadi* cloth, but is every inch a profit-driven businessman, maintaining dubious financial records to hoodwink the taxmen among other things. In another novel, *Waiting for the Mahatma* (1955), Narayan creates a character who is an uninvolved observer of the unfolding political drama. This character, Sriram, is in love with Bharati, a Gandhian activist, and for the sake of her love he himself joins the Gandhian movement, albeit peripherally. His marginality gives him a detached perspective and he can objectively evaluate various followers of Gandhi. He is, for example, surprised by Natesh who conveniently professes patriotism in

Gandhi's presence but otherwise he would not care for his country. Then there is Gropad who has hardly undergone any change of heart but follows Gandhi all the same. While thus Narayan and other writers demystify Gandhi's 'followers' by presenting the other side of the truth, Khushwant Singh somewhat uncharitably calls them '... hired yellers of slogans who spent more comfortable time in jails than in their own hovels. And now want to be compensated with life pensions' (345).

Colonial discourses have sought to essentialize the Indians and their culture, but it has to be noted that the nationalist discourses too in their turn essentialized, dehumanized and demonized the colonial masters. The personal loyalties and emotional bonds professed by many Indians for the British and by the British for the Indians had to be sacrificed in the process. Thus, Mira in Kamala Markandaya's *Some Inner Fury* (1955), who is in love with the Englishman Richard, leaves him at the end of a passionate love affair and joins the nationalist movement, because Richard is an Englishman and therefore cannot be her husband. The moral pressure on the Indians was so tremendous that they could not be on terms other than unfriendly with the English.

The catastrophe in the drama of the British rule in India is constituted by the Partition and the communal riots that preceded and followed it. Contrary to the popular belief, it was not the British who engineered Partition as part of their 'divide and rule' policy. When they no longer wanted to rule India what was the point of dividing it? They wished that the political arrangement they proposed to leave behind should reflect the will of the people. This is where the opportunistic M.A. Jinnah misled them by falsely projecting that the Muslims wanted a separate sovereign state of their own.

It is true that the British encouraged the Muslim League and meted out preferential treatment and offering special privileges in order to counter-balance the growing power of the Congress but the idea of dividing the country was furthest from their mind to begin with or to end with. They were proud of India as a colony, but only as a colony, and in the run up to granting freedom they did everything they could to keep India united. Even the Cabinet Mission through its Plan of 16 May proposed a united Dominion of India as confederation of various provinces. It was the 'two warring parties' which ensured the defeat of this Plan compelling the British to consider other options including Partition.

Who, then, is the chief villain of the piece? Obviously Jinnah, who hoodwinked the British by giving them an exaggerated idea of the popularity and importance of the Muslim League. He, moreover, managed to instill fear psychosis among the Muslims who were otherwise well adjusted to the idea of peaceful coexistence with the Hindus, turned the vague idea of Pakistan into an irreversible demand and finally declared the 'Direct Action Day' which initiated communal riots and created a civil war-like situation. To the British, and later to all other players in the field, Partition appeared preferable to civil war. In the event, Partition did not prevent communal riots and massacres, proving the British policy to be a big failure. It also established that the British were wrong in thinking that the Hindus and the Muslims could be politically and geographically separated by partitioning the country while the fact was that these two communities had lived together for ages in every village, town and city throughout the country and they still do. Partition has done the Muslims no good. It has, on the other hand, needlessly made the Indian Muslims self-conscious as a community and defensive about their religious affiliation and the Pakistani Muslims paranoid about India.

In its long and painful history India had gone through innumerable crises but the Partition was the most traumatic of them all. More than territorial partitioning it meant a widening of the mental divide between the Hindus and Muslims. India has never had peace since this event. War, open or covert, has been raging between India and Pakistan for almost six decades. At least four Indian English novels that have elaborately treated the Partition, namely Kushwant Singh's *A Train to Pakistan* (1956), Chaman Nahal's *Azadi* (1975), Bapsi Sidhwa's *Ice-Candy Man* (1988) and Shauna Singh Baldwin's *What the Body Remembers*, dramatize human suffering at the personal and community level without going into the larger political issues that led to the Partition. Mukul Kesavan's *Looking through Glass* (1994) has some political overtones in that it imaginatively reconstructs the cause of the nationalist Muslims, although their number was not too large, and the way they felt alienated from the mainstream Congress politics. Mulk Raj Anand's *Death of a Hero* (1963) strikes an even different note in that it is set against the background of Kashmir's delay in signing the Instrument of Accession and the enormous tragedy it resulted in and the havoc it still causes in Kashmir on regular basis. The Maharaja of Kashmir hoped to remain independent and dithered till it was too late. Jinnah coveted Kashmir and in less than a couple of months after Pakistan itself came into existence he sent into Kashmir thousands of Pathans from the Frontier Province, fully armed and under the command of the Pakistani army officers. The invaders freely killed and raped, burnt and looted all the way up to Baramula. The Maharaja's own armed forces could offer no resistance because at a crucial moment his Muslim officers and men crossed over to the Pakistani side en masse. At Baramula the invaders did a Nadir Shah by killing more than ten thousand civilians overnight. They were finally checked and driven back by the Indian army which was rushed in there following Kashmir's merger with India. Against this background Anand has woven the story of suffering of the young poet Maqbool Sherwani who hoped to defend Baramula against the invaders but was deserted by his own friends. He was finally captured and brutally killed by the Paksitanis.

This and the novels mentioned earlier unmistakably suggest the failure of the policy of non-violence. All through, this policy obliged Indians to suppress their legitimate anger. Violence, if constructively employed and directed against the colonial interests, could have proved productive. A handful of English rulers, fewer than one hundred thousand at any time, could not have withstood the ire of the 350 million people. India had been at war with itself for thousands of years anyway. One more war could have done it no greater harm and, in fact, it would have been the noblest of all wars—to free the motherland from foreign rule. Recourse to violent means certainly lacks legitimacy at the individual and social levels but when it comes to protecting national interests, national honour and security it should never be shunned. Even the Buddhist nations have fought wars with their colonial rulers and other enemies.

But since violence remained dormant and repressed in the unconscious, it erupted on the occasion of the Partition and turned Indians against themselves. This is precisely the issue chosen for literary treatment in Manohar Malgonkar's *A Bend in the Ganges* (1964). Three idealistic young men—Gian a Gandhian, Debi-dayal a revolutionary and Shafi an underground activist—who wish to lead a peaceful life after Independence are haunted by the violence during the Partition riots. The overall effect of the novel is that the Gandhian policy of non-violence could suppress the brewing anger among the Indians only for a while but betrayed its inadequacy when a provocation presented itself, and finally led to a fratricidal conflict.

The nationalism of most of the activists ended with the gaining of freedom and with their taking to power politics. Their lack of commitment to the nationalist causes is evidenced by their reluctance to dismantle the oppressive colonial power structures, so that there are law enforcement agencies which still brutalize the people and an inefficient administrative machinery which operates on mistrust and thrives on corruption and treats people as worse than colonial subjects. The new ruling class, in association with historians of a certain ideological orientation, continues to falsify Indian history for personal gain and in the process contributes to India's postcolonial confusion.

But life goes on, and in recent times the writers too, following the example of the Indian businessmen who aided the British economic expansion in India in the earliest stages of the empire, have commercialized their art and have taken to commodification of India by turning it into a marketable product. A new wave of colonialism is currently underway and this time it is subtle and invisible but enormously powerful. I am of course referring to globalization, which Indians will surely evolve strategies to deal with, given their long experience of colonialism.

Notes

1. Arvind Sharma, in his book *Hinduism and Its Sense of History*, challenges this contention and seeks to render 'implausible' the assumption that the Hindus lack a sense of history.
2. The comments of Macaulay, denigrating the Indian intellectual and literary achievement, came at a later stage, in 1835, when he was making a case for the introduction of English education in India. The English men who came earlier, and indeed many after him too, viewed India's intellectual achievements in a different light.
3. In his book *The Intimate Enemy* Ashis Nandy explains that many English men of this era married Indian women, settled down in India and never returned home.
4. Among them are: *The Wife and the Ward; or, a Life's Error* (1859) by Edward Money, *First Love and Last Love* (1868) by James Grant, *Seeta* (1872) by Phillip Meadows Taylor, *The Dilemma* (1876) by George Chesney, *The Afghan Knife* (1879) by R.A. Sterndale, *Douglas Achdale* (1885) by Katherine C.M. Phipps,

The Touchstone of Peril (1887) by D.M. Thomas, *Rujjub the Juggler* (1893) by G.A. Henty, *The Great White Hand* (1895) by J.E. Muddock, *The Star of Fortune* (1895) and *The Great White Hand* (1896) by J.E.P. Muddock, *Flotsam* (1896) by Hugh Stowell Scott, *On the Face of the Waters* (1896) by F.A. Steel, *A Man of Honour* (1896) by H.C. Irwin, *Jenetha's Venture* (1899) by A.F.P. Harcourt, *The Peril of the Sword* (1903) by A.F.P. Harcourt, *A Hero of Lucknow* (1905) by F.S. Brereton, *The Devil's Wind* (1912) by Patricia Wentworth, *The Keepers of the Gate* (1911) by Hilda Gregg, *The Disputed VC* (1909) by Frederick P. Gibson, *The Red Year* (1907) by Louis Tracy, and *Rung Ho! A Novel of India* (1914) by 'Talbott Mundy' (Sylvia Anne Matheson).

5. An objective reference work *INDIA—A Country Study* says this about the native rulers:

   Their propensity for pomp and ceremony became proverbial, while their domains varying in size and wealth lagged behind sociopolitical transformations that took place elsewhere in British-controlled India.

6. Among these revolutionaries the following deserve special mention: Aurobindo Ghosh, Bhagat Singh, Bipin Behari Ganguli, Chandrasekhar Azad, Jatindra Nath Das, Khudiram Ghose, Rajguru, Rasbihari Bose and Sukhdev.

Works Cited

Federal Research Division of the Library of Congress. "Post-Rebellion Developments," *INDIA—A Country Study*. Web. 22 JUne 2012. <http://www.country-data.com/cgi-bin/ query/r-5984. html>.

Gidwani, Bhagwan S. *The Sword of Tipu Sultan*. New Delhi: Allied Publishers 1990. Print.

Macaulay, Thomas Babington. "Minute of 2 February 1835 on Indian Education," *Macaulay, Prose and Poetry*. Comp. G.M. Young. Cambridge MA: Harvard UP, 1957. 721-24, 729. Accessible online at "On Indian Education." *Modern History Sourcebook: Thomas Babington Macaulay* (1800-1859). Web. 13 August 2006. <http://www.fordham.edu/halsall/mod/1833macaulay-india.html>.

Nandy, Ashis. *The Intimate Enemy: Loss and Recovery of Self Under Colonialism*. New Delhi: Oxford UP, 1983. Print.

Naoroji, Dadabhai, *Essays, Speeches, Addresses and Writings.* Bombay: Caxton Printing Works, 1887. Accessible online at "The Benefits of British Rule, 1871." *Modern History Sourcebook: Dadabhai Naoroji*. Web. 13 August 2006, <http://www.fordham.edu/halsall/mod/1871britishrule.html>.

Nehru, Jawaharlal. "The Great Revolt of 1857." *The Discovery of India*. New Delhi: Jawaharlal Nehru Memorial Fund, 1986. Print.

Sahgal, Nayantara. *Plans for Departure*. London: Heinemann, 1986. Print.

Sharma, Arvind. *Hinduism and Its Sense of History*. New Delhi: Oxford UP, 2003. Print.

Singh, Khushwant. *Delhi: A Novel*. New Delhi: Penguin, 1990. Print.

Singh, Manmohan. "Address at Oxford University on 8 July 2005." *The Hindu* Online Edition, Web. 14 August 2006. <http://www.hinduonnet.com/thehindu/nic/0046/pmspeech.htm>.

6

Immigration to Emigration: Epitaph for Indo-Fijian Community?

P. SHAILAJA AND M. SRIDHAR

The Indo-Fijian history is full of strange peculiarities and tragic ironies. It is about the odyssey of a people who have made something of themselves, often against great odds. Their entrepreneurial spirit and hard work ensured their gradual ascendancy in the island's economic and professional life. But their success coupled with their cultural insularity led to an uneasy relationship with the indigenous Fijians. One hundred and fifty years after arriving in the islands, the future for the Indo-Fijians looks almost as bleak as it did for their forebears when they had embarked on their unpredictable journey from Calcutta and Madras. Hidden between the pages of history is the fate of these diasporic people. Indo-Fijian literature, though limited, grapples with the Indo-Fijian experiences of colonialism, racial fundamentalism, girmit consciousness and geographical identity. It leads to a complex understanding of the Self as an intersection between history and racial memory.

The Fiji islands were ceded to the Great Britain on 10 October 1874. The new colony, in order to sustain, needed rapid economic development. Sir Arthur Gordon, Fiji's first Governor, prohibited Fijian labour from commercial employment, as his native policy required the Fijians to remain in their own traditional settings under the leadership of their chiefs, away from the harmful effects of external contact. Being bold and imaginative, he decided on a line of action that set the foundations of modern Fiji. Having settled on the plantation system as the preferred mode of economic development and sugar as the main crop, he invited the Australian owned Colonial Sugar Refining Company (CSR) to establish the industry. The CSR arrived in Fiji in 1882 and left in 1973, effectively running the colony's economy for nearly a century. Gordon chose Indian indentured labour to work on the plantations. Indian labour and Fijian land underpinned the Fijian economy in the century between the cession of the Fiji islands to Queen Victoria and its independence.

In response to a request by White settlers in the sugar growing colonies for labour, the British Government turned to India and began recruiting workers. Recruiters (arkatis) working in the Gangetic Plain (populous UP and Bihar) and on the Coromandel Coast (Madras presidency) sent about five million Indians to work in the sugar plantations of British Guiana (Guyana), Dutch Guiana (Surinam), Trinidad, Mauritius, South Africa and finally Fiji. This movement of labour spanned some eighty years, from 1840 to 1917, when the 'new system of slavery' was finally abolished. Thus began the saga of indenture or girmit, as it came to be known by the indentured labourers themselves. The 'agreement' that the labourer signed, through a linguistic transformation, became 'girmit.' The word 'girmit' later came to represent an entire ethos, a legend, a tyranny, and finally a history and an ideology (Mishra 1979).

Indentured emigration was government-controlled. The conditions of employment were stated on a form of agreement—girmit in English, Hindi and Urdu in north India and in Tamil, Telugu and Malayalam in the south. The terms varied in detail according to time and place, but they all specified the conditions of work, pay, accommodation and provision of basic facilities. Typical conditions offered to the Fiji migrants stated that they would be engaged in work related to the cultivation and manufacture of agricultural products; that they would work for nine hours each week day and five on Saturdays, with Sundays and public holidays being free; that men would be paid one shilling daily and women nine pennies. The labourers could return to India at their own expense after five years or at the government's after 10 years of 'industrial residence'. However, there were gaps between what was promised and the practice on the ground, between the rhetoric and the reality of contractual obligation.

Some 60,000 Indians came to Fiji during indenture which began in 1879 with the arrival of 467 labourers on the Leonidas, a labour transport ship. The girmitiyas were followed by traders, lured into the dangerous voyage across the oceans. The indentured recruits were, in fact, a representative sample of rural India, comprising all castes and social groups. More importantly, most of the migrants were dispossessed cultivators or labourers, down and out, looking for a better future. Migration provided a way out. From their local sub-depots, the recruits who had passed medical tests and interrogation by officials were taken to the ports to embark a ship. Cleaned, inspected, and numbered—on a tin circle worn around the neck—the emigrants boarded the ship: single women first, followed by married people with children and finally the bachelors, all 'pleased and amused by the novel experience,' 'decked out in their brightest corals, beads and ornaments' (Lal 2004: 18). Some wept and wailed as the reality of rupture dawned on them. But calm soon prevailed as the ship was out on the sea and with duties assigned like sweeping the deck, cleaning toilets, washing clothes and utensils, preparing food, etc. The recruits were a much maligned lot, disrespected by their contemporaries and despised by their employers. They were assumed by everyone to be a rotten sample of rural India: if men were bad, women were assumed to be worse—individuals with light morals from broken homes, cast adrift by society and beyond the pale of salvation. Indians were often reminded of their low origins by the colonial officialdom as part of the ideological underpinning of European dominance in Fiji.

In the nineteenth century, sailing ships took up to three months to reach Fiji, a month with the advent of steamships after 1904. Whatever the time, the voyage was traumatic. In the crowded confines of the ship's cabins, old rituals and ways of doing things could no longer be sustained. People ate, cleaned, washed and played bound by a shared destiny and a common destination. From the fragments of a common past and a mutual predicament, other bonds emerged. The most notable and enduring was that of 'jahajibhai,' the brotherhood of the crossing, which men cherished well into their twilight as a memory of a shared ordeal and as a bond of solidarity against the alienations and deprivations of a hostile new world. Another remarkable feature was the development of a common language—a variant of Bhojpuri and standard Hindi, which quickly became the language of indentured labourers regardless of their place of origin.

Living conditions on the sugarcane plantations, on which they worked, were miserable. Once in Fiji, and after quarantine, the labourers were allocated to plantations around the country, the majority of which were owned by the CSR. Care was taken not to separate families, but men from the same village or district or having some other distinctive common attribute were separated to prevent trouble—'ganging up'. Conditions varied across the colony. Girmitiyas lived in basic accommodation provided by their employers. Hovels known as 'coolie lines' dotted the landscape. Burton says, 'One of the saddest and most depressing sights, if a man has any soul at all, is a coolie 'line' in Fiji. Vice, wickedness, and abjectness abound. Personal filth is ever in evidence, and life seems to have turned rancid' (1912: 108).

The wet and humid areas of southern islands took a heavy toll on the workers' health, with hookworm, dysentery, diarrhea and anaemic fever creating havoc. The working experience of the girmitiyas on the plantations was excruciating. The absence from work due to infirmity or illness, punishment for the breaches of the contract or insubordination, the heart-rending infant mortality rates, the accidental deaths, the difficulty of forming family and other social networks, the violence and murderous revenge of the girmitiyas have become a part of plantation indenture life. After a hasty breakfast, the workers gathered their implements and marched off to plough and weed the fields, dig drains, feed horses and milch cows, cut and transport the cane to the mills, keep the roads, bridges and tramlines serviceable. This was the routine for five years. The tasks were excessive and were rarely completed on time. Underpaid workers lived on inadequate diets resulting in sickness and absence from work, which in turn led to reduced pay. They laboured for scanty wages and were compelled to perform the hardest agricultural labour but were neglected, when sick.

Women were at the mercy of the overseers and Indian *sirdars*, who allocated and supervised their daily work, harassing, even assaulting, those who refused their sexual advances. Their plight was dramatically brought to light when Kunti's story appeared in the newspaper *Bharat Mitra* on 8 May 1913. In her widely circulated letter, Kunti claimed to have been sent to work in an isolated part of the field by her overseer. The overseer followed her and tried to rape her, but she freed herself, jumped into a nearby river, and was luckily saved by a young desi. When she tried to report the incident to the White plantation owner he said, 'Go away, I don't want to hear about field things' (Reddock 1985: 85–86). 'Field things' were a common occurrence in most plantations, and Kunti's letter dramatized the immorality and brutality of the plantation system. The issues of violence against women, such as rape, murder, and suicide were common. Kunti's story was immortalized in 1914 by Totaram Sanadhya and Benarasidas Chaturvedi in *My Twenty One Years in Fiji.*

Totaram Sanadhya came to Fiji as a girmitiya, in 1893. In 1914, he returned to India and, assisted by an Indian journalist named Benarsidas Chaturvedi, wrote *My Twenty-one Years in the Fiji Islands* in Hindi, which was later translated into English. It is a powerful indictment of the indentured labour system and the treatment of Indians in Fiji. He was the only girmitya who wrote about his experiences in Fiji. The book provides a vivid account of the lives of Indians, indentured and free, in early Fiji: the coolie ships, the coolie lines, the struggles with overseers and law courts, the towns, the bazaars, and Indian religious rituals and festivals; also included are rare and moving narratives of suicide, atrocities and survival. 'The Story of the Haunted Line' is a moving autobiographical story of a man saved from fear and despair by religious devotion and the friendship of ethnic Fijians. It is an account of Sanadhya's efforts to rely on God, in the form of Krishna, while enduring his indenture. In the story, Sanadhya overwhelmed by problems, oppressed by overseer's abuse and near-starvation, is tempted to commit suicide. However just in time,—when he asked God, 'Oh God, take me. Away from You I am disinclined. I do not wish to live now'—a rat bit him followed by a knock on his door (Sanadhya 1991: 135). The moment passed, his thoughts turned toward courage, and then to his duty to his mother in India. He realized that he had to go on, do his duty and rely on God to take care of him and rescue him from his problems.

The plantation was a peculiar cultural institution, with its own complex set of rituals, routines, demands and expectations. For years, it defined the purposes and limits of the girmitiyas' lives. It was also a site of massive social transformation. Plantation work did not respect social boundaries or divinely sanctioned hierarchies. It only rewarded personal initiative and enterprise. The plantation management saw the girmitiyas as 'coolies.' Men and women of different ages, different social, economic and religious backgrounds, often speaking a variety of mutually incomprehensible languages, with contrasting expectations of life, met and mingled. Out of that enforced interaction in the confined and constricting space emerged a new casteless culture. In that new environment, old habits, patterns of thought, associations, understandings about the world and their place in it were shaken. Things collapsed, but not abruptly.

The new culture that was forged during indenture was complex. Culture and religion rather than caste became the basis of identity in the new community. An absence of shrines and images or pundits and maulvis who could give moral and spiritual instruction facilitated an essentially emotional, egalitarian and non-intellectual moral order among the girmitiyas. As Jayawardena observed, 'Religion was an important mechanism in promoting social solidarity among the plantation coolies (during indenture). The powerlessness of the coolies made it necessary for them, in order to protect their interests, to form a tightly knit group which, as far as possible, spoke and acted as one united and unanimous body' (1966: 230).

With the loss of their home and cut off from the motherland, the girmitiyas came to depend on *The Ramayana,* which represented eternal truths in times of crisis and uncertainty. *The Ramayana* of Tulsidas became the 'primary written source for standards of social and personal morality.' Sung to the accompaniment of elementary music, the recital provided spiritual enlightenment as well as social entertainment. It addressed themes of enduring human significance: the importance of righteous conduct in the face of the sternest adversity, the obligations of duty, loyalty and honour. Nandan writes, 'We lived by such stories, our ancient epics—first our grandparents, then our mothers and fathers, now our political leaders. Our fate in Fiji had the echoes of *Ramayana*: exile, suffering, separation, battles, but no return' (1991: 88). The story of Rama's banishment and exile might have made the coolies' exile bearable. The gathering succeeded in reestablishing 'India' in the central consciousness.

The process of retrieval and reconstruction of the Self is vital for an immigrant community. The vernacular version of the Sanskrit classic *Ramayan* acquired the status of 'the holy text' invested with all the moral and spiritual authority among the Hindu Indo-Fijians. The mythology which evolved projected Indian existence in Fiji as an exile like that of Rama. The culture propagated was the old customs of spirituality, domesticity and not the actual life experiences of the girmitiyas. History has become a force and agent of ossification and fossilization when Indo-Fijians indulged in delusory reconstructions of the past. It was into this mire that the Indo-Fijians fell when they wrought a nostalgic past upon the realities of the present. Vijay Mishra says:

> The Indian fragment in Fiji constructed imaginary belief systems for its own self-authentication, self-generation and legitimation. But the Indians themselves were essentially a fragment which had been forcefully wrenched from its centre. For the Girmitiyas (the indentured labourers) their life in Fiji was retrospectively seen as a deception played upon them by recruiting agents (arkatis) who convinced them of future possibilities filled with millenarian expectations. This dual process—the logic of a fragment and the process of millenarianism—led to a Fiji Indian cultural complex which is both specific to that racial group as well as connects it to the larger Girmitiya diaspora around the world.
>
> One of the characteristics of any fragment is that it very quickly becomes fossilised. The principle of dynamic growth which is at the very centre of the contradictions of the land left behind is replaced by a synchronic principle which 'stills' history and constructs a world based upon fantasies which have no real foundation in fact. In this respect the Fiji Indian fragment was no different. (Mishra 1979: 79)

Being 'a fossilized fragment' of an original nation, the Indo-Fijian tried to renew himself through 'a re-fossilization' of his own self. The girmit consciousness is 'a conscious falsification of reality,' created by the girmitiyas themselves. The creation of this conscious falsification originated from 'a conscious misreading of India,' that insulated Indians and provided a blinded vision of the realities of life in Fiji. It created a false sense of security, which enabled exploitation and failed to sustain its stability.

II

The world of Indo-Fijian writers grows out of this historical predicament. The writers did not create an exclusively English/Indian world. This may be because the role of authority in Fiji was deputed to Australians and New Zealanders. Though they were profoundly colonial, authority at second hand does not carry the same weight as when exercised directly. Neither did a return to the ancestral homeland (i.e. India) provide a dominant psychic pull in their writing, may be because there was no surrounding community comparable in exile. Their writing was girmit-driven. Vijay Mishra advances the theory that 'Girmit ideology' informs Indo-Fijian literature, culture and consciousness. It is an ideology shaped by 'thwarted millenarian expectations, by nostalgic links with the cultural traditions of the Indian centre, by perceived threats from the indigenous presence, and the political and social apparatuses of control and manipulation installed and implemented by the British colonial administration in Fiji' (Nelson 1992: xii). Indo-Fijian writing true to this is built around an intuitive grasp of the Girmit ideology. Dislocation and disorientation have predisposed writers to emphasize a sense of dislocation, dereliction, abandonment and towards a treatment of the fragmentation of psyche. The writers have concentrated on the history of Indian indenture—on the trickeries of recruiting, the crossing of the black waters, life in the bhut len, (the haunted lines), sickness, deaths, and the complicated legacy of the indenture period.

Indo-Fijian writing comprises mostly of poetry and short fiction and a few novels. Notable writers like Subramani, Raymond Pillai, Satendra Nandan wrote both in Hindi and English. A central thread in their work is the unjust plight of indentured labourers. Subramani is concerned with mapping the Indian diaspora psyche. He focused on the history of Indian indenture in Fiji, the journey across the black waters to the new land, and the Girmit psyche this history produced. His stories in *The Fantasy Eaters: Stories from Fiji* (1988) encompass nostalgia for an imagined homeland, family breakdown, commitment to their adopted land and betrayal of the promise offered by indenture. Majority of his characters fail to adequately articulate reality to reach a stable sense of adjustment. In his stories 'Sautu' and 'Gamalian's Woman' he not only represents the period of indenture, but the deliberately fragmentary narrative expresses the nature of that history and its contemporary legacy which resulted in what is termed as girmit ideology. The protagonists seem paralysed by antagonistic forces: a wish to take refuge in Indian home and a desire to get in contact with people outside his own community. Dhanpat in 'Sautu' eventually recognizes that his enclave existence is based on a sub-conscious refusal to accommodate forces, ideas, cultures and histories that engirdle him. After such knowledge there is the inevitable loss of reason and final entry into madness.

In his 'Gamalian's Woman,' the background is the indenture period, and Mrs Gamalian is mad at the end of the story. But her madness in a sense sustains her and enables her to recoup in dreams, out of historical time, her indenture losses. Eating the bizarre soup she concocts, from what she thought to be money, Mrs Gamalian is consuming the false promises of wealth on which indenture depended. In a state of living death, she can only adjust to the disruption and psychic fragmentation caused by history through fantasy and madness.

Raymond Pillai's *The Celebration* (1980) portrays the marginality of Indians in tenaciously practicing Indian culture and beliefs, despite their insignificance in the new homeland. In 'To Market, To Market,' a young woman becomes pregnant by her lover. Her parents react differently. Her father is reluctant to condemn her, but her mother refuses to relinquish the idea about arranged marriage. The persistence of traditional beliefs is also the focus of 'A Matter of Conscience,' in which an elderly mother passes on her prejudice against the Whites to her young educated son. In 'The Funeral' the traditional burial customs practiced appear vacuous and irrelevant. The basic social and racial issues remain a focus of several stories.

Satendra Pratap Nandan forces us to see the fractures of indenture history, the parameters of which are too tragic to bear. And by seeing them he himself was transformed from being a writer who sang of personal loss to a writer of national lament. The 'faceless, eyeless' people, writes Nandan, are slowly becoming 'invisible' and 'the outsiders within' (1997). His exposition 'Truth is what you know and do not know' evokes the voices and the concerns that specify the body of his work (1997).

Nandan had been acutely conscious of the weight of the girmit experience, its contradictions and its function as a source of indenture consciousness in the later generations. Nandan's book of poems *Lines across Black Waters* (1997) charts out the diaspora history of the girmitiyas. He expresses the truth of their painful lives, their intense pain and anger. The Girmitiya discourse of leaving home and the exile configures prominently in many poems. He writes about the collapse of the paradisiacal dreams of the coolies on the sugar plantations of the island. Sugar and slavery go together. Nandan ironically comments: 'Sugar and slavery are the Siamese twins of many colonized islands' (1997). The coolies brought from the Indian subcontinent to work on the plantations appear in a variety of poems as ancestral memories of colonial brutality. It is the pastness of the girmit experience and its relationship to the creative consciousness that is expressed when he writes:

> youth I lost here, and grace
> i gave to this island place.
> what more than a man's age
> can one give to history's outrage.
>
> i have lived this exile
> more gloriously than rama

and built kingdoms, you may find,
nobler than ajodhya
in my ancient, eternal mind! (Nandan 1985: 54)

The new kingdoms are nobler but they are fictive. Vijay Mishra says:

> Satendra Nandan's work expresses the agony of banishment in other forms but the narratives are written against the backdrop of this 'primal' banishment. Thus the complete inclusiveness of the village world, its closed world-order and most importantly its myths and idioms are informed, at every point, by a complex transformational process which, finally, left the Fiji Indian with an ideology which was dated and bereft of any revolutionary impetus. A fossil retreated into its memories of a prior narrative which was itself an uncritical glorification of a mythic past, with its sexism, racism and caste ideology intact. (1991: 82)

The indenture background life of his ancestry is a major text for Nandan. He says in his autobiographical writing *Requiem for a Rainbow:* 'One's life is, in the final analysis, the ultimate text' (2001). Nandan's grandparents arrived in Fiji as indentured labourers from India in the 1890s. His parents and all his seven brothers and sisters were born in Fiji. He knew no other country until he left for Delhi in 1958 for higher studies. Throughout Nandan's work are the heard and unheard accounts of voices that recall and confront his childhood, family, nation, coups and exile. The truth of girmit and the socio-political history are linked. Nandan writes: 'politics and personal lives are as interwined in the immigrant and the indigenous as history and destiny' (2001). His diasporic experience as an Indo-Fijian exiled writer in Australia runs as an undercurrent making real the pathetic experiences of the girmitiyas.

III

The second crucial historical 'moment' that permeates the Indo-Fijian writings is the Fijian rebellion of 14 May 1987. Fiji was a tropical island culturally and linguistically dominated by Britain. The Indians had to coexist with a highly developed native Melanesians, numerically in the majority and whose lives had already been affected by European imperialism. Political differences between the two communities, rather than ideological differences, have characterized Fijian politics. The military coup (Rambuka coup) deposed the Indian-dominated government, led to the imprisonment of various officials and scholars, instituted racial quotas in the Parliament leading to a large exodus of Indians from the country. This was followed by 1991 and 2000 coups. The coups shook up the Indo-Fijians. The Indo-Fijians believed that the political act would legitimate his/her existence in a land to which he/she had been banished. The Fijian rebellion brought an end to that possibility and Indians were left in a state of shock. The fictions which they had internalized—the pre-eminence of parliamentary democracy, the obsession with all things colonial and Indian—manifested for what they were, an empty ideology responding to psychological rather than social needs. The cure for the Indo-Fijians lay in political power. This denied, they were left deeply vulnerable with an uncertain future in a troubled and hostile territory. The Indo-Fijians trapped in a cultural time-warp, relapsed into a pathetic rhetoric which could not grasp the real issues at stake.

The pride of an Indo-Fijian being a part of Fiji was replaced by despair and dejection. The sense of being at 'home' in the islands was overtaken by a desperate desire to leave for some other place at the earliest possible opportunity. Since the coups, thousands of people have left bringing the percentage down to 35 per cent from the original 49 per cent of the population. Emotionally uprooted, trapped and terrorized, more would leave if they could. It demonstrated the degree to which the Indo-Fijian diaspora had reconstituted an India that could not dynamically respond to the Fijian reality. The military coups have seriously affected the Indo-Fijian's perception of power and authority and their understanding of reality. The writers who often gave the impression of taking for granted the institutional order of pre-contact Oceania (Ramarajya of *Ramayana*), and for the sake of cultural cohesion were prepared to ignore contesting world views, were beginning to take note of the changed reality.

Nandan's semi-autobiographical novel *The Wounded Sea* (1991) is framed by his experience of imprisonment, cruelty and humiliation as a minister in Bavadra's cabinet, during the two Fijian coups in 1987. He claims that 'indigenous racism, like local liquor, is worse than the imported kind' (1991: 139). He specifically refers to the unfortunate events of Fiji, where he reminds that native sovereignty comes at the expense of the disfranchisement of Indians. The trauma of 1987 lingers in his memory in the image of Fiji as a perpetually 'bleeding, unhealing wound' (1991: 168). The novel compares the uncertainties of a Labour politician in post-coup Fiji, with the peasant certainties of a childhood spent in a village. The narrator attempts to find a way out of the morass of personal, communal and national deceit.

Nandan is primarily known as a poet who writes about the precarious condition of the Indo-Fijians, descendants of indentured labourers brought to Fiji between 1879 and 1916. His poetry collections deal with a transplanted community straddling two worlds and struggling with an unfamiliar landscape and culture while hanging on desperately to the remnants of a tradition that was becoming increasingly meaningless. *Voices in the River* (1985) portrays the infinities of Life and Death as reflected in the minute details of life. He expresses alienation, racism, prejudice, even death, in 'a landscape of little ruins.' The poem 'Inward Death' tells us:

> The death of a king
> A cataclysmic event
> The holocaust
> Of Auschwitz-Shatila-Sabra
> All made by men like you and me
> A shipwreck on Nasilai reef
> A tempest in a Shakespearean sea
> These are not necessary
> For a tragedy
> Happens anywhere, anytime.

After the two Fijian coups, thousands of Indo-Fijians left the country for other lands feeling betrayed, carrying the hurt of history. Nandan himself left to Australia. And this banishment became the defining moment for him. In his book of essays entitled *Fiji: Paradise in Pieces* (2000), he writes that the exiled writers' fate is very painful because he has to create a country of his own.

In contrast, Sudesh Mishra explores a different 'reading' of Fiji. *Tandava* (1992) describes the experience of the 'diasporic Indian,' of one whose very self-hood is defined by the primary fact of its displacement. Most of these tightly written sonnets place the current situation in Fiji in the context of its colonial history. He depicts the nation as a mango tree with 'stretched boughs like David's sling,' which were bound to break at some point or other (1992: 15). By addressing the inevitability of conflict, the poet encounters madness, confusion, dispossession, and later, a new season for the mango tree and a new Diaspora. His analysis is not a regurgitation of seashell mythologies. Nor is it even an ethnicist position. Rather, he performs a class analysis of the Fiji situation, condemning the hegemonic chiefs, the complicit business class, and the positions of all mainstream persuasions alike. It starts with 'Irony,' a self-conscious comparison of the poet with the court jester followed by the 15-poem 'Feejee' sequence. 'Feejee' is dotted with biting criticisms of Rabuka, of the Taukei, of chiefs, of army 'boors', and of the businessman who '[t]allies the annual spoils from his factory.' There's sadness, there's reflection, even hope that since discourse formations are made of words, words might therefore change them.

The Indo-Fijian lived in a timeless world where history was transformed into legend and the indenture became a remembered dream. He presumed that adjustment to a new world was simply an escape from colonial history into a racially hybridized present. He took for granted the institutional order and often ignored the contesting world views. And when the racial present raised its ugly head he was shocked and filled with despair. The 'promised land' of girmitiyas turned into a 'paradise in pieces.' Indo-Fijian experience raises a number of troubling questions: For how many generations does one have to live in a place to be allowed to call it home? Will it be possible for the diasporans to leave their enclave existence? Will future generations see Indo-Fijian presence in Fiji as a nightmarish aberration in the history of Fiji island nation as more and more of Indo-Fijians migrate to settle elsewhere? Is Fiji a temporary stopover for a people condemned by fate to wander the world? These questions can be answered only by time.

Works Cited

Burton, J.W. *Call of the Pacific.* London: Epworth Press, 1912. Print.

Jayawardena, Chandra. 'Religious Belief and Social Change: Aspects of the Development of Hinduism in British Guiana.' *Comparative Studies in Society and History* 8.2 (1966), 211–40. Print.

Lal, Brij V. (ed.). *Bittersweet: The Indo-Fijian Experience.* Canberra: Pandanus Books, 2004. Print.

Mishra, Sudesh. *Tandava.* Melbourne: Meanjin Press, 1992. Print.

Mishra, Vijay. *Rama's Banishment.* London: Heinemann, 1979. Print.

——.'Satendra Nandan: *The Wounded Sea.' SPAN* 32 (1991), 79–82. Print.

Nandan, Satendra. *Lines Across Black Waters.* Adelaide: Centre for Research in the New Literatures in English, 1997. Print.

——. *Voices in the River.* Suva: Vision International, 1985. Print.

——. *The Wounded Sea.* Sydney: Simon & Schuster, 1991. Print.

——. *Requiem for a Rainbow: An Indo-Fijian Journey.* Canberra: Pacific Indian, 2001. Print.

Nelson, Emmanuel S. (ed.). *Reworlding: The Literature of the Indian Diaspora.* New York: Greenwood, 1992. Print.

Pillai, Raymond C. *The Celebration: Collection of Short Stories.* Suva: Mana, 1980. Print.

Reddock, Rhoda. 'Freedom Denied: Indian Women and Indentureship in Trinidad and Tobago, 1845–1917.' *Economic and Political Weekly, Special Issue: Review of Women Studies* (26 October 1985). Print.

Sanadhya, Totaram. *My Twenty-one Years in the Fiji Islands and the Story of the Haunted Line.* Eds John Dunham Kelly and Uttara Kumari Singh. Suva: Fiji Museum, 1991. Print.

Subramani. *The Fantasy Eaters: Stories from Fiji.* Washington, D.C.: Three Continents Press, 1988. Print.

7

Rushdie and '*His*' (Lack of) History: A Study of His Narratology

M. MADHUSUDHANA RAO

For Rushdie, history is 'an act of narration' as he believes that history is no less a form of fiction than the novel is a form of historical representation. For him 'history is an art of narration' (Qtd in Sabrina 2002). He is interested in 'narrative truth' of demonstrating the 'relationship between the act of representation and that which is being represented'. He employs the methods of 'appropriation' as he violently 'possesses' the epistemological facts of the West and 'redefines' them in their Oriental actuality. To this extent, this paper has three parts: in the first part, it broadly discusses the historical, aesthetic qualities of Postmodernism: in the second part, it discusses the idea of history (or lack of it) in the Postmodernist concept; finally, it studies how Rushdie problematizes history (or again, the lack of it) in at least two of his narrative ventures, namely *Midnight's Children* (1981) and *Shame* (1983). In all these cases, Rushdie privileges the subjective self of historical moment (as memory's truth) more than its objectivity.

First of all, let us know what is 'history' *per se* and how it is different from the Postmodernist and Postcolonial points of view. According to Prof. Oakeshott, history is the historian's experience, as it is created by his authentic experience of facts. It implies, therefore, that facts do not come to us 'pure' as they do not coexist in a 'pure form', for they are always 'retracted' through the mind of the recorder. For the historian 'creates' history by his 'imaginative understanding' of the facts themselves. To this extent, the facts of history are nothing but interpretation is everything. To this extent, according to Achebe, a Postcolonial writer is a chronicler as well as a teacher as the Postcolonial poetics is also based, at its intrinsic level, on privileging history which emanates from the subjective self of the colonized, by systematically deconstructing the (objective) history of the Eurocentric view. Rushdie by a process of 'appropriation,' 'reconstructs' Saleem's history. He employs 'memory's truth', as it is a 'remembered truth'. As in a Postmodern way, here he 'narrativises' history as *Midnight's Children* is not 'a some sort of inadequate reference book or encyclopaedia' (Sabrina 2002). For him, even 'nation' is an imaginative trajectory. As in a Postmodernist engagement, in a Postcolonialist poetics, too, history is rendered through the 'unreliable narrator', namely Padma, to become 'an act of narration'; for, Rushdie believes that novel is a 'form' of historical re-presentation', filtered through Saleem's memory, which is a Postmodernist practice.

Postmodernism is a way of representation in art, as it is a condition of mind, and an attitude which describes our social, economic, political and cultural condition of the present times. According to Jencks, it is 'the style of our age.' It is a critique of Modernism (rather than an end of Modernism), as it seeks a continuous redefinition of Modernism. First called 'Postmodernism' by Toynbee in his work *A Study of History* in 1934, it initially appeared in architecture in the works of Charles Jencks, as Felix Guattari and Gilles Deluze described the term of their art in 1950s. It became a cultural theory in late 1980 and later used for describing the altering social reality by late 1980s. It has become an all-inclusive term for all the developments in Europe and North America in its politics, culture as it interacted with Feminism, Postcolonialism and issues of Globalization, History, Environmental Studies, Philosophy and Literary Criticism. According to Toynbee, this postmodernist phase of Western civilization passing through Dark Ages, Middle Ages and the Modern Age reached Postmodernity as a period of decline with the abandonment of the humanist projects of Enlightenment in the World Wars. For, since 1954, a series of fundamental transformations took place in XX century, due to social, economic, military conflicts, globalization and decline of the colonial power. With the development of technology and its ability to displace the existing cultural space, with new media and communication phenomena, and the collapse of religious and political traditions and beliefs across the world and with the looming threat of nuclear war, Postmodernism represents this widely altering mood and attitude to our social, philosophical and political aspirations and ideas of a new life. According to Steven Best and Douglas Kellner, the digitized and networked global economy and society fraught with promise and danger led to uncertainties and fractured view of life, resulting in skeptical ethos and greater radical liberalism and emancipator possibilities of the Enlightenment and Marxism, evaluation of literary art with new definition of taste and categories leading to a culture in which 'any thing goes' so long as it generates profit (1991).

Postmodernism represents certain qualities. They are: it is against any form of rationality or totalization as it is anti-essentialist and anti-elitist. It resists a faith in Enlightenment or belief in any ideology. It believes in anti-canonicity, anti-hierarchical quality as it destabilizes the generic boundaries. It redefines 'reality' in multinational, multi-media globalized context with its multiple levels of plurality. It is eclectic, with its belief in 'any thing goes', which according to Lyotard, is capitalistic in nature. As life is commodified economically, it believes in capitalistic free-trade, deregulation, dispersal and dislocation of securities of tradition and community. As it is a period of playful freedom, it is an occasion of consumer choice. It acquired different meanings of political thinkers, philosophers and historians. For Ihab Hassan, it is a new aesthetic formation; for Lyotard, it is a condition; for Conoor, it is a culture; for Jameson, it is a cultural dominant, for Hutchinson, it is a parodic mode of self-conscious representation, whereas for Eagleton, it is an illusion. However, in its aesthetic manifestation Postmodernism represents the qualities of irony, disruption, difference, discontinuity and playfulness. It manifests the qualities of parody, hyper-reality and simulacrum. It goes beyond the avant-garde experimentation and democratization of cultural studies. It questions some of the modernist practices as Surrealism, Dadaism and Futurism, Imagism and Expressionism. By democratizing art, it breaks down the divide between high and low culture, as it questions Greenberg's argument that art should define itself a domain separate from popular culture, while it does not accept Breton's hatred of bourgeois society. Frederick Jameson discovers 'new depthlessness' due to the invasion of mass media and weakening of historicity (1866). To this extent, parody challenges and subverts the very 'reality' it mimics; whereas, pastiche appropriates different modes and genres for generating its own perfomative style. Hutchinson creates 'historiographic metafiction' through its inquiry into the epistemological and ontological realms of 'reality' (1988).

According to Lyotard, it is a mode of artistic representation (as in Rushdie) as all three modes of representation, namely Realism, Modernism and Postmodernism exist in all these times. While the Realist phase of fictional representation is in the works of Defoe, Richardson, the Modernist and Postmodernist phases are discovered in Virginia Woolf, James Joyce and Barthes, Rushdie, and Alaisdair Gray respectively, resulting in a gradual progression from the restriction of realism to freedom and experimentation in the Postmodernism. However, in any case, all the three forms, of realist texts (*Don Quixote*), modernist texts (*Ulysses*) and Postmodernist texts (*Tristram Shandy*) co-exist in all these three phases. According to Lyotard, the postmodern texts create the feeling of sublime as it indicates a mixed feeling of pleasure and pain, simultaneous attraction and repulsion, awe and terror—for example, Rushdie's grotesque descriptions in *Shame* and the fabulous world of *Grimus* and *Haroun and Sea of Stories.* As in Rushdie's *Midnight's Children's* portrayal of history, it invokes the unrepresentable (the broken silences of fractured historic moments) in presentation in the form of 'absent context'.

According to Jameson, 'Postmodernism is a periodising concept, correlating the formal features of culture with emerging social and economic order' (1866) as in Rushdie's use of hybridity in portraying the cultural plurality in his *Moor's Last Sigh*. Rushdie's *Grimus* and *Haroun and Sea of Stories* and in some of the effects of absence in *Midnight's Children* are illustrations of technological impact in evoking a new paradigm of artistic reality in the manner of Hutchinson's 'historiographical metafiction'. Most significantly, metanarratives in their criteria to judge statements are legitimate, true and ethical for each different form of narrative. In Rushdie, for instance, the supposedly 'same' historical truth has qualitatively and fundamentally different meaning. We do not have grand narrative of persistent meaning as we have metanarrative, where each statement is valid for a particular context. As in Rushdie's portrayal of truth and reality, in the form of 'bits and pieces' of reality (as in advertisement labels and radio messages, etc.), 'True Knowledge' is evoked by means of hyperreality of virtual world of simulacrum in Postmodernism. Here, in postmodernism, according to one view, knowledge becomes a means of profit and power (through technological superiority), leading to pragmatism and efficiency; while, for Steven Connor, science constructs unifying theories to describe the forces known in nature. As in all Rushdie's narrative texts (as in any postmodernist text), the protagonists become 'personages' with the disintegration and fragmentation of their subjective Self. There is no fixed identity of Self, as in Wordsworth, and Descartes' definition of the Self.

With the Baudrillard's simulacrum of truth and 'hyperreality' and Hutchinson's 'historiographic metafiction', we have the postmodernist definition of 'history'. The scope and definition of history as a field of description of human events underwent a radical change since Aristotle's conception of history, poetry and philosophy. According to Aristotle, if philosophy describes a general and universal truth, history a particular truth, poetry combines both, to instruct and please its readers. Sidney in his liberal, humanist imagination described history, as being related to particular truth, whereas poetry like philosophy deals with universal truth. However, the modernist conception of history beginning with the Bible with its idea of 'progress' from the creation to the Establishment of the Kingdom of Heaven on the Earth and stories in Christian theology is linked together as an overreaching story of salvation leading to Hegel's conception of history as the progress of spirit (GEIST). As humanity moves towards a resolution of the conflicts and crises of humanity to a new world, there has been a shift in understanding history from a theological point of view to a secular idea of human progress. For Hegel, there is a relationship between rationality and reality, in the construction of a dialectical movement, as rationality guides the whole structure and development of human knowledge and reason, reality and truth into historical categories, resulting in their change as ideas and institutions come into conflict. However, after the 'modernist' phase of history, there are two theoretical propositions in the postmodernist conception of history. They are from Fukuyama and Baudrillard. Francis Fukuyama, an American critic, believes that modern history acquired its goal of universal freedom in the market-oriented liberal democracy of the USA. For him, this liberal democracy is the legitimate and justified end of history. In his work, *The End of History and Last Man* (1992), he validates liberal democracy and the generation and distribution of wealth by the principle of equality. We are at the Promised Land of Liberal Democracy as it is questioned by Jameson and Lyotard.

However, for Baudrillard, today the real is hyperreal through technology, film and computer. The hyperreal is the abolition of the real by its assumption and elevation 'to the strength of the modes' due to the information technology and so on. Thus, as for Jameson and Ihab Hassan, the postmodern is a world of images whose referents have disappeared; as it is merely a play of surfaces, a playful depthless world. The 'contents' and stuff of history is packaged by media companies and computer-generated simulation. Baudrillard imagines 'an anagrammatic history' (1981). To this extent, these virtual images (as in Rushdie's 'airlanes of history') 'create' 'a poetic alternative to the disenchanted confusion, the chaotic profusion of present events'.

Thus, in the postmodernist conception of history, the interest is on the act of writing history. Rushdie is not a chronicler of history, as he narrativises history, through the subjective identity of his personages. According to Hayden White, as history is a text, and history writing uses emplotment, the encodation of the facts continue in the chronicle and components of specific kinds of plot structures. Histories become 'symbolic structures, extended metaphors'. In this narrativisation of history, events do not generate meaning, but meanings generate events—as Rushdie's use of signifiers in portraying the Jallianwala Bagh events in his *Midnight's Children*. In place of a monolithic historical singularity, we have 'historic pluralism' making history truly 'a subjective foray of one's consciousness of interpreting' an event. As in Rushdie's narrative world, in *Midnight's Children* or *Shalimar the Clown,* history is not a grand narrative of the Absolute as in Aristotle's conception, but 'a field of conflict where different interests and narratives interweave with and question each other', according to Hayden White. For Homi Bhabha, as postmodernist conception of history involves a multiplicity of subjective meanings, a postcolonial writer, like Rushdie, narrativises his own conception of history debunking the Western concept of historiography. Here, Rushdie, in his postcolonial conception of history, narrativises history as cyclical and repetitive. The concept of Time itself becomes an accepted narrative model of the Oriental Time Order. Rushdie, thus, recreates 'alternative histories' outside the purview of the Occidental conception of Time's linearity by indulging in unreliable narrative of Padma and Saleem; mixtures of magical and realistic events. He richly indulges in 'historical pluralism'.

Rushdie's Postmodern Concept of History

Rushdie validates history within the creative ambience of postmodernism by employing the enabling power of hybridity, through the filter of memory. Saleem Sinai provides an individualized history of the Indian sub-continent. *Midnight's Children* begins on the mid-night of 15 August 1947, problematizing history, both retrospectively and prospectively, a period of sixty-three years from 1915 to 1978 to provide 'alternative history' through Rushdie's own narrative voice along with Saleem's subjective self. Salem Sinai, who is merely a twisted symbol of history as he has a twisted destiny—switched at birth with Aziz's biological grandson, Shiva, who is the illegitimate offspring of Vanita. Saleem narrates his history covering the lives of three generations working out his life story and reads it out loud to his friend and co-worker, Padma.

Here Rushdie by narrativizing history, through unreliable memory in bits and pieces, is 'chutnifying' history to evoke a certain alteration, a slight intensification of taste to give it shape and meaning. Rushdie creates Ronald Barthes' mythologies, according to which, myth is constituted by the historical quality of things. For, reality is without historical sense, as we get 'essences' of facts.

Rushdie is historicizing facts to subjectively 'realize' the 'meaning' and 'significance' of facts. He is not a mere chronicler of historical facts, constructed from a Eurocentric point of view. In Rushdie's *Midnight's Children,* history is a timeless myth, as according to Barthes' theory of myth, Rushdie writes an artificial myth. In Rushdie, also, there is no utopia, as there is no existence of the pure and simple, and there is an apocalypse of the present. Truly, in *Midnight's Children*, Rushdie's portrayal of history is a myth—a timeless, ahistorical construct. Saleem's version of the history of the sub-continent is a myth, where the characters, like Aadam Aziz, Tal or Adishankara or Shalimar Gardens are all mythicized (but not 'historical') realities. All these characters impose a sort of meaning through these myths, by erasing history, that is reality.

As Rushdie uses memory by a process of fragmentation, through 'facts' that are distorted and flawed, Saleem creates the special type of history of an unreliable narrator, through his own perspective of history. He is presenting us with his 'memory's truth', that is his version. For him, 'history', that is, its 'essence' is his perspective. For him, the 'present inevitably seems more and more incredible'. For him, throughout the narrative, 'the illusion itself is reality'. His uncle, Hanif's 'realistic' linear documents are unrealistic. He combines 'fiction' with 'facts' to emphasize the ambiguous nature of 'history'. As Saleem's 'history' is not 'pure' as 'fact' is a matter of perspective, he cuts up and retells history to allow him to be its central protagonist. For example, his portrayal of the Jallianwala Bagh depends on his subjective perspective.

In another context, Saleem's interpretation of the linguistic reorganization of states is a matter of identity politics, though he constructs his identity around his childhood version of Bombay. He, however, remains a victim to his myth of the past. Through his version of history, Saleem privileges 'complexity and ambiguity', as Rushdie indulges in exposing 'history' as a hybrid construct. Saleem, in his construction of Midnight Children's Club, consists of 'monsters and evildoers and talented children'. For Saleem, the voices, far from being sacred, turned out to be 'profane and as multitudinous as dust'. The voices that Saleem originally interprets as 'angelic' turn out to be 'impure'.

As Saleem's true identity is a multitudinous character of mixture of races, colours, religions and value systems, he is affected by everyone around him and ultimately is the sum total of his experiences. According to Hawes, Rushdie's method of 'detotalizing' history moves beyond Linda Hutchinson's categorization of Eastern versus Western modes of thought. For Hawes, the novel 'enacts a cultural politics to explore the retrospective fabrication of origins' (1993). Here, Rushdie is re-appropriating the European past for the emerging political and cultural project of postcoloniality. Saleem, by his selective and arbitrary method, invents his identity by self-conscious method. As 'identity' is realized in fluid, in shifting construction, it is made up of fragments of history. As he is a symbolic archetype of 'history', he is 'impure', as he is a conglomeration of experiences, ideas and philosophies and individuals. He begins his life in search of Pure Meaning. By the time he reaches the end of narrative, he realizes that the only meaning available to him is that which he superimposes onto 'reality' and that this 'meaning' of reality is flawed because the process of remembering is open to distortions. *Midnight's Children* is about the process of remembering and pickling. As the mid-night's children disappear, the 'memory' of these multitudes remains. Adam Sinai, born into Emergency, is a 'synthesis' of Shiva and Saleem. He creates new myths, as new myths are needed in India, since the existing myths of 'freedom' and 'religion' and 'money' have all failed. Durga, one such myth, representing newness in the Post-Emergency era tells Adam, 'when a man loses interest in new matters, he is opening the door for the Black Angel'. Durga represents newness as she is not besieged by history. She is a positive, life-giving force as she embodies boundless energy. Durga is fertile. As she beats clothes into cleanliness and symbolically thrashes power out of the well-to-do, she is the opposite of Saleem. Thus, her 'newness' is an alternative opposite of Saleem's connection with the past. To this extent, Durga and Aadam belong to another space with novelty, chance and hybridity. Both Saleem and Aadam are a conglomeration of the history of the Indian colonials and the contemporary India with this difference that Aadam is aware of his hybridity from the beginning and is not interested in going for the meaning unlike Saleem whose entire quest in the novel is towards Meaning and Identity. He has 'cut up' history to suit his nefarious purposes. Unlike him, Aadam's first word is 'abracadabra', a word infused with magical powers. For Aadam, there will be no transcendental meaning as he participates in a variety of meanings and identities.

In *Midnight's Children,* Rushdie introduces many different genres and systematically undercuts each one. By thus not privileging any one genre over the other, he does not allow any 'pure' space to exist in this novel, resulting in a fluid, open text without closure. According to Fawzia Afzal-Khan, *Midnight's Children* is a narrative in which the comic and the tragic, the real and the surreal and the mythic all 'defuse' one another, as it is a 'strategy of liberation' employed by Rushdie (1993). By using myth to liberate his characters from 'the western hegemonic strategies of containment', he is able to avoid 'historical petrification' through the comic/surreal mode. Here, we are always in the narrator's present, as the chapters we read are literally written as we read them. In this novel, writing the future becomes a difficult business.

Thus, Rushdie leaves us with an ending that is not really an ending because it is yet to take place. By subverting the closure of the novel, he is creating an open text. To this extent, what we have is not one narrative, but multiple narratives, thus the 'meaning' of the story of the *Midnight's Children* is not unified, and singular, it has as many trajectories as there are narrators/readers. Here, narrative is not 'a transcendental signified' as 'India' is revealed to be a myth—Time-tinctured and fragmented pieces of 'history' according to the perceiver—Saleem, Aadam or the reader. Thus, 'history' in *Midnight's Children* is postmodern in its purpose, as Rushdie creatively narrativizes history.

According to Sabrina Hassumani (2002), unlike in *Midnight's Children* and later in *Moor's Last Sigh* and in *Shame*, there is 'a rupture in Rushdie's oeuvre', whereas in his other novels (noted above) there is a purposeful hybridity and inclusiveness (as in *Shalimar the Clown*). In *Shame*, Rushdie retells the Pakistani history since independence in 1947, as the story covers three generations and focuses on the lives and families of two men: Razia Hyder, a celebrated General in the military and Iskander (Isky) Harappa, a millionaire-playboy-turned politician. Rushdie bases these 'characters' on 'real-life' Pakistanis: former President Zia-ul-Haq and former Prime Minister Z. A. Bhutto, as Bhutto was deposed in a military coup in 1977. Here, undercutting all levels of characterization and narrative situations, *Shame* is externalized and made to realize by the readers how it becomes the very pathological syndrome of the historical situation on hand. Thus, his characters' as they seek 'to manipulate' history, the world of oppression and repression become the 'motifs' of the narrative. In *Shame*, negative migrations occur because characters either believe they can erase their past or their present, and neither extreme is a viable option. In this novel, repression breeds repression so that women who are kept down by men learn how to dominate others in their turn. Like Bilquis, Omar Khayyam Shakil is a migrant who attempts to leave his past behind, but eventually cannot escape from it. What Omar Khayyam attempts to escape are his three mothers. The Shakil sisters who were imprisoned in Nishapur during their father's life time turn inward. Along with time and identity, another important instance of intermingling in this text is Rani's memory. Thus, in *Shame*, unlike in *Midnight's Children*, 'history' does not present an inclusive moment, as it is a pastiche of diverse events of despair, where memory of the past seeks to 'replace' the 'essence' of the present.

Works Cited

Afzal-Khan, Fawzia. *Cultural Imperialism and the Indo-English Novel.* USA: The Pennsylvania State University Press, 1993. Print.

Baudrillard, J. *Simulacra and Simulation.* Trans. Sheila Faria Glaser. USA: Univ. of Michigan P., 1981. Print.

Best, Steven and Douglas Kellner. *Postmodern Theory: Critical Interrogations.* New York: The Guilford Press, 1991. Print.

Brennan, Timothy. *Salman Rushdie and the Third World.* New York: St. Martin's Press, 1989. Print.

Cook, Rufus. 'Place and Displacement in Salman Rushdie's Work.' *World Literature Today* 68.1 (1994). Print.

Fukuyama, Francis. *The End of History and the Last Man.* New York: Free Press, 1992. Print.

Hassan, Ihab. *The Dismemberment of Orpheus: Towards a Postmodern Literature.* Madison: Univ. of Wisconsin P., 1982. Print.

Hawes, Clement. 'Leading History by the Nose: The Turn to the Eighteenth Century in *Midnight's Children.*' *Modern Fiction Studies* 39.1 (Winter 1993), 147–68. Print.

Hutchinson, Linda. *The Poetics of Postmodernism: History, Theory and Fiction.* London: Routledge, 1988. Print.

Jameson, Frederick. 'Third World Literature in the Era of Multinational Capital.' *Social Text* 15 (Fall 1866). Print.

Jencks, Charles and George Baird. *Meaning in Architecture*. London: Barrie & Rockliff, The Cresset Press, 1969. Print.

Lyotard, Jean-Francois. *The Postmodern Condition: A Report on Knowledge*. Manchester: Manchester UP, 1984. Print.

Sabrina, Hassumani. *Salman Rushdie: A Postmodern Reading of His Major Narratives*. London: Associated University Press, 2002. Print.

White, Hayden. 'The Question of Narrative in Contemporary Historical Theory.' *History and Theory* 23.1 (1984), 1–33. Print.

Woods, Tim. *Beginning Postmodernism*. Manchester: Manchester UP, 1999. Print.

8

Re-presentation of Indian History in Salman Rushdie's *Midnight's Children*

M. PRABHAKAR

> Indian society has no history at all, at least no known history. What we call its history, is but the history of the successive intruders who founded their empire on the passive basis of that unresisting and unchanging society.
>
> —Karl Marx

The postcolonial novel seeks to contest the positionality of history as 'the master narrative'. It demystifies and dismantles the so-called master narrative to situate the historical in the political and social life of a community. According to Laurence Lerner, both history and postcolonial literature are interested in studying the operation of power. The postcolonial novelist is interested in studying how power is sought to be exercised by individuals, whereas the historian is interested in studying the operation of power by groups. Both the historian and the novelist evaluate the operation of power for different reasons through representative figures: 'the historian because he cannot do much with lifeless allegory and needs real people, the novelist because the unrepresentative figure is more interesting and is even better way to breath life into what is representative' (Lerner 1988: 94).

Salman Rushdie does not redeem historical past nor does he annihilate it in his Best of Booker Prize-winning novel *Midnight's Children* (1980). Rushdie goes beyond history, 're-interpreting, revising and appropriating it as a concept for articulating' (Juneja 1995: 106) his colonial consciousness. By using the 'binocular lens of allegory, Rushdie refocuses on our concept of history as post-colonial and post-modernist discourse' (Juneja 1995: 106). History acquires the central stage in Rushdie *Midnight's Children* with the help of postmodern narrative technique of magic realism, parody and allegory.

Rushdie's *Midnight's Children* explores the traumatic inter-relationship between history and the individuals. Rushdie says, 'the history of the twentieth century has been written by mapmakers and that Indian history has been ruthlessly sawed by the Britishers' (Pathak 1988: 28). He feels sorry for the disastrous historical events affecting modern India. His dissatisfaction with the decadent corruption and violation of human rights in modern India is evident in his novel which presents the enduring, heroic resistance shown by Saleem Sinai. Commenting on the inter-relationship between history and fiction in *Midnight's Children,* Pathak says: 'It seems to me that everything his books has to do is with politics and the relationship of the Individuals and history' (1988: 192). The novel is primarily about Indian independence, the power politics and their traumatic effect on the Indian people. The novel focusses on the Partition tragedy and similar historical events like the Reorganization of States in 1956, the 1957, 1963 and 1977 General Elections and the National Emergency by Indira Gandhi.

The reviewer for *The Philadelphia Inquirer* looks at the novel as a 'fascinating history lesson as well as engrossing story'. Robin J. Lewis, an expert in the area of postcolonialism, says: 'Rushdie has altered our vision of the Indian sub-continent in a remarkably short period of time' (1994: 178–79). With his passionate evocation of the recent history of India in *Midnight's Children* Rushdie has surpassed all the previous literary accounts of India by Kipling, Forster, Raja Rao and R.K. Narayan. *Midnight's Children* speaks itself of 'imaginary homeland, India of the mind' (IH 10). Rushdie has succeeded well in bringing home his message of the Indian history. He says:

> Saleem Sinai is not an oracle; he's only adopting a kind of oracular language. His story is not history, but it plays with historical shapes ... the book success—its Booker Prize ... Many readers wanted it to be the history, even the guide book. (IH 25)

Saleem Sinai, the story-teller of Indian history, is the spokesperson of Rushdie. The personality and the voice of Saleem is the fictional translation of Rushdie's own personality and voice. There is close affinity between the protagonist and the writer. Rushdie says: 'The fact that he is called Saleem and I am called Salman ... it's not surprising that the identification is made' (1991: 351). Saleem narrates his 'memory's truth, because memory has its own special kind. It selects, eliminates, alters ... minimizes, glorifies and vilifies also; but in the end it creates its own reality, its heterogeneous but usually coherent version of events' (Rushdie 1991: 211). He claims to be 'mysteriously handcuffed to history' (9) of India through the coincidence of his birth at the stroke of midnight on 15 August 1947, the crucial time when India awoke to freedom from the British colonialism. Saleem possesses magical powers by which he can penetrate into the minds of others.

Midnight's Children opens with the image of bed sheet stained with 'three drops of old, faded redness' (10). The blood-stained bed sheet is the symbol of history written in blood. Referring to the 'Great Killing' (344) in Calcutta on the 'Direct Action Day' Rushdie poses a question: 'what kind of ink is involved here, what sort of pen does it flow from, and how should it be read?' The blood that flows in midnight children is described as 'mercurochrome.' The blood is the result of the violence inflicted on real human bodies. The blood stained 'perforated sheet' is the symbol of our great sacrifice for the nation. 'Midnight's Children' like Saleem wish to keep the soil of India as 'sacred land to be loved and defended, if need be, with the blood of her children' (Wolpert 1989: 262).

Midnight's Children is Rushdie's deliberate evocation of the postcolonial Indian imagination. The novel seeks to present a newer and fresher picture of India and Indianness. As a postcolonial novel it signifies re-presentation of postcolonial India as 'Other, exile, slave, black' (Slemon 1988: 3). The novel also attempts to map the hybridity and the plurality of India through the portrayal of Saleem, a secular Muslim. Commenting on the anti-secular element in the Indian nation, Saleem says: 'Is this an Indian disease, this urge to encapsulate the whole reality? Worse; am I infected too' (75)? The secularism of the Indian nation with its blend of Hinduism, Islam, Buddhism, and Christianity is discernible in Saleem. Out of the dialectics of Rushdie's juxtaposition of magic realism and parody comes his secular novel *Midnight's Children*, 'a hybrid tale of India, incorporating a complex web of Hindu and Islamic (and even Christian) motifs, the philosophies of *maya* and *karma* and Sufism and interweaving private/personal and public/political histories of the Indian sub-continent' (Mujeebuddin 1999: 151).

Like his grandfather Aadam Aziz, the progressive doctor, Saleem the progressive grandson does not believe in the linear time and its linear *karma*. Saleem would like to re-present Indian history through his writing. He is determined to fight against 'the identity and history imposed by [British] colonialism and later after Independence, the *chamcha* politicians' (Brennan 1989: 88–89). He sets up his own blue—print of revolt—' his own web of *maya-lila* as an antidote against what is paraded as authentic history, which is in actuality a mesh of lies, a mirage that deludes by its appearance' (Mujeebuddin 1999: 153). Saleem does not consider the imposed history as the honoured tokens of achievement of the colonizer. Thus, from the postcolonial perspective Indian history becomes what Laming is called 'an intolerable pile' (Slemon 1988: 158). In *Midnight's Children* we are able to perceive how Saleem uses 'history as language, as discourse, as a way of seeing ... to destabilize history's fixity, its givenness and open it up to the transformative power of imaginative revision' (Slemon 1988: 159).

In his narrative, Saleem allegorizes Mrs Indira Gandhi and her emergency. He describes the National Emergency by Mrs Indira Gandhi as an instance of the violation of human rights in India. The imposition of National Emergency in the life of the nation speaks volumes for 'the changing face of India' (Wolpert 1989: 347) and the violation of human rights. He indicts the state-controlled media which keeps silent on the government's atrocities during the emergency. The irony of the situation is that Mrs Gandhi has described the emergency as 'Disciplined Democracy' stressing the discipline by means of 'suspension-of-civil rights and censorship-of-the-press, armoured-units-on-special-alert, and arrest-of-subversive elements ...' (419). There is no denying the fact that people have been deprived of their basic human rights and all fundamental rights during the emergency. This illegitimate censorship leads to doctored news. As

Saleem says: 'All sorts of things happen during an emergency: trains run on time, black money hoarders are frightened into paying taxes, and even the weather is brought to heel and bumper harvests are reaped ...' (434). The state-sponsored media projects Mrs Gandhi the dictator as god. Consequently, she becomes 'Devi, the Mother goddess in her most terrible aspect, possessor of the shakti of the god, a multi-limbed divinity with a centre-parting and schizophrenic hair ...' (438). Mrs Gandhi relays her fascist slogan, 'Indira is India and India is Indira' (427) over the media as if to get rid of all the atrocities of her government. Saleem raises his voice against Indira Gandhi's power politics and the violation of human rights. Thus, Saleem narrates how the emergency is the greatest threat to India's democracy and its ideals under the rule of Mrs Gandhi.

In his re-presentation of Indian history, Saleem sees Indira as his main rival. He ridicules matching Indira's own projection of herself as 'Bharat Mata', the image of Mother India in spite of her unquenchable thirst for power over human lives. The plural identity of Saleem as secularist, Marxist and human rights crusader makes Indira the goddess afraid whose Hand [the election symbol of the Congress I] maintains, '*millions* of gods .... For the masses, our Lady is a manifestation of the OM' (438). Saleem empowers himself as 'Brahma,' (Brennan 1989: 99) the creator and as 'Vishnu,' the preserver. Thus, Saleem emerges as the 'all-knowing, all-seeing and all-wise narrator' (Mujeebuddin 1999: 154) who 'chutnifies' his own version of postcolonial India in his humble pickle factory. Saleem, who is a secular Muslim, identifies himself with the elephant-headed Hindu god Ganesh because of his nose, his love of writing and his insider-outsider position. Like Vishnu, Saleem appears in various avatars such as 'Snotnose, Stainface, Baldly, Sniffer, Budda and 'Price-of-the-Moon' (9).

Saleem's history is poised against the colonial history of the postcolonial Indian nation. According to Saleem, we have not only inherited political power from the British colonial masters but also preserved intact many of their peculiar colonial trappings such as the houses of the Parliament, the bureaucratic structure and educational modes even after Independence. In his narrative, Saleem points out the criminalization of politics and deterioration of values during the elections. He takes pity on the gullible and illiterate voters exploited by the power mongers whose sole aim is to secure power. Saleem shows how power-hungry groups resorted to all sorts of malpractices during the elections regardless of the inconvenience caused to the poor. He exposes how Sanjay Gandhi is militaristic and has implemented family planning programmes forcefully and inflicted atrocities on common people by bulldozing slums.

The bodyguards of Sanjay Gandhi arrest Saleem. He undergoes stress and becomes subnormal psychologically due to the traumatic effect of the historical forces. The fast moving historical forces destroy Sinai's memory. He forgets his past. He is seen as the Buddha because of calmness on his face. Mrs Gandhi comes to know of Saleem's magical powers. She also knows about the other Midnight's Children and destroys all of them except Saleem. The 'Midnight's Children' possess special powers as their fate is linked to the fate of modern India. They can change the destiny of the nation positively. But the historical forces do not allow them to lead India to prosperity and glory, but 'like the dreams of 'Suraj after Swaraj' they deteriorate and degenerate into a helpless pack of scapegraces' (Salunke 1992: 186). Saleem is determined to continue his battle with the historical forces. He says:

> I'm prepared to ... re-write the whole history of my times purely in order to place myself in a central role ... I cannot judge. I'll have to leave it to the others. For me there can be no going back. (153)

He contests 'the history of the successive intruders who have founded their empire on the passive basis of that unresisting [Indian] society' (Marx) through his power of writing. Commenting on the vibrant vision of Saleem, Mathur says:

> Saleem is a crystallization of an evolving mood, a distillation of a vision, nostalgic, critical and philosophical. He is a camera eye, which is itself cracked and fragmented. He is able to project what may be called a sort of prismatic vision of reality, partial, fissured and fragmented but highly absorbing and deeply meaning. Afraid of absurdity, he is frantically engaged in a quest for meaning. (1993: 113)

The life and history of Saleem comes to an end by creating his own 'Universe'. Saleem ends his narrative with a note of hope that a new generation will understand and preserve or chutnify Saleem's own marginalized identity and history of India. Saleem is quite optimistic that his son will inherit 'Abracadabra'—magic and art, the inheritance of his mother, Parvati, who is a Marxist and has lived in the Marxist magician's ghetto. His son, who is named after his grandfather Aadam Sinai, signifies the optimism or progress that is symbolized by his grandfather Aadam Aziz.

Thus, Saleem Sinai's account of Indian history in *Midnight's Children* is re-presentation of Indian history or 'an alternative history, a tale of marginalized who preserve in spite of the attempts by centers of power to sweep them under so-called history' (Mujeebuddin 1999: 163). It is an assertion of the plural identity of Saleem Sinai's secularism, Marxism and human rights as an Indian. The novel subverts every form of convention and authority. According to Rushdie, human rights are under threat from the forces of anarchy, oppression and social injustice.

As a cautionary tale *Midnight's Children* seems to warn what Margaret Atwood, the most prominent postcolonial writer, says: 'If we cease to judge this world, we may find ourselves, very quickly in one, which is infinitely worse' (1982: 333). Expressing his deep sense of feeling of love for his country, Rushdie says:

> The novel *Midnight's Children* is written to sort of reclaim my roots, that part of my life ... the writing of the book was a kind of high romantic way of paying a debt to India I felt owed. (1981: 6)

Midnight's Children is a sprawling work which will be best remembered not only for its exposure of facts and figures, experimentation with style and language but also for its forebodings.

Works Cited

Ali, Tariq. *An Indian Dynasty: The Story of the Nehru-Gandhi Family*. Introduction by Salman Rushdie. New York: Picador, 1985. Print.

Atwood, Margaret. *Second Words: Selected Critical Prose*. Toronto: Anansi, 1982. Print.

Brennan, Timothy. *Salman Rushdie and the Third World: Myths of the Nation*. London: Macmillan, 1989. Print.

Dharkar, Rani. Interview with Salman Rushdie. *New Quest* 42 (1983), 351–60. Print.

Juneja, O.M.P. *Post Colonial Novel: Narratives of Colonial Consciousness*. New Delhi: Creative Books, 1995. Print.

Lannoy, Richard. *The Speaking Tree*. London: Oxford UP, 1974. Print.

Lerner, Laurence. *The Frontiers of Literature*. Oxford: Basil Blackwell, 1988. Print.

Lewis, Robin Jared. 'Salman Rushdie: *Midnight's Children*.' *Masterworks of Asian Literature in Comparative Perspective: A Guide for Teaching*. Ed. Barbara Stoller. Armonk, New Delhi: M.E. Sharpe, 1994. Print.

Mathur, O.P. 'A Metaphor of Reality: A Study of the Protagonist of *Midnight's Children*.' *Images of India in Indian Novel in English*. Eds Sudhakar Pandey and R. Raja Rao. Delhi: Orient Longman, 1993, 113–14. Print.

Mujeebuddin, Syed. '*Midnight's Children* and Its Indian Con-Texts.' *Journal of Commonwealth Literature* 29.2 (1994), 95–108; Reprint *Rushdie's Midnight's Children: A Book of Readings*. Ed. Meenakshi Mukherjee. Delhi: Pencraft International, 1999, 149–64. Print.

Pathak, R.S. *History and the Individual in the Novels of Rushdie*. Eds G.R. Taneja and R.K. Dhawan. New Delhi: Indian Society for Commonwealth Studies, 1988. Print.

Rushdie, Salman. *Midnight's Children*. 1980. London: Picador, 1982. Print. All page references in parentheses are to this edition.

——. *Imaginary Homelands: Essays and Criticism 1981–1991*. London: Granta, 1991. Print.

——. Interview. *The Sunday Standard* (14 June 1981), 1–6. Print.

——. Interview. *Kunapipi* 7.1 (1985), 1–19. Print.

Salunke, V.B. 'Salman Rushdie and India.' *The Novels of Salman Rushdie*. Eds G.B. Taneja and R.K. Dhawan. New Delhi: Prestige Books, 1992. Print.

Slemon, Stephen. 'Modernism's Last Post.' *Past the Last Post*. Eds Ian Adam and Helen Tiffin. London: Harvester/Wheatsheaf, 1991. Print.

——. 'Post-colonial Allegory and the Transformation of History.' *Journal of Commonwealth Literature* 23.1 (1988). Print.

Wolpert, Stanley. *A New History of India*. 1977. New York: Oxford UP, 1989. Print.

9

Silencing Subaltern Voices: Pakistan in *Shame*

MUJEEBUDDIN SYED

Writing about 'Commonwealth' literature, Salman Rushdie in one of his numerous essays severely criticizes the appellation and condemns academics and critics for having created this 'chimera.' He attacks the notion of authenticity that critics look for in literary works and points out that it is absurd to apply these criteria to Indian literature. He says, 'the very essence of Indian culture is that *we* possess a mixed tradition, a mélange of elements as disparate as ancient Mughal and contemporary coca cola American. To say nothing of Muslim, Buddhist, Jain, Christian, Jewish, British, French, Portuguese, Marxist, Maoist, Trotskyist, Vietnamese, Capitalist and, of course. Hindu elements.' 'Eclecticism, the ability to take from the world what seems fitting and to leave the rest,' is the hall-mark that has '*always*' been an important factor of Indian tradition (Rushdie 1991: 67; emphasis added).

What such a panegyric to Indian eclecticism tends to ignore in its enthusiastic sweep is the severe fissiparousness that has rocked India all through its modern history—right from the blood-soaked Independence that India achieved through its 'non-violent struggle' to the present-day, extremely violent so-called liberation struggles in numerous states and the communal clashes that sweep the country periodically. It mouths, on the other hand, in a rather unproblematic manner, the age old adage, used by both the visionaries and the rogues alike that have ruled independent India, of its mythical Unity in Diversity. While upbraiding the critics for their fallacious search for authenticity, Rushdie himself falls into the trap of a notion long emptied of its meaning.

Actually Rushdie's position here, one might justify, reveals his propensity for rejecting the oppositional, binary, black/white spaces that marks most nationalist discourse and indicates his preference for polyphonic discourse and hybridity. This might also validate Rushdie's position as an 'original' postmodernist who borrows the hybrid structure of his works from the Indian oral tradition (specifically from the story-teller of Baroda) and not only from Marquez, Grass and company whose names are strung around the neck of his work like a 'kind of garland' (Rushdie 1991: 67).

However, Rushdie's intellectual and artistic formulations are, in fact, as Aijaz Ahmad argues, essentially modernist but which distinguish themselves as postmodernist 'primarily by celebrating human inability to experience reality as a totality ... .' Rushdie himself has acknowledged his debt to many western influences not the least being the Modernist/Post-modernist streams. By insisting on placing such disparate traditions within the same frame of reference Rushdie would appear to be bridging Manichean spaces that impose hindrances and restrict creative freedom.

Yet Rushdie's work is about more than an artist's creativity. Timothy Brennan maintains that Rushdie's use of the dominant literary mode of Modernism and its attendant 'complexity,' 'subtlety,' 'irony,' and 'understatement' also involves at the same time 'a vision of democracy, freedom, popularity, truth—(largely lost or devalued in the metropolis seen as an arena of disintegration and postmodern decentering)' and forges a work of art which informs the 'First World audiences about what they persist in refusing to see (1989).'

But Rushdie's work which exhibits 'a political-aesthetic that is itself double,' and which apparently would manifest a resistance to submission to 'values branded on to the skin of (his) culture' is also fraught with an ambivalence that can be counter-productive (Brennan 1989). The Rushdie text, which is unarguably a splendidly poignant reading of the Third World and its cultures, can yet yield to the very imperatives of the imperialistic meta-narrative that it had originally set out to displace, namely, an usurpation of the subaltern's articulation of difference. I hope to show the occurrence of this phenomena in the following 'note/s' on Rushdie's *Shame.*

Talking about the beginnings of *Shame,* Rushdie tells us how he was determined *'not to allow a mere character to usurp me'* as had happened in *Midnight's Children.* He says that he wanted the hero of his second novel to be as different from Saleem as possible in order to make him a peripheral man so that writing about him would mean writing about many other people because 'actually all adopt the history of this one man.' 'I also thought,' he further says, 'that it was a way of making sure that he was not taken to be me' (Rushdie 1985).

Rushdie does hold his own persona in the novel, in spite of a passage couched in admirable irony in which he conflates himself, his hero and the 'translatedly' popular but vastly misunderstood 'real' Omar Khayyam. His interventions in the novel, though reminiscent of the traditional story teller, are also significant for his pronouncements on his characters in the book, as they offer to the reader a clarification of the author's studiedly ambivalent and intentionally polemic position/s about his book and its characters.

> Outsider! Trespasser! You have no right to this subject! ... . I know: nobody ever arrested me. Nor are they ever likely to. Poacher! Pirate! We reject your authority We know you, with your foreign language wrapped around you like a flag: speaking about us in your forked tongue, what can you tell but lies? I reply with more questions: is history to be considered the property of the

participants solely? In what courts are such claims staked, What boundary commissions map out the territories? Can only the dead speak? (*Shame* 28)

'What can you tell but lies? … . Can only the dead speak?' (*Shame* 23) Rushdie here initiates a dialogue across the barrier which separates the 'post-colonized' from the 'post-colonizers.' The oblique question hints at his recognition of the powerlessness of the native tongues and more importantly the chosen silence of the Pakistani intellectual, the imprisoned poet, who was hung upside down by his ankles and beaten, as (if) 'a new-born baby whose lungs had to be coerced into action so that he could squeal' (*Shame* 28). But the poet does not 'squeal,' neither does Omar Khayyam Shakil, the peripheral hero, and the mantle passes onto the 'translated' writer Rushdie, 'so here I am instead, inventing what never happened to me' (*Shame* 28).

Rushdie's ambivalence here, as also his avowed 'existence at a slight angles to reality', his 'necessary' off-centeredness, his 'Fitzgerald-Khayyam' persona and his projection of himself as a voyeur rather than a participant, in spite of the irony that informs the statements, is all offset by a syntagmatic defence mechanism. His learning of Pakistan by slices, his floating 'upwards from history, from memory, from Time, his last words on the 'East,' to which he is 'still joined by elastic' bonds' (*Shame* 28) and his sketchy knowledge of Pakistan—all this smacks of too meticulous an attempt to ward off an anticipated criticism that there is much missing from this judgment of his last words.

The picture of Pakistan that Rushdie constructs in the book needs examining here: Pakistan, 'insufficiently imagined,' is presented as a maimed Utopia, 'a dream that went wrong,' 'the wrong miracle' (*Shame* 88). Far from being the land of the pure that its name implies, it is 'Peccavistan.' As Ahmed suggests, the sense of Pakistan as a trap no one can flee, a claustrophobic prison or cage is very strong. The portrayal of a lack of vision and ideas/thought in Pakistan or Pakistanis brought about by religious dogma and/or dictatorship almost deserves a place in orientalist discourse on areas of darkness.

Only it is Rushdie himself here who has escaped the prison— 'to fly and to flee: both are ways of seeking freedom'—and is now able to celebrate his floating 'upwards from history, from memory, from time' (1991: 86–87).

The postcolonial space depicted in *Shame* then, is, to invert Foucault's term, a 'reverse-heterotopia'—not a counter-site of Utopia which 'enacts a visible self-criticism or self-creation' of any given culture (Foucault 1984)—but a space which shows all the negative aspects that a culture is *better off without*—in plain terms the metropole talking down to the subaltern. Given Rushdie's much-acclaimed 'hybridity' and 'cosmopolitanism,' this view may seem odd but considering Rushdie's insistence on imposing a vision and his veering clear of typical or representative fictions, one finds his version of this part of the Third World very much in compliance with metropolitan terms (Spivak 1991). For, the very cosmopolitan terms he sets out for his works deny the subaltern a voice (and in *Shame* even a place). The enunciation of the problematic of the Nation that he undertakes is unproblematic in that it precludes *any* possibility of resistance in the general sweep of despotic fundamentalist fervour that informs the spirit of nationalism and forgets that like any other discourse nationalism too rarely has 'a pure virginal quality about it' and people are *not* always 'reluctant to see (it) discredited, disenfranchised, mocked' (Loomba 1991). What Rushdie falls prey to is a multiculturalism that constantly celebrates the other space as just one moment in the Metropolitan state that celebrates the migrant and the hybrid at the expense of the subaltern.

The epistemic wasteland that Rushdie indicates in his novel is even for a work of fiction, of magic realism, too much to digest in as much as it is supposed to be a novel of gigantic proportions of hybridity but does not foresee any positive political action from within the polity itself; the only release lies in the *same* class and in its macabre violence. But resistance, as Bhabha says 'is not necessarily an oppositional act of political intention ... but the effect of an ambivalence produced within the rules of recognition of dominating discourses ...' The master 'text' when placed within 'other discourses, texts, cultures, and social formations' prompts and shapes the questioning of the received truths of the text, contradicting though these might be in themselves and in their enunciation (1985)'. That Pakistan can come into touch with any other discourses is doubted by Rushdie (and so he, the metropolitan-cosmopolitan has to do the job for them), and his critique of Pakistan ends up ignoring the lasting influence of poets like Iqbal, Faiz Ahmed Faiz, and the other popular forms of art like Indian films (which are very popular in Pakistan) and modern Pakistan TV to name just a few. Serials like 'Ankahi' and 'Tanhaiyan' in the past have always carried a feminist message to their women audiences (through in a coded manner, which is how feminism even in the progressive West sometimes works) providing much needed role-models. Even more so his enunciation of Pakistan, through the monologic structure that he encases his 'hybrid' discourse in, denies *even* (much in his own tradition) atheistic poetry (Ahmed 1991). Above all his pluralism denies monoism a space to argue its own grounds, fixing it with its liberal gaze. His declaration that 'Pakistan is not Iran' and his dismissal of the Islamic Movement in Pakistan as confined to the Jamaat's Maulanas and college students is typical of his refusal to examine whether this might not be a valid aspiration of the people, and configures a lack of critical insight on his own part, that denies alternative ways of being and seeing. Aijaz Ahmad points this out when he says that 'Rushdie's work is marked by an inability to believe in any community of actual praxis, hence the belief in the universality of betrayal which is lost in those readings of his work which locate it primarily in the problematic of the nation and the Third World (1991).'

The postcolonial space that Rushdie has chosen to situate his work in, is where many men and women have to intervene in structures established through past and present histories of domination. Needless to say such acts of disruption are difficult and confined to small sections of people and highly ineffective—and to a metropole like Rushdie might even seem to be absent. But to say that they never 'squeal' and that it is only the metropolitan high culture that could speak for them is to impose a new unsavoury silence which is as crippling, as suffocating and as demeaning as the older colonial/orientalist impositions were, on the Third World's subalterns.

Works Cited

Ahmad, Aijaz. 'Salman Rushdie's *Shame.*' *Economic and Political Weekly* (15 June 1991), 1467–71. Print.

Ahmed, Rukhsana (tr.). *We Sinful Women: Contemporary Urdu Feminist Poetry.* London: Women's Press, 1991. Print.

Bhabha, Homi. 'Signs Taken for Wonders.' *Critical Inquiry* 12 (1985). Print.

Brennan, Timothy. *Salman Rushdie and the Third World: Myths of the Nation.* Palgrave: Macmillan, 1989. Print.

Foucault, Michael. 'Of Other Spaces: Utopias and Heterotopias.' *Architecture/Mouvement/Continuité* (October 1984). Print.

Loomba, Ania. 'Overworlding the Third World.' *Oxford Literary Review, Special Issue: Neocolonialism* 13 (1991), 164–92. Print.

Rushdie, Salman. 'Commonwealth Literature Does Not Exist.' *Imaginary Homelands.* London: Granta Paperbacks, 1991. Print.

——. Lecture/Interview. *Kunapipi* 7.1 (1985). Print.

——. *Shame.* London: Picador, 1984. Print.

Spivak, Gayathri Chakravarthy. 'Neocolonialism: An Interview with Robert Young.' *Oxford Literary Review* 13 (1991), 220–51. Print.

10

Historical Element in Salman Rushdie's *Shame*

M. NARENDRA AND V. NAGARANI

History is but an interpretation of the historical which implies a synopsis of data of dates, names, battles, coups, political happenings, religious and traditional paraphernalia, social situations, cultural phenomena, and other details relating to events. The historical brings about an understanding of the past and its relation to the present. In Salman Rushdie's third novel *Shame*, most of the specific details are not historically true, but the main characters in the story resemble the historical personages. As Uma Parameswaran rightly points out, '*Shame* is a history, but it is only skeletally historical' (1988: 80). Rushdie adopts many strategies to overcome the problems of a historical novelist like using surrealism and symbolism in the place of realism, violating chronology, intertwining the past and the present and using allegories. Another important strategy adopted is shaping the narrator of *Shame*, like that of *Midnight's Children,* as a symbol of the country he belongs to. Thus, the writer presents the history of the nation with a lot of human interest.

Time and space impose certain restrictions on history. Rushdie has produced a creative work which is not chronological. *Shame* is not written in a chronological order. It jumps forward and backward in time. Rushdie rejects historical time and takes recourse to memory, dream and finally to fantasy. He documents history by creating an illusion of fantasy and unreality. Rushdie's art and vision can be clearly understood, if one can study his method of intertwining the present and the past in the narrative. In the novel, Rushdie tries to explain that he is not writing a realistic novel about Pakistan; but calls his fictitious country Peccavistan.

> My story's palimpsest-country has, I repeat, no name of its own .... There's an apocryphal story that Napier, after a successful campaign in what is now the south of Pakistan, sent back to England the guilty, one-word message,

> 'Peccavi', I have Sind. I'm tempted to name my looking-glass Pakistan in honour of his bilingual (and fictional, because never really uttered) pun. Let it be Peccavistan. (*Shame* 88)

Rushdie avows he is not writing a realistic novel for fear of being dumped and banned. He further observes, '... The book would have been banned, dumped in the rubbish bin, burned. All that effort for nothing! Realism can break a writer's heart. Fortunately, however, I am only telling a sort of modern fairy-tale, so that's all right .... What a relief!' (1991: 70). As in the case of Gabriel Garcia Marquez and the other Latin American writers, Rushdie chooses the fantastic and magic realistic mode of telling the story to present the contemporary reality. His fear of choosing such a mode is not warranted as his later novel *The Satanic Verses* was banned in a number of countries.

The Partition of the subcontinent into India and Pakistan becomes the core of the novel. Rushdie narrates the communal stirrings in Delhi before Partition. As S.K. Tikko has rightly opined, 'Although, historically speaking, the causes of the partition were many, Rushdie presents only a casual picture of the communal disturbances that were to be witnessed on the eve of the great divide when bombs had begun exploding in different places' (1992: 125). By delving deep into the thoughts of the individuals, who have been victims of the Partition, the novelist draws out their innermost senses of shame, shamelessness, hope, despair, ambition and anguish besides banking upon their optimism at the rise of a new country. After the creation of Pakistan on 14 August 1947, every effort was made to wipe out its past history and rewrite it. Rushdie knows that Pakistan made a vain attempt to reject its past which was 'open' and 'pure' and tried to garb itself in a history; a kind of concocted pseudo history based on religious fanaticism. The re-written history of Pakistan represents characters as heroes and martyrs and makes religion legitimate.

Rushdie critiques the history of Pakistan through selected events from its past. According to him, Pakistan is 'a peeling, fragmenting palimpsest' (1995: 87). The act of covering up what exists underneath is technically called a 'palimpsest'. Rushdie uses this word metaphorically to reflect the attitude of Pakistan in trying to repress its past by re-writing official history. He uses motifs like violence, betrayal, death, revenge, shame and shamelessness that help in the reality of narration. They indicate that the development of the country is moving in the wrong direction. The gradual growth or development of these motifs results in the central theme of the novel-repression. Into these themes and patterns of tragedy, Rushdie successfully configures history. *Shame* is a mixture of politics, history, satire, fantasy and allegory. It is a novel of fictional distortions. It offers an inner, thematic, fanciful jumbling of historical items. Geography, history and persons are imaginatively recreated to form part of a modern fairy tale. Thus, the novel covers up an underlying theme of shame; while shamelessness pervades it unobtrusively. The political, religious and cultural events that contribute to the entirety of historical events form the backdrop of the novel.

The novel *Shame* covers the history of Pakistan over a period of thirty-six years—from 1947 to 1983—from the birth of Pakistan to the present, the year of the publication of the novel. Rushdie fictionalizes the factual events collected from history. He tactfully portrays the shameful activities like obscenity, permissiveness, debauchery, untruths, ill treatment of women or gender bias, smuggling and lack of patriotism as a guise to present the historical events of Pakistan. The novel concentrates on three related families—the Shakils, the Hyders and the Harappas. The novel reflects the historical facts of Zulfikar Ali Bhutto and Zia-Ulhaq (in the novel Iskander Harappa and Raza Hyder respectively), the two presidents of Pakistan who represent civilian and military authority, respectively. The other characters in the story also represent the great names in the political history of Pakistan—Marshal A. as General Ayub Khan, General Shaggy Dog as Yahya Khan, Sheikh Bismillah as Sheikh Mujibur Rahman and Arjumand Harappa as Benazir Bhutto. The characters in the novel have derived traits from the historical ones, though the factual and fictional biographies differ in many ways. Ensuring a strong factual base from the historical data secured, comparisons can be drawn with the events also.

The canvas of the narrative covers the events from the Partition in general, but more precisely from the time of the East-West conflict. The subsequent events like the overthrow of the President Ayub Khan, the martial law of General Yahya Khan, the rise of Zulfikar Ali Bhutto, the military action against the tribesmen of Baluchistan in the 1970s, the military coup and the downfall of Bhutto, the dictatorial regime of General Zia and his attempt to Islamize the country are all woven into the texture of the narrative. Rushdie comments on Soviet aggression of Afghanistan, the genocide in Bangladesh, the fundamental Islamic revolution of Khomeini against the monarchy of the Shah of Iran and of his family and its exodus from India to Pakistan after the Partition, the general elections in Pakistan, the Bangladesh war, etc. As T.N. Dhar has rightly pointed out, 'In Rushdie's estimation both Bhutto and Zia represent the worst period in Pakistan's history for they grew bigger and uglier as the country started growing fast in a stupid way' (1999: 199). Therefore, the major part of the shameful history of Pakistan gets connected with their rise to power.

Thus, Rushdie fictionalizes the real and justifies his imaginative treatment of history. Rushdie portrays the characters in a complex way by intertwining realism and symbolism. Iskander Harappa's wife Rani Harappa embroiders the shawls that depict the political oppression and cruelty of Isky's regime. The shawls, woven by Rani Harappa, symbolize not only Iskander Harappa's infidelity and violent conduct, but also the abuse of political power. The eighteen shawls she embroiders that are entitled 'The Shamelessness of Iskander the Great' encompass realism and symbolism that makes the work allegorical. As Brendon Nicholls rightly observes, these shawls are 'the best indication of the seamlessness of oppression. The shawls with their secrets function as an aspect of the theme of repression. They are patiently worked expressions of how chauvinism and political suppression converge' (2007: 115). They are all concentrated expressions of the fact that Pakistan has followed the wrong direction. Thus, Rushdie reflects his perspective through Rani Harappa who sees Pakistani history as a grotesque nightmare. Taking recourse to history, Rushdie in his collection of essays, *Imaginary Homelands:*

Essays and Criticism comments that Benazir Bhutto in her book *Daughter of the East* was unwilling to admit that her martyred parent committed any sin. Rushdie observes: 'The resulting omissions from the story are as revealing as the bits she puts in. She manages, for example, to get through her entire account of her father's government without once mentioning the little matter of genocide in Baluchistan ... . She fails entirely to mention Bhutto's strenuous efforts at election rigging in 1977 ... . Worst of all, she falsifies Bhutto's role in the events leading to the secession of Bangladesh ...' (1991: 53). Rushdie in his *Imaginary Homelands: Essays and Criticism* confirms that the other ruler portrayed in the novel, Zia-Ulhaq, Islamized Pakistan constitutionally. He 'was one of the cruellest of modern tyrants ... . Pakistan under Zia has become a nightmarish, surreal land, in which battlefield armaments meant for the Afghan rebel are traded more or less openly on the country's black markets' (1991: 53). Rushdie further adds, 'The medieval misogynistic stultifying ideology which Zia imposed on Pakistan in his 'Islamization' programme was the ugliest possible face of the faith and by which most Pakistani Muslims were, I believe, disturbed and frightened' (1991: 54). Rushdie's portrayal of General Raza Hyder is very much similar to that of Zia-Ulhaq. Raza Hyder's origin and early career deviate from Zia's; but Raza's resemblance to the historical character increases as he enters the political scene. General Zia, a religious bigotry, believed that only religion could improve the state of affairs and put his ideology to severe and unrestrained practice. Similarly, the strategy Raza applies in reaching his goal is Islamization.

Rushdie has been very much disturbed by tyrants and tyranny from the beginning of his career. In his first three novels, *Grimus, Midnight's Children* and *Shame*, Rushdie makes an attack on the power-hungry tyrannical leaders of India and Pakistan. As a postmodern writer, he tries to find an effective action against tyrants. In *Shame* he observes, 'How does a dictator fall? You try and get rid of a dictator some time' (1995: 257). As a creative writer, Rushdie takes it up as his responsibility to present a critique on the politics of the Indian subcontinent. He aims at presenting a proper perspective of religion and politics. In an interview with John Haffenden, Rushdie says, 'I do think that if the state has a chance of surviving, it has to remove religion from itself, and when it does that it has a chance of removing the generals' (1985: 258). He strongly propagates the great ideals of French Revolution—Liberty, Equality and Fraternity and considers them alternatives to Islamization. He avows, 'Few mythologies survive close examination ... only two options: disintegration, or a new dictatorship ... no, there is a third ... . The third option is the substitution of a new myth for the old one. Here are three such myths, all available from stock at short notice: liberty; equality; fraternity. I recommend them highly' (1985: 251). In spite of presenting all the negative facts, Rushdie lures the readers into reading the book. He achieves the impossible by using historical allusions and magic realism with great aplomb. As the narrator wants to give an image of the country and of its past, the ancient history of the country is evoked throughout the novel in the names and actions of the characters. Timothy Brennon is of the opinion that, 'Shame hides history in allusive references to the past which are buried in casual place names and family titles and ironic reincarnations of figures from legend' (1988: 211). The ex-major general Iskander Mirza of Punjabi bureaucracy returns in the figure of Iskander Harappa. He is alluded to in *Midnight's Children* also as Brigadier Iskander. The surname 'Harappa' alludes to the ancient Harappan civilization. The famous Macedonian conqueror Alexander who invaded India in 326 B.C. is referred to in a chapter entitled 'Alexander the Great' that deals with the rise of Bhutto. 'Hyder' refers to the legendary hero, Hyder Ali of Mysore (1761–1782), a free booter from the South. Omar Khayyam Shakil takes his name from the famous medieval Persian poet, astrologer and also, by legend, a doctor. The name Sufia is based on the Muslim mystical sect 'Sufis'. Rushdie alludes to some of the great Mughal rulers like Babur, Aurangzeb and Humayun. Pinkie Aurangazeb, Iskander's mistress; and Babar, Omar Khayyam's brother, recreates the last great Mughal monarch Aurangazeb and another emperor Babur, respectively. Mahmoud, Bilquis's father alludes to Mahmud, the founder of the Ghaznawid dynasty who conquered Lahore in 1010 A.D. All of these names '... exhibit a kind of nearness to history, but escape becoming entangled within the formulas of historical narrative ... (and) obliquely suggest the archaeological sediments of once-absolute power, whose fragmented legacy is unearthed or re-articulated in the present as ironic decline. There is here an unmistakable hint that any autocracy—civilian or military, secular or Islamized—might heed such cautions from history and exercise restraint in the interests of longevity' (Nicholls 2007: 114).

Besides historical allusions, Rushdie uses magic realism lavishly to heighten the effect of narration. Though history is always considered to be scientific and authentic, no historical document is out of ambiguity and irregular. As it is the Victorian who always writes and records the history, it is always one dimensional and partial. The selfishness and the parochial temperament of the historians are responsible for making history more creative than authentic. So Rushdie observes, 'History is always ambiguous. Facts are hard to establish and capable of being given many meanings. Reality is built on our prejudices, misconceptions and ignorance as well as on our perceptiveness and knowledge' (Rushdie 1991: 25). In a way many historians have made history more a fantasy than a reality. But Rushdie uses fantasy to present the reality in an amazingly perceptive method. And in some novels, he dovetails history and fantasy which ultimately turn to magic realism.

The birth of Omar Khayyam appears more a fantasy than a reality. His father is hinted to be a British and the identity of his mother is also a mystery. He is said to have been conceived by one of the three Shakil sisters. His conception or birth is not truly revealed. Rushdie successfully clubs the birth of Omar Khayyam to the fantastic thought, thereby making it appear real. Reality is, thus, revealed in an exaggerated manner. Rushdie uses magic realism to portray his ideas and thoughts through the character of Sufiya Zinobia, daughter of Raza Hyder. She grows physically, but remains retarded psychologically. The manner in which she kills the turkeys of Pinkie Aurangazeb, attempts to strangulate her brother-in-law by twisting his neck, four unidentified, decapitated youths, etc. are all a figment of fantasy thawed into reality. The birth of children to Sufiya's sister Naveed in profusion is likened to the growing population of the country. This profuse birth of children appears quite unbelievable. Unable to bear the strain, Naveed commits suicide; maybe in a way symbolizing what lies in store for Pakistan. The birth of children is acceptable as reality, but the profusion and the steady increase only mystify the reader. The clairvoyancy of Talvar Ulhaq is magnified to fantasy level. It enables him to root out thieves, murderers, dons and political plotters from carrying out their schemes. Throughout his narration, Rushdie, thus, attempts to combine the unreal and the fantastic with the historical facts of Pakistan. Rushdie not only dramatizes his disgust and anguish at the negative aspects of the political and cultural history of Pakistan, but also asserts that someday people would be drawn to the old myth of liberty, equality and fraternity.

Works Cited

Brennon, Timothy. 'Shame's Holy Book.' *The Journal of Indian Writing in English* 16.2 (July 1988). Print.

Dhar, T.N. *History-Fiction Interface in Indian English Novel.* New Delhi: Prestige, 1999. Print.

Haffenden, John. *Novelists in Interview.* London: Methuen, 1985. Print.

Nicholls, Brendon. 'Reading Pakistan in Salman Rushdie's *Shame.*' *The Cambridge Companion to Salman Rushdie.* Ed. Abdul Razak Gurnah. New York: Cambridge UP, 2007. Print.

Parameswaran, Uma. *The Perforated Sheet: Essays on Salman Rushdie's Art.* New Delhi: East-West Press, 1988. Print.

Rushdie, Salman. *Shame.* London: Vintage, 1995. Print.

——. *Imaginary Homelands: Essays and Criticism 1981–1991.* London: Granta Books, 1991. Print.

Tikko, S.K. '*Shame:* A Modern Comic Epic in Prose.' *The Novels of Salman Rushdie.* Eds G.R. Taneja and R.K. Dhawan. New Delhi: Indian Society for Commonwealth Studies, 1992. Print.

11

Insurgency as History in Rushdie's *Shalimar the Clown*: A Note

K. PURUSHOTHAM

Shalimar the Clown (2005), Salman Rushdie's ninth novel, like his earlier ones, deals with history. Rushdie employs postmodernist technique to delineate the theme of borders and borderlessness. According to postmodernism, the contemporary reality is without borders thereby every part becomes a part of everything else and vice versa. The locale of the novel, therefore, encompasses parts of the world from America to Kashmir. The protagonist's story is no longer his story *per se*. Kashmir, which was earlier idyllic and serene, is no longer so; it is not immune when different parts of the world are at collision. In the subsequent period, Kashmir gets afflicted with terrorism. Rushdie portrays in the novel how the people of Kashmir betrayed it paving the way for destruction.

Pachigam, a serene village in Kashmir, becomes the centre of destructive activities. When a teenaged Muslim boy called Shalimar falls in love with and makes love to a young girl named Boonyi, the elders of the village, true to the tradition of brotherhood in Kashmir, bless the young couple upholding the values of Kashmiriyat practice. They perform their marriage. But Boonyi, being unhappy with the development, decides to wait for a chance to leave Pachigam in search of becoming an accomplished dancer. Boonyi is on the lookout for an opportunity to dance in a performance for Max Ophuls, the American ambassador to India. With the help of Max, she leaves Pachigam to lead a new life. Max and Boonyi get closer to each other, 'My body will be yours to command and it will be my joy to obey' (Rushdie 2005: 316).

Their relationship, based on infatuation and being superficial, begins to wane. Boonyi's search for fulfilment and accomplishment is not realized. Having lost her physical attraction, she no longer attracts the attention of Max. Confined to solitude, she becomes addicted to chewing tobacco and opium consumption that provide her means of daydreaming and escape from reality. Meanwhile Max decides to send her back home at a time when Boonyi reveals to him of her being conceived. The relationship, having assumed the proportion of a scandal, attracts the attention of the media. The personal becomes the public. President Zakir Hussain expresses a sense of unhappiness about the way the American Ambassador conducts himself, 'angry statements in private about the godless American's exploitation of an innocent Hindu girl' (2005: 339). As a result of this, Max is withdrawn as the American ambassador. Max's wife makes arrangement for Boonyi's safe delivery of the child, and makes arrangements for her to reach Pachigam. Boonyi comes back to Pachigam as a failed woman. She realizes that the freedom she chose was only an illusion.

Back home, Shalimar becomes a part of *jihad*, the holy war against the infidel forces. He is determined to take revenge against his wife, Max and the daughter of his wife. Having killed Boonyi, Shalimar then sets out to America and kills Max at his daughter's place, India Ophuls's house. The latter learns that her father's killer is none other than her mother's husband, Shalimar.

II

The author represents through Shalimar the drastic transition from innocence to betrayal among the inhabitants of Kashmir. Over a period of time, the Kashmiriyat values of the valley are degraded. The serene and idyllic Kashmir is home for destruction, terrorism and militancy. The two cultures of Kashmir are separated by a temporal boundary. The innocent, beautiful, multicultural and hybrid world of old Kashmir is temporally demarcated by the violent, betrayed and divided world of the contemporary Kashmir. Shalimar, who was innocent in the beginning of the novel, becomes violent as the events unfold. He crosses over to the other side to avenge his wife because of the betrayal. Shalimar seems to be fighting for a religious cause, but in reality, he uses the religious veil as a platform to kill his wife's lover.

Pachigam becomes home for extremists. The armed forces use the gun against the people of Pachigam. Everyone being killed indiscriminately, bloodshed replaces love that Pachigam was earlier known for. 'The village of Pachigam still existed on maps of Kashmir, but that day it ceased to exist anywhere else, except in memory' (2005: 309). Rushdie portrays in the novel how the Kashmiris are subjected to the atrocities of the terrorists as well as the armed forces leaving them no option, having been 'undone by the twin forces of nationalism and religious fundamentalism. As usual in Rushdie's novels, these forces are not the enemies of enlightenment as much as they are the enemies of freedom' (Roth 2005: 19).

India Ophuls, daughter of Max and Boonyi is shocked at the developments. Having assumed a new name Kashmira, she decides firmly to avenge the murder of her father. Kashmira leaves for Kashmir in search of her identity. She survives the death of her Indian mother and American father killed by Shalimar. The twist in Shalimar's revenge is the survival of Kashmira. Her survival leaves Shalimar's revenge incomplete. She vows to herself to avenge the death of her mother and father. Targeting Shalimar, she plans to kill Shalimar's ego which she believes is the cause of her parents' death. Kashmira at last realizes about her true identity. The realization on her part symbolizes a new beginning. She is an embodiment and symbol of hope and regeneration emerging from betrayal. At symbolic level, the survival of Kashmira indicates that Kashmir problem will find an amicable and peaceful solution.

III

Though the motif in the novel is revenge, one form of revenge is destructive and the other is redemptive. Shalimar avenges by means of *jihad* and blood. But Kashmira does not resort to mindless violence, 'She was not fire but ice' (2005: 382). The novel being a lament of peace, innocence and brotherhood, Rushdie shows hope by the end of the novel. Cowley writes in this regard, 'Shalimar looks to several beginnings: reflecting on what has been lost in Kashmir; it also looks forward to a time when the words Muslim and Hindu will once more be merely 'descriptions' rather than 'divisions'' (2005: 27). The novelist focuses on the movement from innocence to betrayal. The end of the novel, however, hints at heralding the strength of hope and human spirit.

Ever since the Partition, a lot of sustained ill-will has been in place between India and Pakistan with Kashmir as the never ending bone of contention. Yet Kashmir retains the positive qualities that it has been known for especially of its people, their attitude and culture. Rushdie is critical of religion as a subterfuge for spreading terrorism. This could be one of the reasons as to why he is acceptable to the West, but rejected by the Islamic countries. Undaunted, Rushdie's conviction and world view continues to be represented in novel after novel, and *Shalimar the Clown* is another one in a row that represents is conviction and world view.

This aspect is symbolically suggested through the character Kashmira, who transforms from India to Kashmira. She embodies a new beginning from chaos, turmoil and terrorism to the beginning of a new dawn beckoned by hope. Kashmira's presence in the novel is indicative that Kashmir is not going to be destroyed but will hopefully regain her past glory that it has been known for.

Rushdie portrays the aspect of terrorism in a poignant way. He chooses two Kashmiri villages for the purpose. The villagers are involved in communal violence. They turn against one another. Shalimar, who turns a terrorist, is a part of the machinations of terrorism. The betrayal of the people of Kashmiri villages is suggestive of the destructive potential of terrorism. The plunders, destruction and total lack of regard for human rights are a consequence of terrorism.

Rushdie uses Max Ophuls to castigate the American international policy vis-à-vis the Third World. Max is a critical embodiment of the role of America in perpetrating terrorist activities in the Third World countries. Max happens to be the anti-Nazi war hero in the novel. America supports the terrorist activities in Kashmir through its Ambassador. In the novel, Max supports terrorists. The international policy of America is essentially governed by the motto of pitting one nation against the other within the Third World, and reap benefit out of the differences. Peace and harmony in South Asia and the Arabic region is disturbed by this kind of American policy. Through Max, who encourages terrorism in Kashmir, Rushdie castigates the American policy of using the Third World countries for its self-aggrandizement. Shalimar's anger against Max is, therefore, not only because of his liaison with his wife Boonyi, but also because of Max's support to terrorism in Kashmir.

Works Cited

Cowley, Jason. 'From Here to Kashmir.' Review of *Shalimar the Clown. Guardian Weekly* 173 (14 September 2005). Print.

Roth, Marco. 'Give the People What They Want.' Review of *Shalimar the Clown. The Times Literary Supplement* 5345 (9 September 2005). Print.

Rushdie, Salman. *Shalimar the Clown.* London: Jonathan Cape, 2005. Print.

12

Gandhian Movement in Chaman Nahal's *The Crown and the Loincloth*

M. RAJAGOPALACHARY AND K. YADAGIRI

Chaman Nahal's *The Crown and the Loincloth* (1981) re-presents the freedom movement of the period 1915–1922 with meticulous attention to detail and humane understanding of people and situations. The title of the novel suggests the conflict between the British Government, represented by the crown, and the national movement for Independence, represented by the loincloth, which stands for Gandhi. The variety of characterization and action, the deft mingling of the historical with the fictional, the powerful play of the tragic and the farcical and the moving multiplicity of sense and incident, all combine to make *The Crown and the Loincloth* 'a forceful recordation of the first of the three phases of the Age of Gandhi' (Reddy 1994: 168).

The Crown and the Loincloth deals with the socio-economic, political disturbances and effects of the freedom struggle. It is one of Nahal's novels of Gandhian Quartet, the other three being *The Salt of Life, The Triumph of the Tricolour,* and *Azadi. The Salt of Life* deals with the Salt Satyagraha to achieve freedom for India besides the fight against social evils like drinking of liquor and untouchability. In *The Triumph of the Tricolour,* Nahal refers to both the violent and non-violent movements of freedom struggle when the Gandhian struggle was paralysed for some time during the Quit India movement. *Azadi* shows the horrible consequences of Partition and suffering of both Hindus and Muslims. *The Crown and the Loincloth* articulates in fictional terms the victory of Gandhi and Gandhian ideals in counteracting the British Government on the one hand and vindicates the nobility of non-violence over terrorism on the other. Gandhi is the guiding force in the novel drawing people into the national movement like a magnet and influencing their lives. The novel projects Gandhi at the macro-level and Sunil at the micro-level each carrying out his own destiny. In the words of K.R. Srinivas Iyengar, 'It is verily the story of the transmutation of the ordinary one to the heroic extraordinary (and Sunil's end is almost a foretaste of what Gandhi's is going to be)' (1981: 77).

The destiny of the characters in the novel is invariably linked with the Gandhian movement. The personal and social lives of the protagonist Sunil coalesce with each other throughout the novel. The central meaning and vision of the novel lies in Sunil's quest for fulfilment in love and Gandhian ideology. Though the novel depicts the whole gamut of Sunil's experience with the dutiful and wifely love of Kusum, the spiritually stirring and maddening love of Rehana and the intensely physical and passionate relationship with Priti, Sunil's active participation in the Gandhian movement and the consequent transformation to be a true Satyagrahi assumes a greater significance. Deeply influenced by the Gandhian spirit, Sunil seeks the meaning of life in social emancipation of the untouchables, commitment to the spinning wheel, attempts at preserving the unity of workers against their exploiters and spontaneous and humane act of sacrifice to protect a British in the true spirit of a Satyagrahi. Sunil succeeds in his death to inspire his wife Kusum to live for the cause of freedom of India.

II

Gandhi is one of the major characters of *The Crown and the Loincloth*. His main concern was to drive the British out of India. He discards violence as a weapon to fight against the British. He adopts the principles of non-violence and truth to achieve freedom for India. Nahal portrays Gandhi as an ordinary human being ridden with conflict who rose to the extraordinary stature with his steadfast commitment to moral principles. The conflict in Gandhi's mind, his doubts about himself, and his leadership as well as his faith in himself and his principles to a certain extent are parallelled by the conflict in Sunil's mind, his active support to the freedom struggle, his disillusionment with its leaders and finally his humane act of rescuing a foreigner at the cost of his life. Nahal depicts in detail Gandhi's Non-cooperation movement against the British. Though the Government arrests Motilal Nehru and his son Jawaharlal Nehru, it hesitates to arrest Gandhi when he launched the movement. Gandhi still wanted to put non-cooperation into practice and initially he was worried about its success.

> Non-cooperation. No more loyalty to this government, no more allegiance. But how to give it a practical shape, a shape that may be understood by the millions in the villages, a shape that may register some response with authorities? These details Gandhi had yet to work out, but the vision before him was clear. They would break some law and fill the jails. If only he had the full support of his countrymen, India would win its swaraj in under a year. Might sound preposterous—considering the adversary they were pitched against—but it *was* possible. (Nahal 1981: 129–30)

When Jallianwala Bagh tragedy took place, Gandhi was hurt deeply. Though Gandhi opposed the British, he had extended his hand of friendship to them all along and identified himself with the British in the fond hope that they would give India an equal status in the empire, and time and again he had placed his services at their disposal. Now, with Jallianwala Bagh massacre, he regrets his misplaced trust. He has lost all his faith in the Englishman. The Englishman has undone himself with the ghastly act against the innocent people at Jallianwala Bagh. 'That General Dyer had fired a bullet into him as well, though he wouldn't know it; he had killed Gandhi's faith in the Englishman' (Nahal 1981: 126). This compels Gandhi to fight back the British with a new weapon of non-cooperation. And he gives a call to the people to follow him in the cause of the motherland. Consequently, Motilal Nehru aligns with the Congress. Jawaharlal Nehru gives up his practice in 1920 and becomes a full time worker for the Congress. The Indians give up the British titles they have received.

> In 1920, Gandhi presented a new constitution for the Congress, enlarging its scope to make it a party of the masses. In July 1920, Tilak, the last of the old guards passed away, leaving Gandhi in undisputed command. In the same year, the Congress formally passed the resolution on non-cooperation, and week after week Gandhi explained in *Navajivan* and *Young India* what the movement meant. The coming year, 1921, saw the implementation of the movement. (Nahal 1981: 325)

Gandhi influences Sunil to start a very special type of store in Ajitha as a full time worker by resigning his teaching job. He asks Sunil to learn spinning, a new language, which touches the chords of Indian villages everywhere in the nook and corner of India. Once peasants follow Sunil in spinning, they follow him in everything, including politics.

> You will learn and teach the other villagers, how to spin, and you will buy the thread spun by them. You will then give this thread to the weavers and buy the material woven by them. And then you will try and sell this material. You will persuade the people to wear this instead of foreign mill-cloth. Other dedicated men like you might start similar stores in other villages and towns, but you must proceed on the assumption that even if not a single other individual comes forward, you'll do it alone (Nahal 131).

Thus, Gandhi appears as a character as well as a force to reckon with throughout the novel.

III

Sunil, the protagonist of *The Crown and the Loincloth*, is a replica of Gandhian movement. The author shows Gandhian philosophy through him in the novel. Sunil, a school master drawn to Gandhiji like many other obscure men, becomes an active political worker. Though he confesses to Gandhiji that he is an ordinary man, he rises later to be heroic and extraordinary through his death in saving the Prince of Wales. He is concerned for the poor. He wants to improve their economical condition, and lead them out of slavery from the British. Sunil plays a few characteristic roles as husband and father, lover cheated of the desired consummation with Rehana, and sensualist losing himself in polyandrist Priti, and also khadi salesman, and itinerant medicine man and satyagrahi.

Sunil actively participates in freedom struggle and wants his wife also to join him in response to Gandhi's call for *hartal* against the Rowlatt Bills. He tells his wife: 'Under these laws they can arrest us at will, without warrant, and try us in courts without a jury. Gandhi had given out a call that sixth of April be observed as a hartal by the entire nation (Nahal 51). Gandhi was to address the public meeting at Jallianwala Bagh on 13 April 1919. Sunil actively encourages people to attend the meeting. But he is caught by the police and brought before Dyer. During the interrogation Sunil exhibits rare courage and confidence and Dyer understands that Sunil is a true follower of Gandhi:

> Dyer could see the man was not a peasant. There was a cultivated air about him, and his bearing indicated breeding; he also spoke such prefect English. That was all the more dangerous, from Dyer's point of view. That meant he was one of those petty leaders who had pledged themselves to Gandhi. (Nahal 87)

Dyer wants to teach him a lesson by punishing him severely. Mr Kenneth Ashby, the Asst. Commissioner of Amritsar district who knows the loyalty of his father Thakur Shanthi Nath tries to protect Sunil. But Sunil does not relent and expresses his readiness to take part in the nationalist activities once again if he has a chance, thus braving the trouble.

Sunil becomes the first volunteer in the movement of Non-cooperation. He sets up in Ajitha the first of the Khadi Bhandar stores denoted to homespun cotton material, that were soon to spread all over India. Many of Thakur Shanti Nath's workers leave him and join hands with Sunil. In addition to running the store, he takes active part in enrolling members into the Congress. Sunil's new house is in a predominantly Muslim populated area of the village. His neighbour, Muzaffar actively helps Sunil in the spinning programme. Rehana, Muzaffar's wife and other women work for the Congress and help Kusum in running the store. Under the influence of Gandhi, Rehana discards the *purdah* system. She accompanies Sunil to the different houses of weavers or spinners in the village. Though Rehana and Sunil are attracted to each other, Rehana forbids physical union with him as it goes against the Muslim law.

In connection with the visit of Duke of Connaught, there was a boycott by the Congressmen. Sunil and Muzaffar are sentenced to two months' imprisonment for their demonstration in Hall Bazaar against the Duke of Connaught. During the two months in jail period, Kusum and Rehana run the Khadi Bandar in Ajitha. Sunil's imprisonment, consequent estrangement from Kusum and his unconsummated love for Rehana lead him to the mission of solving the feud between the labour and timber merchants in Simla hills. Sunil seeks fulfilment in fighting for a social cause. He organizes protests against the merchants. On every Sunday there is a slogan-raising procession going through the bazaar at Rohru, shouting, 'Down with the timber merchants; we want justice'. The district officials sense the danger of the problem. As a result, the government bluntly tells the merchants to come to an agreement with the labourers, and there is a compromise.

> The principle of a standard wage, adequate medical treatment, leave, travel allowance back and forth from the place of recruitment, had all been accepted by the merchants. They had even agreed to pay the *mukhyas* their salary for the period they were in Rohru, deeming it as duty. (Nahal 219)

Sunil trains Amin Chand in Satygraha and explains it to others, so that the movement may continue even after his departure from the hills.

Sunil's reaction against the segregation of the habitations of the untouchables is Gandhian. In the hills and at different places, Sunil observes a peculiar phenomenon of untouchable villages called Dom's villages. The sweepers, the barbers, the cobblers, the washer-men and such outcasts live there. Sunil feels ashamed to be a Hindu for this blot of untouchability. He writes a letter to Gandhi about this. Gandhi suggests that he could either live in the midst of untouchables or bring one of them to live with him. Sunil adopts a young boy of fifteen years from one of the Dom's villages much to the consternation of the Timber merchants. Concerned about the health of Doms, Sunil becomes an itinerant medicine man within a week's training and helps the poor untouchables.

> He now went around with a bag in which he carried bandages, surgical scissors, a knife, a bottle of tincture benzine, some methylated sprit. And such simple medicines as quinine, aspirin, sulphadiazine, sulfgua-nadine, eye lotion. To these he added indigenous remedies, like Castor oil for constipation, mulathi for a cough, garlic and soda for indigestion. (Nahal 234)

Sunil also organizes relief for the outcasts with the help of Amin Chand and Duni Chand, the new recruits in the Congress. His infatuation for Rehana, however, interrupts his social service and he goes to meet Rehana on the day of her release from prison. His relations with Kusum get strained after his confession to her about his love for Rehana. Rehana's accidental death in Nainital places Sunil back on the tracks of the movement.

Sunil's visit to Lahore to see his distant relative and also the Prince of Wales bring about a turning point in the story. On the invitation of Kenneth Ashby, Assistant Commissioner of Amritsar district, Sunil visits the Fair and sits in the special enclosure near the dais. While the prince was watching the tonga race, suddenly three tongas rush straight towards the dais in an attempt to kill the prince as pre-planned by the revolutionaries. Sunil sees Rakesh disguised as a policeman whipping out a pistol and rushing towards the Prince. He jumps at once between Rakesh and the prince to rescue the latter braving the bullets fired by Rakesh and courting death in the hospital later. This act of Sunil's sacrifice reveals the spirit of a true Satyagrahi. 'Indeed while fighting the British, it was the duty of every Indian to protect the life and property of every single Britisher. Sunil had acted in the true spirit of a *Satyagrahi'* (Nahal 407).

A true satyagrahi, according to Gandhi, is inspired by humanism and acts with courage and conviction to protect the fellowmen beyond sex, creed and race. Sunil becomes a hero in the eyes of both the Indians and the British. He seeks fulfilment in freedom fight following Gandhian ideals of truth, non-violence, satyagraha and service to the humanity. Thus Chaman Nahal re-presents fictionally the Gandhian movement in the freedom struggle and its influence on the Indians through the protagonist Sunil.

Works Cited

Goyal, Bhagwat S. 'The Possibilities of Human Existence: A Note on Nahal's *The Crown and the Loincloth.*' *Culture and Commitment: Aspects of Indian Literature in English.* Meerut: Shalabh Book House, 1984, 128–30. Print.

Iyengar, K.R. Srinivas. Review of *The Crown and the Loincloth*: *A Novel. The Literary Criterion* 16.3 (1981), 76–79. Print.

Mathur, O.P. 'The Novels of Chaman Nahal: A Penultimate View.' *Studies in Contemporary Indian Fiction in English.* Ed. A.N. Dwivedi. Allahabad: Kitab Mahal, 1987, 319–33. Print.

Nahal, Chaman. *The Crown and the Loincloth.* New Delhi: Vikas Publications, 1981. Print.

Reddy, K. Venkata. 'The Novelist as Affirmationist: The Achievement of Chaman Nahal.' *Critical Studies in Commonwealth Literature.* New Delhi: Prestige Books, 1994, 163–78. Print.

13

An Anglo-Indian '*Nama*': History in *The Trotter-Nama: A Chronicle*

G. SUJATHA

The Trotter-Nama is a humorous, all encompassing narrative complete with a self-centred, grotesque, omniscient, omnipresent narrator. It is a mock-epic family saga spanning two centuries and over seven generations of an Anglo-Indian family. It is not just a novel; it is an illustrated chronicle of the events that occur in an Anglo-Indian family and perhaps also the first novelized history of the Anglo-Indians. By writing an epic-narrative using eastern and western modes of narration, I. Allan Sealy breaks the boundaries between genres. He also breaks geographical boundaries when Eugene Trotter, the protagonist-narrator, travels throughout the world in search of information regarding the Trotters, thus, bringing into the novel the concept of transnationalism.

The journey of a solitary hero in a novel through a nation's social landscape fuses the world inside the novel with the world outside and unifies the nation to construct the notion of an 'imagined community' **(**Sealy 1999:**)**. In *The Trotter-Nama,* Eugene Trotter's journey throughout the world, however, fuses the entire world creating a transnational community. As Eugene Trotter says, '... we came from all over, not just England, and went all over not just to England' (7). With the geographical boundaries waning, *The Trotter-Nama* becomes a narrative that spreads beyond boundaries.

Narrating the important events in the history of the Anglo-Indian community, Eugene's contempt for European historiography and history becomes obvious in the constant abuse that he heaps upon history and historians. He favours the chronicle—a contrast to history:

> The foul substance is called history
> And its opposite

Is the Chronicle
Which may be illustrated?
Profusely
Is it colourful?
In the extreme
Has flavour?
Honey in the mouth, honey in the belly.

... Its supreme exponent?
You.
Does it usher in a new age?
It ushers in an age of promise
Which is the end of what lie?
It is the end of Historie.
Go up, Cup-Bearer. (375–77)

Again, he describes the historian as

INTERLOPER! SNAKE IN THE GRASS! DUST DEVIL! ARCH FIEND! ARCH TEMPTER! SERPENT IN THE GARDEN! SEDUCER! LECHER! CAD! THUG! DECIVER! FATHER OF LIES! BANDED KARAIT! SNAKE IN THE DUST! BANDIT KARAIT! INTRUDER! IMPOSTER! PRETENDER! POSTURER! BOGUS SALESMAN! PETTY CROOK! CHARLATAN! WHITED SEPULCHRE! ASP IN THE BOSOM! LYING TOAD! PHARISEE! DISSEMBLER! MOUNTEBANK! HUMBUGGING TUTOR! CURRUPTOR! FALSE FRIEND! CUCKOO! HAWK CUCKOO! CROW IN PEACOCK'S FEATHERS! IN DOVE'S FEATHERS! DESPOILER! DEFLOWERER! HISTORIAN! (383)

European historiographers like Arnold J Toynbee define the method of recording history as ascertainment and recording of 'facts' (Anderson 1983: 35). Facts lay the foundation to any historical document. As E.H. Carr says 'it [history] is a continuous process of interaction between the historian and his facts ...' (Toynbee 1965). Thus, history relies on facts but is based on the individual perception of those facts by the historian. Behan McCullagh says that when a historian finds any other story that could bring ambiguity to the existing fact, then he prefers not to include that story (quoted in Tej Ram Sharma 1987). In short, historians try to locate facts that would confirm their accepted theories (McCullagh 1998). Thus, history becomes a one-sided opinion of the historian. Criticizing the method of recording history, Kelly Oliver says that history as recorded until now looks at events from a 'Eurocentric view of law' (2001: 41). Sealy's *Trotter-Nama* makes light of history's tendency to adhere to facts and seems to suggest that there is a definite difference between the narration of historical facts by just anyone and the narration of history by those who have lived through it (Oliver 2001: 54). Eugene, the narrator, traverses through time and space to become the omnipresent narrator who narrates the experiences of his community, while Montagu, the anti-Trotter, cannot write history of the Trotters as he is an outsider, a fake Trotter. Eugene writes regarding Montagu:

His principal name?
The Anti-Trotter.
His other name
Theobald Horatius Montagu
Was he a Trotter of the flesh?
In no part, form, or substance. (Sealy 1999: 375)

Eugene dismisses Montagu's method of writing history, based as it is on mere facts and corresponding dates, and writes the Trotters' history in the form of a 'Nama' because it allows him the freedom to not just write history but also to create legends, myths and stories around that history. The word 'Nama' suggests not just the writing of history but also that of writing a letter, a diploma, a work, a book, an exemplar, a model and a type. The word 'Nama' also means a mirror, a looking glass, a flood, a torrent, an hour book, a letter announcing victory as well as an epic (Oliver 2001: 51). The 'Nama', unlike history, not only records events and corresponding dates but also includes local tales, myths, genealogical details, journal entries, personal details, verses and illustrations. The form does not narrate events in a continuous manner but is interrupted several times to include interpolations, which may or may not have a connection with the main historical narrative. However, the form, despite its affinities with the epic, is still not an epic for, after the interpolated narrative ends, the chronicle continues, actually indicating that the 'historical narrative (has) resumed.' Hence, the form of the 'Nama' gives Eugene a flexibility that allows him to narrate his history, write his book, pen his epic or create a work that combines all these forms in one. The 'Nama' also gives him the scope to narrate *his* version of the community's history by accommodating myth, fantasy and legend.

However, in *The Trotter-Nama,* apart from the 'Nama' elements such as myth and genealogical details, Eugene also includes dictionary meanings, information from encyclopaedias, advertisements, journal entries, table talk, scientific calculations and archives thereby transcending the generic boundaries of 'Nama' itself. The Cup-Bearer, who stands for the imagined reader, interrupts the Chronicler whenever he starts rambling, questions whenever he attempts to exaggerate and interrogates whenever he ventures to lie. In short, the Cup-Bearer intervenes whenever the narrative slips. The 'authenticity' of the narration formed by the intrusion of the Cup-Bearer in the story is evident in the following quotes:

Bidi in his hand, he marched off round the saltpeter hill–
–*When horses without number were his for the riding, Narrator?*–
–rode off around the saltpeter hill and across the burning plain he had once used for target practice. (149)

The Trotter-Nama, thus, no longer remains a chronicle or history or novel or an epic but goes beyond the boundaries of these genres to establish a new kind of writing that defies all accepted norms of writing history and fiction.

Sealy seems to uphold the Eastern method of recording history, for history as recorded by the West does not allow inclusion of myths as it is against the basic precepts of rationalism and adheres to plain facts and corresponding dates. Sealy believes that there are countless Indian forms that can be 'revived and intelligently reworked so that Indian modernism need not be a wholesale imitation of foreign objects (1999).' In the preface to *The Trotter-Nama,* Sealy acknowledges that he wanted to recreate an Indian *Tin-Drum;* however, it was Abu'l Fazl's *Akbar-Nama* that finally gave him the inspiration to write *The Trotter-Nama.*

Akbar-Nama is a biographical account of Akbar the Great written by Abu'l Fazl who begins the *Nama* in customary praise of Allah (Fazl 1989). He also praises God who has given him the opportunity to write the chronicle and explains the labour involved, the responsibility and honour bestowed on him to write the biography and who has created 'Word' and 'Speech,' which will help him complete the arduous task of writing *Akbar-Nama.* After showering praises on God and paying respects to saints and others who have helped him, he opens *Akbar-Nama* by giving an account of secret annunciations and holy manifestations, which took place before Akbar's birth. Fazl says that according to reliable sources, innumerable miracles occurred before the birth of Akbar. He narrates, for example, an incident where Miriam Makani while carrying Akbar expresses her desire for a mango. Her half-brother, Khwaja Mu'azzam, sees a glorious light shining upon the forehead of Miriam Makani, when he returns with the mangoes (Fazl 1989: 44–45). He takes this miracle as an indication of the celestial, majestic presence in her womb. He narrates various miraculous incidents that occur before the birth of Akbar.

The narrative is interrupted here to include Akbar's genealogical tree which Fazl traces from Adam, the first man created by God, according to Quran and places him at the fifty-third generation after Adam. Fazl uses honorary epithets to address people related to Akbar. Miryam Makani is addressed as 'cupola of chastity,' Her Majesty Alanquwa as the 'veil of purity' and deceased people like Adam and Seth, who according to Fazl are the first and second generation in Akbar's genealogical tree, are mentioned with respect indicated by the words 'Peace be upon Him', a form of address reserved only for the highest in Islam.

He employs verses to give a poetical touch when the narrative gets prosaic and uses them as a means to eulogise the people close to the emperor. He also includes an ode, written by the court-poet Faiyyazi at the birth of Akbar's sons, in its entirety. When the ode ends, Fazl, asks his reader: 'Where was I? Whither has the plenteous flood of words carried me?' (1989: 462). Fazl continues to narrate how Akbar established an empire in India, founded a religion called Din-i-Illahi and also details the life of young prince Salim, whose erratic lifestyle forced Akbar to take the extreme step of sending him away for rigorous training at a very young age. *Akbar-Nama* ends with Fazl giving details of the peaceful regime established by Akbar.

Sealy, too, uses phrases like 'cupola of chastity,' 'veil of purity' every time he mentions the name Sultana Trotter, Justin Aloysius Trotter's first wife and the mother of Mik Trotter. The words 'Peace be upon Him' are used whenever Sealy mentions the Great Trotter. Sealy employs ornate language for exaggerated flattery describing the Great Trotter, in the same style as Fazl does when he praises Miriam Makani. An excerpt from *The Trotter-Nama* will substantiate the comparison:

> Great Trotter, Beloved of God, Cynosure of Mankind, Builder of Sans Souci, Feeder of One Lakh, Who Sweetens the Melon, Who Will Shortly Walk in the Sky, Whose Tower Scrapes the Heaven, Valiant One, Who Plucks the Liver of Crocodiles, Namer of Stars by Day, River-Course Changer, Holy One, Sleek Master, Heralder of the Ice Age, Causer of Lakes to Appear, Causer of Water to Run Uphill, Virile One, Beloved of Many, Who Fathered a Fat Son, Who Is Himself Fat, Who Eats Jakfruit [sic] Whole, Shapely One, Who Cannot be Outeaten ... (240–41)

Sealy's narrator Eugene Trotter, like Fazl, asks his Cup-Bearer at various places in the novel the question 'Where was I?' and the Cup-Bearer directs him to the previously narrated event.

The *Babur-Nama* (Ghazi (tr) 1998), unlike the *Akbar-Nama,* is autobiographical, hence ornate language and extensive use of superlatives are missing (Ghazi 1998). Babur's memoir is a simple and honest narrative of a soldier, beginning with the invocation of God: 'In the name of God, the Merciful, the Compassionate' (1). After this customary beginning, Babur writes 'In the month of Ramzan of the year 899 (June 1494) and in the twelfth year of my age, I became the ruler in the country of Farghana' (1). Following these few lines, the chronicle is interrupted and Babur gives an account of the geographical description of the country Farghana. While describing Farghana, he narrates a story associated with the creation of Ha Darwesh, a small town in Farghana. The end of this interpolation is indicated by these words: 'Historical narrative resumed.' The *Babur-Nama* is also interrupted intermittently to include genealogical details of not only his family but also his close relatives (19). He also intersperses the narrative with short verse written by either him or recollected verse of others suitable to the event he describes.

The *Babur-Nama* incorporates various forms of writing, including the diary format. It takes the diary format from 925 AH—3 January to 23 December 1519 AD to be precise—when Babur takes the fort of Bajaur. Then, the *Babur-Nama* takes the form of a scientific survey with Babur describing the flora and fauna of India. *The Trotter-Nama* follows *Babur-Nama* also in its narrative style. *Babur-Nama* deviates from the chronicle of events intermittently to describe unrelated items only to resume the narrative with the words: 'Chronicle resumed.' Example of this style are the inclusion of interpolated accounts— 'Concerning an alleged painter, one Zoffanij.' A note on the crocodiles of Hindoostan,' 'The black partridge (Francolinus francolinus) praises sugar' etc.

Writing in the style of the 'Nama', Sealy also includes verses in the chronicle that complement the mood of the event being described. *The Trotter-Nama* follows the diary format in the same manner as Babur records his military exploits when Mik attempts to record his military achievements: 'The Military Memoirs of General Mik Trotter (translated from the Persian)' (272). *The Trotter-Nama* at times looks like a translated work with footnotes and additional notes when the narrator wishes to inform the reader regarding the lacunae and misinterpretation in earlier works.

Eugene Trotter, like the translator of *Babur-Nama*, translates some of the words and offers explanations and additional notes on those words. When he mentions the word *Tire* on the weekly menu for breakfast at Dr Bellow's School, Madras, he adds an additional note explaining *Tire: 'Tire, O Wedding Guest, is called dahi this side of India. It is soured milk or curds.'* He also gives the Latin names for indigenous flora and fauna (as mentioned earlier) as part of the narrative.

Apart from liberally imitating the style used in the 'Nama', Sealy employs the style used in 'Ain' of Abu'l Fazl's *Ain-i-Akbari* to write interpolated narratives. The word *Ain,* in this context means, 'fit or proper time,' thus the title of the text means 'The Time of Akbar' (*A Comprehensive Persian-English Dictionary* 132). In the *Ain-i-Akbari,* while describing the reign of Akbar, Abu'l Fazl inserts information such as 'The Manner of Refining Gold' (*Ain* 7, 21) or 'The Method of Refining Silver' (*Ain* 7, 23). Again, in the *Ain,* he gives the recipes of some favourite dishes cooked in the 'Shahi Bawarchi Khana' of the Emperor Akbar such as 'Zard Biring, 'Qabul', 'Khushaka', 'Khichri', etc. Abu'l Fazl also includes the statistics of the prices of certain articles (*Ain* 27, 65) and writes detailed notes 'On Perfumes, On Flavours and recipes of Oil' (*Ain* 30, 79), *The Trotter-Nama* details 'How the gypsonometer is made' (73), 'How a fortune is made (150), 'On the correct manner of harvesting ice in Quebec and Massachusetts, North America (95) and the recipe of the Trotter curry (363). Furthermore, the protagonist of *The Trotter-Nama* Eugene, like the poet in Akbar's court Fayyazi, commands the cup-bearer or Saki (in Persian) to bring him the choicest wine while narrating his story/history.

In content also, Sealy parodies, imitates or alludes to *Akbar-Nama, Babur-Nama* and the *Ain-i-Akbari* as well as other literary works. Beginning with the *Akbar-Nama*, the character of Justin Aloysius Trotter or The Great Trotter is akin to Akbar the Great. Like the miracles that preceded Akbar's birth, Justin's birth, in a ship in the middle of the Mediterranean, causes a raging storm to subside. Eugene describes the birth of the Great Trotter: 'A glistening globe, he greets the world like all great men from Akbar to Zoroaster, with a laugh' (113). Justin's and Akbar's mothers share the name, Miriam, derived from the name, Mary; Akbar and Justin, both have sons who were irresponsible, pleasure-seeking young boys and were sent away on rigorous training at a very young age; Justin and Akbar establish their own new religions, which were the combination of the precepts of different faiths. While, Akbar founded *Din-i-Illahi,* (which was practiced seriously only by Akbar and his court jester Birbal) Justin established *Din Havai.*

The adventures of the Great Trotter's son Mik are also similar to the adventures of Kim, the protagonist of Rudyard Kipling's novel of the same name. The protagonist Kimball O' Hara or Kim (Mik is an anagram of Kim), the orphaned son of a sergeant in the Irish regiment, spends his childhood as a vagrant until he meets an old lama from Tibet who accompanies him in his travels (Ganapathy-Dore 1995: 69). He falls into the hands of his father's old regiment where his aptitude for secret service is recognized by Colonel Creighton of the Ethnological Survey and he starts his life as a spy. Likewise, Mik, the son of Colonel Justin Aloysius Trotter, entrusted by his father to the Tibetan plinth-master to get educated, sees in his journey through the Indian landscape the conditions in India, in much the same manner as Kim's journey through the Indian landscape gives him a vivid glimpse of India. However, Mik's journey does not stop with India, he continues to travel to England, France, Persia. Mik, like Kim, is recruited to become a spy in the Royal Military Academy at Woolwich following recommendations from an old colonel and Sir John. Regarding Mik's interview at the Royal Military Academy, Eugene writes: 'In addition, he had a brief for covert activities. 'He will make us a capital spy,' beamed the major with rubicund cheeks, for he had found his swarthy protégé to be formidably sharp and resolutely foolish' (200).

Sealy takes the combat between the Great Trotter and Mik, from Firdausi's epic poem *Sohrab and Rustum* (Ganapathy-Dore 1995: 69). Sohrab, leader of Tartars, challenges his father Rustum who believes that his own child is a girl. Unaware of the identity, both father and son engage in fierce battle. Rustum recognizes Shorab as his son after Sohrab receives mortal wounds at the hands of his father. In *The Trotter-Nama,* the father and son combat is depicted when the war between the Company and Marathas ensues and the Great-Trotter, fighting under the flag of the Company, comes face-to-face with Mik, who, ousted from Company Services joins the Marathas. Initially, the Great Trotter doubts that the rival challenging him is his son; however, the doubt is dismissed when he finds that the locket, he had fastened on his son's neck at his birth, is missing. The battle between the father and the son leads to Mik losing his hand and suffering defeat at the hands of his father.

Sealy's *The Trotter-Nama* is also similar in its style and content to Salman Rushdie's *Midnight's Children.* As both the books were written almost during the same time, it may not be justifiable to say that *The Trotter-Nama* has been influenced by *Midnight's Children,* even though the latter was published in 1981. However, the similarities do remain. Originally, in *The Trotter-Nama,* like in *Midnight's Children,* Sealy had the narrator born at the midnight hour of India's independence, but dropped this idea when he read Rushdie's novel (Nanawati and Kar 2000: 35). Coincidence again has both Rushdie (in *The Satanic Verses*) and Sealy quote the song sung by Raj Kapoor in his movie *Shri 420:*

> My shoes, they are Japani
> These pants are Englishtani
> My red hat is Russi
> *But my heart is Hindustani.*

Sealy quotes the song to depict the hybridity is an Anglo-Indian's identity that yet bears an affinity to India. Both *Midnight's Children,* and *The Trotter-Nama* have their protagonists handcuffed to history. The lives of both Eugene and Saleem mirror the fate of the nation just as the personal and the public space gets intertwined in the case of both the narratives. Both Eugene and Saleem are illegitimate children with mixed blood of two separate communities and both narrate their histories celebrating their chaotic multiplicity. Both novels use the concept of duality; while in *Midnight's Children* it is Saleem and Shiva as the two opposing forces, in *The Trotter-Nama* it is Eugene Trotter, the chronicler, and Theobald Horatius Montagu, the historian. The very birth of Eugene Trotter and his writing *The Trotter-Nama* is to counterbalance the effects of Montagu's historical works. So, when Eugene is born, Montagu dies. In fact, *The Trotter-Nama* itself is the opposite double of Montagu's history. Apart from these similarities, both make allusions to multiple texts. If in *Midnight's Children,* it is *The Thousand and One Nights* narrated by Scheherazade that forms the core narrative anchor, in *The Trotter-Nama* it is *Akbar-Nama* and *Babur-Nama.*

The Trotter-Nama, thus, is a blend of works from Europe, Persia and India just as the community is a synthesis of many cultures.

II

The Trotter-Nama: A Chronicle begins with the prologue where the protagonist-narrator, Eugene Trotter, in a Tristam-Shandian manner, introduces himself and tries to build a rapport with the reader (Sterne 1996; The manner in which Tristram Shandy, the narrator, introduces the novel to an imaginary reader, impels him to join in a conversation and question him.). In fact, Eugene Trotter persuades the reader to be a part of the narrative by including his opinions and queries rhetorically forcing him to become a fellow passenger not only in the journey to Sans Souci (which in French means free of care) but also in the journey through Anglo-Indian history. The prologue ends with the narrator reaching Nakhlau with the reader-cum-fellow passenger and they both enter the journey leaping back through time into the chronicle of the Trotter family.

The Trotter-Nama, the tale of the Trotters, as pointed out earlier, is the history of Anglo-Indians novelized. As Eugene Trotter says, *'But most of it happened here in India, in Nakhlau. In Sans Souci—Home of the Trotters, Anglos, same thing. You'll see in a minute'* (7). Each character of the novel is handcuffed to Anglo-Indian history and their life mirrors each event and change in their history.

Writing in the mode of the historical novel, *The Trotter-Nama* takes its setting and characters from historical events and details events from both Anglo-Indian and Indian history that become important to the central narrative. Thus, this historical novel or fictionalized history begin with the birth of Mik Trotter, the son of the Great Trotter (who himself is born of a Franco-Swiss father and a Coptic mother) and Sultana Trotter, a Muslim lady supposedly of the Prophet's line, with a khaki body and a blue spigot (Anglo-Indians were also known as Khakis and were considered to have blue gums and nails). Mik's life reflects the changes that occur in Anglo-Indian history and their condition during the eighteenth century.

This can be seen, for example, when during Mik's journey he is admitted into the Lower Military Orphanage. Lower Military Orphanages were established in Calcutta and Madras during the early part of the eighteenth century to care for and educate the Anglo-Indian children of British officers and soldiers, while civil asylums dealt with the children of non-military personnel. Here, Mik finds scores of Anglo-Indians like him. But, unlike them who want to become writers—a profession once dominated by Anglo-Indians—Mik wants to become a surveyor, another profession which was also dominated by the Anglo-Indians. Later, Mik's entry into the Military is barred by the three vicious decrees of 1786, 1791 and 1795 that made it illegal for Anglo-Indians to join the service of the Company except as fifers, drummers and farriers (Caplan 1998). Mik becomes a victim of these decrees, ousted from the Company services and is rendered jobless. Anglo-Indians during this period suffered a lot and were forced to join native princes, in the same manner as Mik joins the Marathas. Later, the British decreed it illegal for Anglo-Indians to join the native princes and threatened Anglo-Indians of dire consequences, if they violated the decree (Abel 1988). Mik is ousted from the services of the Marathas following this decree. The discrimination against the Anglo-Indians by both the natives and the British becomes apparent when giving details about his job for the Henry Salt Commission that came to enquire about the death of the Great Trotter, Mik says:

> 'I have travelled and fought battles.' Mik shook his empty sleeve with a soldier's bland arrogance.
> 'Under which flag?'
> 'Under more than one flag. *Both my masters chose to disown me, the foreign and the native.*' (emphasis added) (255)

This statement by Mik clearly explains the condition of the Anglo-Indians, discriminated against and disowned by both the parent communities, left jobless with no food and money. Eugene Trotter also mentions the other Anglo-Indians whom Mik meets after being ousted from the Company Services; people like Skinner, Powell and Hearsay. These names are actually, historically, some of the most important Anglo-Indian families who helped Britain retain its principalities in India. Among these, the most famous was Col. James Skinner. Col. Skinner's mother was a Hindu Rajput Princess and his father was a Scot. Skinner commanded his own mercenary force of irregular cavalry, with which he had fought for both Marathas and Moguls, before finally taking service under the Company. Skinner's Horse (the name of the irregular cavalry that Skinner commanded) enabled the East India Company to secure great parts of Northern India and were said to have scarlet turbans, silver-edged girdles, black shields, and bright yellow tunics as uniforms, and were believed to be the most useful and trusty men in India. It is believed that Skinner's Horse never lost a battle (Abel 1988: 19).

The turning point in the history of Anglo-Indians came with the *Petition of East Indians to the House of Commons* in 1830, which highlighted the problematic legal status of the community and helped draw the attention of the administration towards the plight of Anglo-Indians. In *The Trotter-Nama*, this petition is put forward by Henry Luis Vivian Fonseca-Trotter (the son of the barber-cum-kahani master, Fonseca, and Farida Wilkinson-Trotter, the mistress of the Great Trotter who nevertheless claimed that she was the Great Trotter's second wife) and Jackob Kahn-Trotter (son of the Chief Steward Yakub and Elsie or Jarman Begaum the Great Trotter's second wife). While, according to

Anglo-Indian history, this petition was led by John Rickett in 1830, in *The Trotter-Nama,* the petition is taken to London by Jacob Kahn-Trotter. To depict the similarity between the historical figure and the character in the chronicle, Sealy creates Kahn-Trotter with rickety legs and gives him the nickname 'Cricket.'

The petition submitted by John Ricketts/Jackob Kahn points out that the Anglo-Indians' legal status is anomalous 'sometimes recognized as Europeans, and sometimes as natives, as it serves the purpose of the government' (Lyons 1999). It also made the point that there were three kinds of Civil Laws in operation in the courts: the Hindu Laws applicable to the Hindus, the Muslims came under the Mohammedan law for the Muslims and English Civil Law for the British. In criminal matters, they were amenable to the Mohammedan law— 'a law' Ricketts points out 'in itself barbarous and imperfect' (Abel 1988: 23). Anglo-Indians were amenable under no personal laws but were amenable to English Civil Laws only if they lived in Calcutta. Ricketts' petition drew the attention of the British Parliamentary House to the lack of the laws for Anglo-Indians concerning regulation of marriages, legitimacy or illegitimacy of their issues, succession of their progeny, bequeathing of property, and property rights in case of intestacy (Abel 1988: 24).

In *The Trotter-Nama,* Mik becomes the victim of an anomalous legal identity, due to the lack of personal laws for Anglo-Indians. Thus, when his father dies and the will is lost, the Henry Salt Commission, entrusted to solve the mystery behind the Great Trotter's death, declares that Mik, 'in a uterine nine months', must find the lost will if he has to succeed to his father's property. Eugene speaks for the entire community when he says: 'The fact of intestacy remained and there his birth dogged him: he had no rights because as a country-born he had no laws' (256).

The next request in the petition dealt with the lack of jobs for the Anglo-Indians, as they were excluded from all superior and covenanted offices in the civil, military and marine services in the East India Company. The decrees of 1786, 1791 and 1795 had rendered the Anglo-Indians jobless, as they were also forbidden to join the native princes. *The Trotter-Nama* sets Mik's life as an example of this, for, being the son of a native he was not allowed to join Company Services and being born of an European, the Marathas did not trust him and considered him a traitor. The petition highlighted the discriminatory policies of the Company with Anglo-Indians being rejected to hold covenanted offices in the Civil Services because they were not Europeans and could not qualify for civil positions because they were neither Europeans nor natives. Thomas Henry Trotter, the son of Charles Augustine Pote Trotter and the Grandson of Mik Trotter, is unable to qualify for the covenanted services because he was not an European and is finally forced to join as a clerk in the Writer's Building on the recommendation of his grandfather Mik Trotter.

The petition successfully culminated in the Reform Bill of 1832 and laid the foundation of the Charter Act of 1833, Section 7 which declared that no native would be debarred from employment on the basis of his religion, place of birth, descent or colour (Abel 1988: 24).

Another period when there was a crisis of identity for the Anglo-Indians was the time when the prospect of India's Independence materialized. It was a testing time for Anglo-Indians—a transition phase—where Anglo-Indians were asked to decide upon their loyalties and to make a choice about residing in India or leave for England. Young Paul, in *The Trotter-Nama,* an ophthalmologist turned a politician and who institutes an organization for Anglo-Indians and Domiciled Europeans, alludes to the historical figure Dr J.R. Wallace who founded the Imperial Anglo-Indians Association in 1898 and like Young Paul suffered the restriction imposed on Anglo-Indians in the medical service (Abel 1988: 26). Young Paul demands a separate land for his people, in case India is granted independence; one of his proposals is to shift the entire community to Andaman and Nicobar Islands. Many of the Trotters agree with the proposal, but it is rejected because the Trotters who went to the Islands could not survive the harsh conditions there. He also demands reservations and quotas for his community in government jobs following Independence. Historically, the proposal to shift Anglo-Indians en bloc to Andaman and Nicobar Islands was put forward by Henry Gidney in the 1920s; however, Anglo-Indians rejected the proposal due to the inhospitable living conditions in the Car Islands (Abel 1988: 41). The efforts of Frank Anthony, in the post-Independence India are synopsized in the efforts of the character Marris to secure reservations for Anglo-Indians in jobs, for operating English-medium schools, declaration of English as one of India's official languages and the reservation of seats in both the houses of Indian Parliament and State assemblies for Anglo-Indians (Gideny 1934: 42). *The Trotter-Nama* also mentions the mass exodus of the community to other countries with many of the Trotters settling abroad as they fear discrimination and foresee their status as being marginal in a caste-conscious, narrow-minded Indian society.

In the colonial history of India, for example, the role of the Anglo-Indians in helping the British control many revolts has been ignored. The first revolt against the British came in the form of the Indigo revolt in Champaran where indigo farmers (Nilaris of central India, a tribe that specialized in growing and extracting indigo) revolted against the colonial indigo planters (Mills 1999). This revolt was the precursor to the Sepoy Mutiny in 1857. In *The Trotter-Nama,* the indigo revolts begin in Sans Souci with the nilchis (tribals who worked for the Trotters from the time of the Great Trotter) revolt, demanding to be paid for their work in the indigo farms, as they had not been paid for one year.

Anglo-Indians played an important role in the Revolt of 1857 also. Reflecting this, Mik plays an significant role here, as he foresees a revolt among the sepoys when they are issued greased cartridges. He sends a letter, warning the Company officials of the consequences of using greased cartridges, which gets lost in the maze of files in government offices.

The character Cyril Brendish, the son of Mik Trotter and one of the Alexander sisters, who saves many British people by sending a prompt telegraphic message to the British about the outbreak of the mutiny, alludes to George Brendish, who remained at his post in Delhi during the mutiny and managed to send a warning message across Punjab. The Trotters being lodged in the Nakhlau Residency and its siege refers to the Siege of Lucknow mentioned in history. This period, denoted as the most turbulent period for the community, was also the time when many Anglo-Indians contributed their services to the British. Regrettably, these contributions by Anglo-Indians in controlling the mutineers remain unnoticed even by

British historians. The mutiny episode also reveals the ambiguous status of the community with Anglo-Indians being victimized by the natives. Both Indian and British versions of the Revolt of 1857 do not record the trauma that the Anglo-Indians went through during the period of the revolt.

In the pre-Independence Hindu-Muslim riots, Eustace, the sixth Trotter who is a policeman, loses his life trying to control the group of people that comes for a peaceful march for religious integration but turns completely violent. Eugene also makes mention of the many Trotters in the defence services who fought in the Indo-Pak war and earned medals from the President of India. *The Trotter-Nama* highlights the contributions made by the Anglo-Indians, which otherwise in the context of history, go totally unnoticed and a micro-minority community of India that rarely finds its due place in the socio-political set-up of India would remain in the oblivion with its unsung heroes.

By recreating Anglo-Indian history in *The Trotter-Nama,* Sealy helps Anglo-Indians to locate their past, ignored by both British colonial and nationalist historians. Eugene Trotter's distrust for either of the histories is revealed when he says: 'The Monkey story is told by mendacious Indians. Another concerns the Elephant. For that you must go to the deceitful British. But who will trust either? Trust me: I will tell a better tale than both' (40).

Ranajit Guha, writing on the historiography of colonial India, has argued that the historiography of Indian nationalism has been dominated by elitism—colonial elitism and bourgeois nationalist elitism. He points out that elitist colonial historiography of the colonialist or neo-colonialist presented Indian nationalism as the effects and responses to British institutions, opportunities, resources, etc. created by colonialism. Thus, colonialism is the root cause or in other words the foundation of nationalism in India. On the other hand, the nationalists and neo-nationalists presented Indian history as a product of their untiring efforts to liberate the subjugated subaltern from the clutches of the colonial powers (Guha 1999). In either histories, the ordinary people and the marginalized communities rarely find a place. *The Trotter-Nama* attempts to creatively resurrect the Anglo-Indian past that would otherwise be misunderstood or totally lost to posterity. Eugene's attempt to write a subaltern history that mixes the 'facts' of history with fiction thus helps pull the Anglo-Indians out of past oblivion and questions and challenges the given 'truth/s' of history.

Works Cited

A Comprehensive Persian-English Dictionary. 1380. New Delhi: Oriental Books. Reprint 1981. Print.

Abel, Evelyn. *The Anglo-Indian Community: Survival in India.* Delhi: Chanakya Publications, 1988. Print.

Anderson, Benedict. 'Cultural Roots.' *Imagined Communities: Reflection on the Origin and Spread of Nationalism.* London: Verso Editions and NLB, 1983. Print.

Anthony, Frank. *Britain's Betrayal in India.* New Delhi: Allied Publishers, 1969, 53–61. Print.

Caplan, Lionel. 'Colonial and Contemporary Transnationalisms: Traversing Anglo-Indian Boundaries of the Mind.' *The International Journal of*

Anglo-Indian Studies 3.2 (1998) (24 February 2003) <http://www.alphalink.com.au/~agilbert/cap0399.html> Web.

Derozio, Henry. *Poems*. Calcutta: Writer's Workshop, Red Bird Publications, 1972. Print.

Fazl, Abu'l. *The Ain-i-Akbari*. Trans. H. Blochmann. Ed. Lieut. Colonel D.C. Phillott. Delhi: Low Price Publications, 1989. Print.

——. *The Akbar-Nama*. Vols. I, II and III. Trans. H. Beveridge. Delhi: Low Price Publications, 1989. Print.

Ganapathy-Dore, Geetha. 'Allan Sealy's *The Trotter-Nama:* Post-Colonial Synchronicle.' *Journal of Commonwealth Literature* 36.1 (1995), 69. Print.

Ghazi, Zahiru'd-din Muhammad Babur Padshah. *Babur–Nama*. Vols. I and II. Trans. Annette Susannah Beveridge. New Delhi: Munshiram Manoharlal Publishers Pvt. Ltd., 1998. Print.

Gideny, Henry. 'The Future of the Anglo-Indian Community.' *Asiatic Review* 30 (January 1934), 27–42. Print.

Guha, Ranajit. Introduction. *Subaltern Studies: Writing on South Asian History and Society*. Vol. I. Ed. Ranajit Guha. Delhi: OUP, 1999, 1–2. Print.

Hawes, Christopher. *Poor Relations: The Making of a Eurasian Community in British India 1773–1833*. Surrey: Curzon Press, 1996. Print.

Lyons, Esther. 'A Note on Some Famous Anglo-Indian Families by Esther Mary Lyons.' *The International Journal of Anglo-Indian Studies* 4.2 (1999) (24 February 2003) <http://www.alphalink.com.au/ ~agilbert/lordsk~ 1.html.> Web.

McCullagh, C. Behan. *The Truth of History*. London and New York: Routledge, 1998. Print.

Mills, Megan Stuart. 'Some Comments on Stereotypes of the Anglo-Indians.' *The International Journal of Anglo-Indian Studies* 4.2 (1999) (24 February 2002) <http://www.alphalink.com.au/~agilbert/jmills1. html.> Web.

Nanawati, U.M. and Prafulla C. Kar (eds). 'After Midnight: The Indian Novel in English of 80's and 90's.' *Rethinking Indian English Literature*. Delhi: Pencraft International, 2000, 35–43. Print.

Oliver, Kelly. 'Witnessing Otherness in History.' *What Happens to History: The Renewal of Ethics in Contemporary Thought*. Ed. Howard Marchitello. London: Routledge, 2001, 41–66. Print.

Sealy, Allan Irwin. *The Trotter-Nama: A Chronicle*. New Delhi: India Ink, 1999. Print.

Sharma, L.P. *History of Modern India*. Delhi: Konark Publishers, 1994. Print.

Sharma, Tej Ram. 'The Meaning and Definition of History.' *The Concept of History*. Delhi: Bharatiya Vidya Prakashan, 1987. Print.

Sterne, Laurence. *The Life and Opinions of Tristram Shandy Gentleman*. Hertfordshire: Wordsworth Editions Limited, 1996. Print.

Toynbee, Arnold J. *A Study of History*. Abridged. D.C. Somervell. Vols. 1–5. New York: Dell Publishing Co. Inc, 1965. Print.

Wright, R. Dean. 'The Life and Times of Henry Louis Vivian Derozio: A Legend Among Anglo—Indians.' *The International Journal of Anglo-Indian Studies* 5.2 (2000) (24 February 2002) <http://www.alphalink.com.au/~agilbert/derozi~1.html.> Web.

14

Myth and History in Shashi Tharoor's *The Great Indian Novel*

T. VISWANADHA RAO

'What is here may be found elsewhere,/what is not here, may not be found elsewhere' (*'yadihasthi tadanyathra yannehasthi na tat quachit'*), claims Veda Vyas, the author of the *Mahabharata*. The epic of Veda Vyas has many versions, many translations, many transcreations, and many adaptations. The novel, as Bakhtin opines, is open-ended, but epics like the *Mahabharata* are as open-ended as a novel. This gives the desired advantage to Shashi Tharoor in giving the ancient work its modern version to embody contemporary events of Indian history. Like the original, it also covers a vast span of time, dealing with the pre-Independent as well as the post-Independent scenario in India. Veda Vyas's claim mentioned earlier, makes sense as it has some substance in it.

During the course of an interview, Shashi Tharoor is reported to have remarked that the *Mahabharata* 'struck me as a work of such contemporary resonance, it helped crystallize my own inchoate ideas about issues. I wanted a vehicle to transmit some of my political and historical interests in the evolution of modern India. I saw the recasting of the *Mahabharata* as a perfect vehicle for the two Indias' (Chowdhury 2003: 682). Shashi Tharoor also believed and rightly too that history is in a state of constant evolution. 'Life is Kurukshetra. History is Kurukshetra' (1989: 391) says the author, attesting as it were the universality not only of the appeal but also of the perennial problems of human life which the epic intends to discuss at length, and which become the body of the novel as well.

The Great Indian Novel is a fictional narrative on the birth of independent India, narrated by Ved Vyasa. Vyasa, like Tiresias the seer and prophet of *The Wasteland*, narrates the long and complex phenomenon of Indian independence from the clutches of the British colonial empire, what is, what was and what should have been, as the narrator observes. If Tiresias and Vyasa were seers who could read the past and the present to envision the future, Ved Vyasa the narrator of this novel is eminently equipped with political experience and statesmanly vision of shape of things to come.

The novel is a highly satirical portrait of the attitude of the colonizer as well as the colonized. Rightly, therefore, does the novel begin with a disclaimer that India is no underdeveloped country, 'They tell me India is an underdeveloped country ... stuff and nonsense, of course .... I tell them that they have no knowledge of history .... India is not an underdeveloped country but a highly developed one in an advanced state of decay' (17). Veda Vyasa, the old sage of the epic, becomes the old politician of the novel. The ancient epic becomes a modern novel in the hands of the writer. The mythical character of Vyasa, whose age cannot be ascertained, becomes here an octogenarian whose first person narrative claims, 'This is my story, the story of Ved Vyas, eighty eight years old and full of irrelavancies, but it could become nothing less than the Great Indian novel' (18).

The style and expression of Tharoor serve him well in keeping the interest of the reader alive by tickling his imagination fully. The story of Parasara and Matsyagandhi is brashly interpreted as a down-to-earth union of a fisherwoman and a Brahmin and the description of ancient saints like Parasara as 'the twice-born travelling salesmen of salvation' (19). The stinking body odour of Matsyagandhi the fisherwoman is euphemistically characterized as 'olfactory inconvenience' (19). The supernatural contrivances of the sage are reduced in the narrative to 'a thick copse of trees' and 'a mist around the island' and the claim of Satyavathi of a magic cloud setting on the island is dismissed as a figment of imagination, a mere 'female hyperbole' (19) as the writer ingeniously puts it.

The great Bhishma of the Mahabharata becomes the Ganga Datta of the story, Gangaji as he is to be described later in the narrative. The historical parallels are not too far to seek. The political Bhishma or Gangaji is no other than Mahatma Gandhi who in political astuteness, professional strategies, and the practices of austerity merits an unobtrusive comparison with the Bhishma Pitamaha of the Mahabharata. Veda Vyasa of the original becomes the oldest politician-narrator of the novel. Subhash Chandra Bose is King Pandu of the epic while Pundit Nehru is the Dhritharashtra of the epic. Indira Gandhi who was lovingly called 'Priya Darshini', as one can easily notice, becomes the Priya Duryodhani or Dussala of the novel. Karna becomes Jinnah. Keeping Dalhousie's Doctrine of Lapse in mind, the novelist brings in the threat of annexation of Hasthinapur. In the original story, it is an understandable eventuality of a great dynasty of kings being disinherited as a result of lack of progeny to sustain the monarchical line, that being the reason why Veda Vyasa had to be called upon to ensure the required continuity. It is easy to see the approval of the British Government parallels that of Bhishma and others of the original narrative.

Salva, the king of the original story, is modernized into a Cambridge Blue. The anger of Amba on being rejected by all including her former lover Salva, propels her into a vengeful figure aiming at no less than the head of Bhishma. The original story of even Parasurama no other than the Guru of Bhishma himself being unable to defeat his disciple is cleverly modernized as Amba's search for hired assassins, a search all in vain as 'no assassin in the whole of India was willing to accept her contract' (29).

Like Julius Caesar of whom it is proverbially narrated that he came, he saw and he conquered, 'vini, vidi, vici', Ved Vyas also says that in the case of his mother, he had to rush to the rescue of the childless Ambica and Ambalika, 'I rose. I came', he says.

The novelist's use of Draupadi as a metaphor of democracy is yet another remarkable use of mythical characters. She is made to stand for secular democracy; many religions and the religious freedom in India being represented by the many husbands she has accepted. Draupadi said, 'I prayed to Shiva, to Jehovah, to the Virgin Mother of my adoptive parents, to the Allah of the Muslims and to the Archbishop of Canterbury' (316). Polyandry, thus, becomes a convenient symbol of secularism.

Besides, the novelist establishes his work as an autobiographical novel and quotes the autobiographical tradition in Indian writing in English laid down, as the writer feels, from Rajaji to Chagla. But he voices his mild concern at what might look like verbal excesses on his part, which do not fall into the line established by the autobiographical tradition just now referred to.

The character of Dhritarashtra, on the other hand, is akin to Pundit Nehru's. Described as a Fabian socialist like Bernard Shaw, he is reported to be a product of King's college, Cambridge. Narrating the story in modern terms, the novelist substitutes the Sun-God of Indian mythology with his Greek namesake Hyperion or Helios as he calls him and a foreigner of 'immense presence and warmth' (44). Modernizing the myth in his characteristic vein, Tharoor observes 'it is easy to imagine how an impressionable and inexperienced young mind could be taken in by the blandishments of this plausible stranger' (44).

As in an invocation of an epic, Ved Vyas, the narrator, addresses Ganapathi the scribe with expressions like 'shall I tell', 'shall I sing', and 'shall I speak', all in connection with the weapon of disobedience, the civil disobedience or Satyagraha of Mahatma Gandhi. The greatest tribute, however, is paid to the Mahatma in brief but pithy words when it is said of him, 'while he was alive, he was impossible to ignore, once he had gone, he was impossible to imitate' (47).

In the process, the novel takes all the care necessary to persuade or convince the incredulous readers of the present about the heroic attributes of people like the Mahatma. 'The hyperbole of the old, the heroism of the nostalgic, that's what you think it is. You can't know, you with your ration cards and your black markets and the cynical materialism of your generation, what it was like in those days, what it felt like to discover a cause, to belong to a crusade, to believe' (52).

The novel is, thus, analytic and interpretative rather than merely being descriptive. As in an epic narrative, concepts of existence are commented upon and Gandhiji's method is explained formulaically as law versus conscience.

Ved Vyas's modernization as a character is evident when the novelist makes him say, 'I read the Vedas and quote the laws of cricket' (65). To enrich the prose descriptions of the novel, and as though to remind the reader of the epic origins of the saga in question, the novelist intersperses his prose narrative with a few poems in between. These short lined rhymed verses are crisp and humorous by turns.

Yet another remarkable feature of the novel is the writer's sense of humour. Speaking about the amatory adventures in Arjuna's peregrinations, the writer says, 'in Hardwar, for instance, by the sacred Ganga, there was Ulupi, a Naga beauty who taught him underwater pleasures omitted in his adolescent swimming lessons' (322). The writer's description of the Ambassador car is a remarkable piece of humour. He describes it as 'this graceless contraption of quite spectacular ugliness' (331). Speaking about the call for elections by Indira Gandhi in the aftermath of the emergency, the author observes that it was widely believed that she consulted an astrologer before taking the decision, and adds with a characteristic sense of humour, 'An Indian without a horoscope is like an American without a credit card, and he is subject to many of the same disadvantages in life' (389).

The eventual annexation of Hastinapur becomes symbolic of the onset of the imperialist yoke. The Jallianwala Bagh massacre invokes just the kind of response we expect from the novelist. His comments are virulent and corrosive, coloured with brutal irony, when he speaks of the British colonel responsible for the historical savagery, 'perhaps he just acted in the way distorted by the simple logic of colonialism, under which the rules of humanity applied only to the rulers, for the rulers were people and the people were objects .... Yet the civilizing mission upon which Rudyard and his tribe were embarked made savages of all of us, and all of them' (80).

The novelist rightly accuses the British that they invented our poverty by creating the Indian landless labour and by killing the Indian artisan. He exhibits a savage sense of humour and blunts the edge of tall western claims, while seeming to be casual in his pronouncements, 'great discoveries, Ganapathi, are often the result of making the wrong mistake at the right time. Ask Columbus' (97).

Comparing the average attitude of western women to their Indian counterparts, he comments, 'where a western woman misses a meal in the interest of her figure, her Indian sister dedicates her starvation to a cause' (103). What is even more, he characterizes going in fast as 'an act of/affirmation rather than a blackmail' (103).

'The recounting of history', the novelist opines, 'is only the order we artificially impose upon life to permit its lessons to be more clearly understood. So it is, Ganapathi, that in this memoir we light up one corner of our collective past at a time, focus on one man's action, one villages' passions, one colonel's duty, but all the while life is going elsewhere' (109).

The writer is also highly critical of the tax system under the colonial rule. The British, he says, have stolen everything they need for centuries successfully from India and yet, surprisingly they wanted to impose taxes of all kinds on the already looted and overburdened Indians. Employing a caustic figure of speech, he berates the British, 'they taxed property, and income and harvests, and they taxed our petrol, our patience, and even our passing to the other world' (116).

No wonder the author realizes the efficacy of tactical modes as opposed to idealism fit only for ivory towers when he praises the Mahatma in unmistakable terms as a master tactician, 'don't ever forget, young man', Ved Vyas tells Ganapathi the scribe, 'that we were led not by a saint with his head in the clouds, but by a master tactician with his feet on the ground' (122).

To add sauce to the wit of his imagination, the novelist chooses to give a twist to well-known aphorisms like 'humanity cannot bear too much reality', by altering it with a tongue in cheek, 'and colonialism, as the poet said, cannot bear very much hilarity' (125).

Other modernizations include Mohammed Ali Jinnah becoming Mohammed Ali Karna. A serious deviation from the Mahabharata epic is the story of Ekalavya. Ekalavya of the novel refuses to pay *'Gurudakshina'*—the fees the teacher Drona demands from Ekalavya for his having listened to him secretly standing outside the room where Drona taught the Pandavas and the Kauravas.

The Pandavas are described as the Famous Five, Enid Blyton-like. In an amiable anachronism, the Pandavas are credited with a cricket ball which they lose to be retrieved by their teacher Drona. Amba's gender conversion under strange circumstances in the myth is very conveniently described in the novel as being effected with the help of a surgeon.

The novelist is also against many digressions as they tend to destroy the homogeneity of the narrative and the centrality of focus. Indian Independence and the role of the Mahatma in it, therefore, occupy a major chunk of the fictional narrative. All this, the novelist argues, is in keeping with the tastes of the present day readers, the young readers of the day in particular, 'In the olden days our epic narrators thought nothing of leaving a legendary hero stranded in mid-conquest while digressing into sub-plots, with stories, fables and anecdotes within each. But these, Ganapathi, are more demanding times. Leave Ganga to his devices and start telling fables about Devayani and Kacha, and your audience will walk away in droves' (133).

Keeping in view the situation prior to the declaration of Emergency by Indira Gandhi, the author compares her to Frakenstein's monster, as all the while 'more and more laws went on to the statute books empowering Priya Duryodhani to prohibit, proscribe, profane, prolate, prosecute or prostitute all the freedoms the national movement had fought to attain' (357). Commenting on the elections, the author says there are no victors in such a battle, and adds, 'This election is not Kurukshetra; life is Kurukshetra. History is Kurukshetra. The struggle between dharma and adharma is a struggle our nation, and each of us in it, engages in on every single day of our existence. That struggle, that battle, took place before this election; it will continue after it' (391).

With a sense of Shavian humour, the author makes Ved Vyas speak to Ganapathi wherein the former claims that Democracy is, perhaps, the most arrogant of all forms of government, but according to him, 'democracies that turn authoritarian go a step beyond arrogance; they claim to represent a people subjugating themselves. India was now the laboratory of this strange experiment. Our people would be the first in the world to vote on their subjugation' (391).

The novel ends in Ved Vyas's vision being broken, and the writer wants to begin again at the beginning as it is a never-ending saga of epic proportions.

Works Cited

Chowdhury, Kanishka. 'Revisioning History: Shashi Tharoor's *The Great Indian Novel.' World Literature Today* 69.1 (Winter 1995), 41–48. Print.

Genoa, Pamela A. (ed.). *Twayne Companion to Contemporary World Literature*. Vol. 1. New York: Twayne Publishers, 2003. Print.

Tharoor, Shashi. *The Great Indian Novel*. New Delhi: Penguin India, 1989. Print.

15

Re-charting History in the Recent Indian English Fiction: A Study of Shashi Tharoor's *The Great Indian Novel* and Vikram Seth's *A Suitable Boy*

B. KRISHNAIAH AND M. RAJAGOPALACHARY

Indian English fiction has earned recognition of its own in the world literature of the recent past particularly since 1980. R.S. Pathak aptly observes: 'In the growth and development of the Indian novel in English the 1980s occupy the most significant position ... . It is during the eighties that Indian English novelists and novels earned unheard of honours and distinctions in the Western academic world' (1994: 14). It has expanded its technique from the imitative, realistic, psychological, philosophical and realistic stages to the experimental. Meenakshi Mukherjee traces three different stages in the evolution of Indian English novel since 1930, viz., the first stage of the historical novel from 1920s to 1930s, the second stage of the socio-political novel during 1930s and 1940s and the third phase of the narrative of self-identity, including the psychological novel, from 1950s to 1960s. The postmodern novels, beginning with the publication of Rushdie's *Midnight's Children* in 1981, could be regarded as the fourth stage in the art of Indian English Fiction. Rushdie gave a new direction and verve to the Indian English Fiction with *Midnight's Children* which fetched him Booker Prize and James Black memorial prize in 1981, and the Booker of Bookers in 1993. It was considered the best among Booker Prize winners in twenty-five years since the inception of the coveted prize in fiction. *Midnight's Children* shook the very base of the monotonous approach of writing. Commenting on the impact of *Midnight's Children* on Indian English Fiction, Viney Kirpal points out that 'Salman Rushdie lay in the new voice and narrative technique he had brought to the old themes of history, politics, gender and self-identity all of which he had pulled together into one novel' (1996: 1). Rushdie's sensational international literary success has paved the way for numerous Indian writers of calibre to follow in the footsteps of their master to earn them the epithet 'Rushdie's Children' by the *New York Times.* The Indian English Fiction has taken a new direction with its novel experimentation in the hands of these writers of second generation.

Surprisingly, the Indian fiction writers of second generation are obsessed with the history of very recent India. In fact, these writers evidence a search for their roots. Madhusudhan Rao rightly points out: 'History is a matter of the soul's search for finding one's roots in its essential human significance. In such an imaginative capturing of its essence, history is richly humanized' (1992: 155). Saleem Sinai, the narrator of *Midnight's Children,* feels that 'he had been mysteriously handcuffed to history, my destinies indissolubly chained to those of my country' (9). The fiction of this period attempts to re-present Indian history of the recent past in general and India's Freedom Struggle, the trauma of Partition, political history of the aftermath of Independence and the Emergency in particular. However, the treatment of history is not new in the history of Indian English Fiction. But, what sets them apart from the earlier writers is their ripeness in selection and treatment of theme, manipulation of point of view, use of innovative methods of narration, magic realism and linguistic improvisation such as hybridization, chutnification of language, intertextuality. Belliappa opines that 'History and Magic Realism seem to have become the major concerns of many Indian English novelists due to the phenomenal influence of *Midnight's Children*' (2002: 7).

Referring to the radical change in the process of fiction writing in this postmodern phase, Balaswamy says: 'Among the process of disintegration, dissolution and explosions in this genre, one perceptible development over the recent decades has been the gradual demise of literary realism and the conscious use of the non-realistic modes such as allegory, myth, archetype, etc. Referred to, for the sake of convenience, as the mode of fabulation, it has given rise to the writing of, what is paradoxically called, Fables of Fact' (1998: 228). The present paper seeks to examine re-presentation of recent Indian history in Shashi Tharoor's *The Great Indian Novel* (1989) and Vikram Seth's *A Suitable Boy* (1993). Tharoor re-presents history by employing the mythic structure, while Seth presents it in the mode of conventional narrative method.

II

The Great Indian Novel is a part of postmodernist-deconstructive sensibility. It has taken a multidimensional form and impressions like the magic realism, intertextuality, metafictionality, the presence of deconstructive markers and practices. Tharoor employed this method as it enabled him to merge myths, fairy tales, legends and contemporary realities into a single component. The *Mahabharata* provides Tharoor a suitable allegorical background to re-present modern India's political history. His caricaturing of characters is rightly fitted into the mythic structure. He dexterously interweaves the freedom struggle and post-Independence India's political history with the *Mahabharata* events and characters. In other words, Tharoor superimposes the modern politics on the ready-made structure of the myth. In the words of M.L. Pandit, 'Tharoor wittily superimposes the structure of the Mahabharata on the history of the Indian freedom struggle and thereafter, hence, distorting the original text' (1996: 62). In his structural complexity, Tharoor re-presents the political history of India of the twentieth century through the mythical story of the *Mahabharata.* Commenting on the novel, Lal says that *The Great Indian Novel* presents the 'multiple realities' and 'multiple interpretations of reality,' that is India. He explains:

> The *Mahabharata* has come to stand for so much in the popular consciousness of Indians: the personages in it have become household words, standing for public virtues and vices and the issues it rises, as well as the values it seeks to promote, are central to an understanding of what makes India. To take characters and situations that are so laden with resonance and to alter and shape them to tell a contemporary story, was a challenge that offered a rare opportunity to strike familiar chords while playing an unfamiliar tune ... . (1990: 5)

Shashi Tharoor delineates the relevance of the ancient India's epic in the postmodern context through the narrative. He asserts: 'It is precisely the epic's appeal to non-Sanskrit scholars that has ensured the *Mahabharata*'s present day relevance and given me material for my novel .... I found the *Mahabharata* the perfect vehicle for an attempt to retell the political history of 20th century India, through a fictional recasting of its events, episodes and characters' (*The Hindu*). Tharoor revisits the past with objectivity and irony. He attempts to draw analogy between the mythical events and the contemporary political history by re-presenting the past in the present. In the words of Lal, 'Its characters still walk the Indian streets, its animals populate our forests, its legends and the myths haunt and inspire the Indian imagination, its events are the disturbing warp and woof of our age' (Qtd. in *The Hindu* 3). Like Rushdie's *Midnight's Children*, Tharoor's *The Great Indian Novel* deals with the events of national history since colonial times such as peasants movements, Jallianwala Bagh massacre, the Partition of India, wars between Indian and China, India and Pakistan and the precarious conditions of the Emergency. It reflects the characteristics of the postmodernist historiographic metafiction that problematizes history. Explaining its characteristics, Balaswamy says:

> Historiographic metafictional works problematize history, by portraying historical events and personalities only to subvert them. They attempt to re-write/re-present the past in fiction so that the past can be opened up to the present; by this they prevent the past from being conclusive and teleological; such metafictional works posit no single 'truth' but *truths* in the plural, never one Truth. It is just your version of truth against someone else's truth, so there is no falseness *per se.* Also, such truths are relative to the specific place and culture. (1998: 229)

Ved Vyas dictates the epic *Mahabharata* to Lord Ganesh in eighteen *parvas.* Shashi Tharoor makes Ved Vyas dictate his story, thoughts and memories at length to Ganapathi, an amanuensis, in eighteen books. Some episodes are taken from the myth to represent the events of the twentieth century political history. The defeat of Hidimba by Bhima stands for the liberation of Goa from the Portuguese rule; and the episode of tearing off of the body of Jarasandha into two by Bheema reflects the formation of Bangladesh from Pakistan. In the original episode of Bheema-Bakasura wrestling match, Tharoor replaces Bheema by Sahadeva. It represents the defeat of India in the Indo-China war.

Tharoor burlesques the epic characters as men and women in the narrative. Bhishma of the *Mahabharata* is renamed Gangaji who reminds us of Gandhiji in every word and action. The common trait of the two is an 'obsession with celibacy.' The blind Dhritarashtra is pictured as Jawaharlal Nehru. Queen Gandhari, mother of Kauravas, gives birth to Priya Duryodhani equal to the strength of hundred evil sons. Priya Duryodhani represents Indira Gandhi. Pandu is Subhash Chandra Bose, Vidur—Sardar Patel and Drona—Jayaprakash Narayan, Yudhistir—Morarji Desai, Amba Shikandi—Godse, Karna—Mohammed Ali Jinnah. Bhima—the army and Arjuna—the Press. Shishupal is Lal Bahadur Shastri. Draupadi Mokrasi represents 'democracy'. The Kaurava clan is presented in the powerful 'Congress party' and Lord Krishna is caricatured as a local M.L.A. of the Kaurava party and secretary for a remote taluk in Kerala. Tharoor, thus, meticulously builds parallelism between the *Mahabharata* and the contemporary political history. In the narrative, Gandhi serves as the crucial connecting link between the past and the present by 'immersing himself increasingly in the great works of the past and the present, reading *Vedas* and Tolstoy with equal involvement, studying the innumerable laws of Manu and the eccentric philosophy of Ruskin' (2005: 25).

The narrative begins with the princely state of Hastinapur and its annexation to the British, and moves swiftly through incidents of the freedom struggle such as the Jallianwala Bagh massacre (Bibigarh Garden massacre), peasants' and industrial workers' movements, Gandhi's Dandi March (Great Mango March) and Partition, Independence and the dark period of Emergency and its consequences.

In the *Mahabharata,* Bhishma takes a vow to remain a celibate throughout his life to fulfil his father Shantanu's desire to marry Satyavathi, a fisher woman. Gandhi at the age of 45 takes a decision to cultivate sexual self-restraint like Bhishma. He explains it in his autobiography, *My Experiment with Truth*:

> After full discussion and mature deliberations I took the vow in 1906. I had not shared my thoughts with my wife until then, but only consulted her at the time of taking the vow. She had no objection. But I had great difficulty in making the final resolve. I had not the necessary strength. How was I to control my passions? The elimination of carnal relationship with one's wife seemed then a strange thing. (1927: 191–92)

Gandhi prefers simple and natural life. His habits such as vegetarianism, nature therapy are usually considered Gandhian fads. Sumit Sarkar, a celebrated historian, gives an account of Gandhi's simple style of political life:

> Travelling third class, speaking in simple Hindustani, wearing a loin cloth only from 1921 onwards, using the image of Tulsidas's *Ramayana* so deep rooted in popular religion of the North Indian Hindu rural masses. (1983: 181)

Tharoor describes the same lifestyle of Gandhi in a subversive and ludicrous manner:

> Thin as a papaya plant ... peering at you through round-rimmed glasses that gave him the look of a startled owl. And the rest of his appearance was hardly what you would call prepossessing. He had by then burned his soup-and-fish and given away the elegant suits copied for him from the best British magazines by the court master-tailor; but to make matters worse, he was now beginning to shed part or most of even his traditional robes on all but state occasion. People were forever barging into his study unexpectedly and finding him in nothing but a loincloth. (1989: 35)

During freedom struggle, Gandhi (Ganga Datta) was instrumental in bringing out a change in the politico-economic life of India. His message inspired everyone to participate in the freedom struggle. Truth, satyagraha and non-violence were his weapons in the battle against the British Raj. Gandhi's struggle and his way of organizing the people nonplussed the British. Gandhi's participation in the peasant movement at the village level attracted the politics at the national level which contributed to the birth of 'nationalism' in the country. Champaran in the Northwest Bihar and Kheda in Gujarat are the best instances for this. At Champaran there had been a sporadic resistance during 1860s against the *tinkatia* system 'when European planters had involved the cultivators in agreement that forced them cultivate indigo on 3/20th of their holdings (known as the *tinkatiya system*)' (Chandra 1989: 178). Gandhi explains *tinkatiya* system in his autobiography 'as three kathas out of twenty (which makes one acre) had to be planted with indigo (1927: 371). *Ved Vyas* tells it to Ganapathi: 'under the colonialist laws, ... three tenths of every man's land had to be consecrated to indigo, since the British needed cash-crops more than they needed wheat' (50). Gandhi's enquiry and the publicity gathered for his enquiry compelled the Raj to constitute a committee to enquire into the matter. The Committee recommends for compensation to the peasants and abolition of *tinkatiya* system. Tharoor re-presents this movement with admiration for Gandhiji: 'Imagine it for yourself, Ganapathi, frail, bespectacled Gangaji defying the might of the British Empire, going from village to village proclaiming the right of the people to live rather than grow dye' (1989: 51).

Gandhi's Salt Satyagraha was an effective tool of the Civil Disobedience Movement. The Congress working committee met at Sabarmathi (on 14–16 February 1930) and empowered Mahatma Gandhi to launch the 'Civil Disobedience Movement' at any place and time of his choice. He first chose to defy the salt tax which he considered the most inhuman act of the British. He began a march on 12 March from Sabarmathi Ashram to Dandi along with 78 ashram participants drawn from all parts of India. The march acquired the form of a 'padayatra'. It reached Dandi on 6 April 1930. By picking up a handful of salt, Gandhiji inaugurated the Civil Disobedience Movement, 'a movement that was to remain unsurpassed in the history of the Indian national movement for the country-wide mass participation it unleashed' (Chandra 1989: 272). He called upon the people to manufacture and auction salt. He declared the week from 6

April to 13 April as national week and called the people to picket liquor shops and boycott foreign cloth. Many legislators and government employees resigned their positions and many people violated salt laws and peasants evaded taxes and debts. The country was in an open revolt. During the movement, Gandhi appealed to the people not to indulge in violence. Tharoor has re-presented this historical struggle as 'The Great Mango March' to pluck the 'forbidden fruit' in the novel parodying quite humorously the great achievement of Gandhi: 'The Crowd cheered, and yelled, and swarmed around Gangaji as he stepped off the platform. The mango he had plucked, that first fruit of India's liberation, was instantly auctioned to enthusiastic acclaim, for the princely sum of sixteen hundred rupees' (1989: 124).

Tharoor re-presents Jallianwala Bagh massacre as Bibigarh Garden Massacre or Hastinapur Massacre. Regarded as the gloomy day in the history of freedom struggle, this incident shook the nation on the afternoon of 13 April 1919. Dyer's orders of firing on the unarmed crowds in the meeting left about five hundred persons killed and twelve hundred wounded. In protest, Tagore renounced his Knighthood and Gandhi returned the Kaiser-I-Hind medal given to him during the Boer War. Tharoor refers to the Sepoy's Mutiny of 1857, considered the first freedom struggle in the history of Freedom Movement. The national revolt, carefully disparaged by imperial historians as the 'Sepoy Mutiny', was put down (135). He regards the Quit India Movement of 1942–45 as a landmark in the history of India's struggle for freedom since the 1857 revolt. He deprecates the communal riots and anarchy during the Partition which he thinks was instigated by the British. He questions 'the killing, the violence, the carnage, the sheer mindlessness of the destruction ...' (226). Tharoor re-presents the assassination of the Father of the Nation by a Hindu fanatic in the mythical story of mahaguru Bheeshma's death. He exposes the power hungry nature of Jinnah and Nehru who rejects Gandhi's advice to offer the premiership to Jinnah in order to keep India united.

Tharoor compares Priya Duryodhani's misuse of power in the Emergency to the episode of 'disrobing Draupadi' in the myth, which reflects denuding the dignity of freedom of the Indians. When her election was set aside by Allahabad High Court in 1971 on charges of misuse of official machinery for political campaign and an agitation was brewing against her on the call given by Lok Nayak Jayaprakash Narayan, she imposes 'internal emergency' under article 352 of the constitution on the advice of her legal advisor Shakuni Shankar Dey (Siddartha Shankar Ray). Ved Vyas laments that Priya Duryodani was empowered 'to prohibit, proscribe, profane, prolate, prosecute or prostitute, all the freedoms the national movement had fought to attain during all those years of my Kaurava life' (357). Mohan Dharia, a Member of Parliament, criticizes it 'as the blackest day in Indian Democracy and in the history of our country (Qtd by Nayar 1977: 68). It is the press during the Emergency that takes up cudgels against the disrobing of democracy. Tharoor represents Arjun as the symbol of the Press. The marriage of Arjuna to Draupadi is the union of democracy and the press—the voice of the people. While in the myth Yudhistir loses everything to Duryodhana in a deceptive dice play with Shakuni, Tharoor makes Arjun, the

Press, play the final dice with Priya Duryodhani to regain country's self-respect and freedom (382). Dice play here symbolizes the general elections held in the aftermath of the Emergency.

Ved Vyas holds that the ancient politics and epic battle like Kurukshetra are intended for noble causes whereas in modern India politics is motivated by moneymaking and selfishness. He laments that 'Today's India is a land of adulteration, black-marketing, corruption, communal strife, dowry killings, you know the rest, and that this is the only India that matters' (412).

The Great Indian Novel, thus, re-presents the recent political history of India in the garb of a mythical story. While Shashi Tharoor re-presents history in the postmodernist way in this novel, Vikram Seth presents history in his magnum opus, *A Suitable Boy* in a conventional manner.

III

Vikram Seth presents the political history of newly-born Independent India of 1950s in his novel *A Suitable Boy* (1993). It covers the events such as the rift in the Congress party, the Zamindari Abolition Act of 1951, the religious contentions, the cultural life of that period and the political power games. Like Shashi Tharoor's *The Great Indian Novel*, it also deals with the events and situations like Gandhi's leadership and his personality, and Nehru's era which started with new hopes and promises in the independent India—land reforms, elections, communal politics, secularism and untouchability. Seth meticulously intermingles the political and social struggles with the daily domestic affairs of the four families—the Mehras, the Chatterjees, the Khans and the Kapoors. There is much of history and politics accurately portrayed in the novel and Seth takes care not to allow the novel to turn into a document of mere historical facts. Seth emerges as a reliable spokesman of India's cultural heritage and national identity. Commenting on the impact of the novel on the world literary scene, Kerstin W. Shands says:

> Many Western readers, not surprisingly, have seen this novel as a good introduction to India—or at least to those aspects of Indian history and culture that are conveyed through a narrative that, moving through an impressive array of dissimilar and disparate discourses, touches on historical, cultural, and religious issues ranging from the caste system, the Land Reforms Act aiming to abolish the Zamindari landowner system, the tensions between Hindus and Muslims, and the political struggle of post-Independence India. (2003: 98)

Against this political backdrop, Seth dexterously interweaves the story of searching for a suitable boy by the protagonist, Latha. However, the re-presentation of political history in *A Suitable Boy* differs from that of Shashi Tharoor's *The Great Indian Novel*. While Tharoor adopts the postmodern mode of narrative technique and borrows the ready-made structure of the epic the *Mahabharata* to allegorise the recent India's political history, Vikram Seth adopts the traditional mode of narrative technique—linear mode of description, and fictitious representation of the characters and situations of political history of the 1950s in general. In the words of Seema Paul: 'Seth has neither exoticised' India nor criticized it, he has merely presented it as he knows it' (1993: 8).

Seth brings out the power politics of the two groups within the Congress party itself during Nehru's regime soon after Independence. This period has turned agitators into rulers, bureaucrats into public servants. Contrary to Gandhi period, selfishness, corruption, distortion and decay started creeping into politics in Nehru period. Seth describes the long feud between the Nehruites and the Tandonites. At the state level, Mahesh Kapoor, the revenue minister, is a supporter of Nehru and L.N. Agarwal, the home minister, a defender of Purushotham Das Tandon. S.S. Sharma, the Chief Minister of Purva Pradesh, P.C. Ghosh from Bengal, Kidwai of Uttar Pradesh, Kripalani of the Kisan Majdoor Praja Party (KMPP) are the other notable political characters in the novel.

In the political stunt between Nehru and Tandon, Seth exposes the weaknesses and strengths of political personages. Tandon is known for his discipline and political ability. Despite his gigantic stature, Nehru often stoops to political manoeuvring for power. Both Nehru and Tandon were 'vying with each other for power on the national stage' (953). Tandon, the president of Congress Working Committee, simply opposes Nehru's policies and his followers. Therefore, Nehru looks for a flexible president as Tandon 'proved to be a formidable opponent in his own right .... And on every important issue his views were diametrically opposed to those of Nehru or his supporters-men such as Kripalani and Kidwai or, closer to Brahmapur, Mahesh Kapur' (954). As a political strategy Nehru resigns abruptly from the Congress Working Committee and the Central Election Board as he 'feels that the congress is rapidly drifting away from its moorings and more and more the wrong kind of people, or rather people who have the wrong kind of ideas, are gaining influence in it' (989). The Tandonites 'smacked of the build-up to a show down' (991). In a gentle action and having known well 'the impropriety of Nehru's tactics' (992), Tandon resigns his Presidentship. Immediately Nehru takes over as Congress President. 'It was in effect a coup; and Nehru had won' (992). Nehru takes on the Tandonites with his 'most uncharacteristic unwillingness to back down, to understand their point of view, to postpone unpleasantness, to compromise' (991). Seth portrays Nehru as a secularist and protector of the rights of the minority community. He says 'we must give full protection to our ministers. This means also that we must not permit any propaganda on the part of Hindu or Sikh communal organizations' (977). He champions the cause of world peace.

Mr Mahesh Kapoor continues to be an unselfish social worker even after Independence. He keeps his freedom struggle ideology intact. Politics for Mahesh Kapoor is progressive and secular while for Agarwal, a 'coal trade' (323). Mahesh Kapoor laments: 'previously politics was not profitable .... Now politics is profitable and naturally the kind of people who are interested in making money are keen to join the game' (324). Though a Hindu, he condemns revivalism. Mahesh Kapoor reveals his progressive and anti-feudalistic attitude in getting Zamindari Abolition Bill approved at the cost of his friendship with Nawab sahib 'for the greater good of millions of tenant farmers' (264). He rejects the offer of the ruler Marh, 'a wad of money ... to soften the provision of Zamindari Bill.' Fed up with the corruption of politicians, Kapoor decides to quit the party: 'This is not why I spent years of my life in prison. I am sick of the congress party and I too am thinking of leaving it' (753). It brings out the clear difference in the approach to politics between the freedom fighters and the present day selfish politicians. In spite of his integrity, Kapoor becomes a victim of corrupt politics and loses the election. His main rival, Waris employs foul methods to win the elections, 'he threw feasts and distributed sweets and liquor, he coerced whoever he could and cajoled whoever he could, he promised whatever was necessary' (1243). He indulges in character assassination of Mahesh Kapoor one day before the election in an anonymous pamphlet in Urdu.

The power in the hands of the selfish politicians gets abused. L.N. Agarwal as a Home Minister of Purva Pradesh had 'enjoyed the power that went along with being Home Minister, and he knew that it was not a portfolio that could be given to anyone else' (822). Since he hailed from trading community, he never neglects his community. Once some Jatavs picket the shop owners in Misri Mandi, a part of which lay in his constituency. L.N. Agarwal transgresses his power to save his people. He even orders young District Magistrate to open fire to restore order at Misri Mandi if the Jatavs do not disperse. He rejects alternative possible ways suggested by the Magistrate to solve the problem of Jatavs.

Seth portrays how these politicians victimize the common men in their power games. In communal riots 'at least five people were killed by the police in the firing near chowk' (251). Agarwal is more worried about his vote bank than the deaths.

> What will be the effect of all this be on the Jatav vote and the Muslims vote? The General Elections are just a few months away. Will these vote-banks swing away from the Congress? If so, in what numbers?. (242)

Officials become targets in power politics. Jha, the chairman of the Upper House of the state legislature asks Sandeep Lahiri, Sub Divisional Officer (SDO) of Rudhia, to mobilize funds for him. When Lahiri refuses to do so, he transfers him with 'immediate effect from the post of S.D.O. of Rudhia sub division to a post in the Department of Mines at Brahmapur the same day' (969).

Seth throws light on communal violence in the novel. He suggests that religious fanaticism and bigotry lead one nowhere but to destruction. The temple committee of Hindus headed by Raja of Marh prepares to construct a temple of lord Shiva contiguous to the west of Alamgiri mosque. Home Minister L.N. Agarwal supports the committee. The Imam suspects 'they could be hatching their designs to prevent our evening devotion by blowing their conches to drown out the call to prayer' (234) and Alamgiri Masjid Hifazat committee instigates the crowds. Ultimately it leads to communal riots and police firing.

Seth questions the hypocrisy of the religious leaders. The comments of Kedarnath, a shoe merchant who survived the trauma of 1947, are quite perceptive.

> Certainly I cannot understand people like the Raja of Marh. He imagines himself to be a new Ganesh whose divine mission in life is to lead the armies of Shiva to victory over the demons. And yet he's besotted with half the Muslim courtesans of the city. When he laid the foundation stone of the temple two

> people died. Not that this meant anything to him, he's probably had twenty times that number murdered in his time in his own state. (199)

When Rasheed, an Urdu teacher and a progressive thinker, determines to bring about some social change to a centuries-old land-tenure system and compels the village Patwari to transfer the ownership of his own piece of land to Kachheru, his father himself threatens him: 'Your communist schemes will not work here' (678). It shows how the landlordism exploited the innocent poor in rural India.

Seth presents the social evils such as 'untouchability' and the social conditions of the downtrodden in the novel. Some conservative thinkers have the opinion that if anybody is attached to the shoe-making business and tannery work he will be polluted and will lose his caste. Haresh Khanna's uncle in Delhi considers him 'polluted,' and that he has 'lost caste by working with leather' (577). Jagat Ram, a shoemaker, is a spokesperson for untouchable community. He does not agree with Gandhi, who 'believed that people should continue in their hereditarily ordained professions; a cobbler should remain a cobbler, a sweeper a sweeper' (1039). He understands Gandhiji's 'dignity of labour' as 'a misleading condensation' (1039). There is nothing worthy in cleaning lavatories and standing in a foul-smelling tanning pit. He expects a social change, but not in the near future. Before that 'a few more generations would continue to be crushed under the wheels of the great chariot before it finally ground to a blood stained halt' (1039). Jagat Ram thinks that the passing of the constitutional provision abolishing untouchability is more due to Ambedkar's pragmatism than Gandhi's legalism.

Seth attacks the domination of upper caste people and their intolerance of the untouchables at the countryside. When an untouchable youth asks an upper-caste woman for some water to drink, he was 'forced to eat human excreta. His brain and bicycle had then been smashed to bits' (1038). The upper caste people cannot brook the freedom and progress of the underdogs or the downtrodden in the lightest manner.

Both Tharoor and Seth, thus, present the deteriorating ethical values in politics. They 'apparently challenge the system, but actually infuse it with new life and vigor' (Karunakaran 1994: 97). They re-present contemporary Indian history with great skill.

Works Cited

Balaswamy, P. 'The Presence of the Past: Shashi Tharoor's *The Great Indian Novel* as Historiographic Metafiction.' *Indian Literature Today*. Vol. II. Ed. R.K. Dhavan. New Delhi: Prestige, 1998, 229–36. Print.

Belliappa, K.C. 'Problematising Indian History in English.' *The Journal of Indian Writing in English* 30.2 (July 2002). Print.

Chandra, Bipan. *India's Struggle for Independence*. New Delhi: Penguin, 1989. Print.

Gandhi, M.K. *An Autobiography: The Story of My Experiments with Truth*. Ahmedabad: Navajivan Mudranalaya, 1927. Print.

Karunakaran, Supriya. 'Games the Novelists Play: The Subversive Rebellion of Vikram Seth in *The Golden Gate* and Shashi Tharoor in *The Great Indian Novel.*' *Fiction of the Nineties.* Eds Veena Noble Dass and R.K. Dhawan. New Delhi: Prestige, 1994. 93–97. Print.

Kirpal, Viney. *The Postmodern Indian English Novel: A Study of the 1980s.* Ed. Viney Kirpal. New Delhi: Allied Publishers, 1996. Print.

Lal, P. 'Mod-Bharata.' *Littcrit* 16.12 (June–December 1990). 9–12. Print.

Mukherjee, Meenakshi. *The Twice Born Fiction: Themes and the Indian Novel in English.* New Delhi: Arnold-Heinemann Publishers, 1974. Print.

Nayar, Kuldip. *The Judgement.* New Delhi: Vikas, 1977. Print.

New York Times (16 December 1991). Print.

Paul, Seema. Interview of Vikram Seth. 'The Great Indian Novelist.' *The Telegraph* (21 February 1993). 5–10. Print.

Pandit, M.L. 'Subversion of Faith as Fiction: Salman Rushdie's *The Satanic Verses* and Shashi Tharoor's *The Great Indian Novel.*' *New Commonwealth Writing: A Critical Response.* New Delhi: Prestige, 1996. Print.

Pathak, R.S. Introduction. *Recent Indian Fiction.* New Delhi: Prestige, 1994. Print.

Rao, M. Madhusudhan. *Salman Rushdie's Fiction: A Study.* New Delhi: Sterling, 1992. Print.

Rushdie, Salman. *Midnight's Children.* Great Britain: Jonathan Cape Ltd., 1981. Print.

Sarkar, Sumit. *Modern India: 1885–1947.* New Delhi: Macmillan, 1983. Print.

Seth, Vikram. *A Suitable Boy.* New Delhi: Penguin, 1993. Print.

Shands, Kerstin W. 'Coming Together: Shoes and the Seduction of Rational Love in Vikram Seth's *A Suitable Boy.*' *Indian Writing in English.* Ed. Mohit K. Ray. New Delhi: Atlantic, 2003. 98–113. Print.

Tharoor, Shashi. *The Great Indian Novel.* New Delhi: Penguin, 1989. Print.

——. 'Timeless Epic.' *The Hindu Literary Review* (2 January 2005). 3. Print.

16

Eloquence of Silence: The Scourge of Violence in Amitav Ghosh's *The Shadow Lines*

K. DAMODAR RAO

In his much-acclaimed novel, *The Shadow Lines,* Amitav Ghosh focuses on three forms of violence that marked the course of the last century: violence witnessed during periods of war, violence resorted to by extremist organizations in pursuit of their goals, and the faceless violence that erupts during communal riots. In fact, this s(co)urge of violence in all the above gory manifestations was so pervasive that it appeared it was the only common language that bound mankind together. It is in its overarching fold that the major events of the twentieth century unfolded: The World Wars, The Nazi genocide, Hiroshima, Liberation struggles, Vietnam, Palestine, the civil wars, Latin American dictatorships, Partition of India, rise of fundamentalism, and the aggression on Iraq. In an ironic twist of history, the turn of the new century was greeted with the attacks on New York WTC twin towers by the al-Qaeda terrorists. In its aftermath some oft-quoted lines[1] from W.H. Auden's poems that deal with his recurring theme of desolation and loss of hope and faith in the face of man's self-destructive agenda were in circulation in many newspapers. Again, one is reminded of the play by Wole Soyinka, *A Dance of the Forests*[2] that projects violence as so ominously ingrained in human nature, as so much visceral that it blinds the protagonists to its devastating effects. The problematic of violence has been handled by creative writers in many effective and different forms and much commented upon by critics. Commenting on the scars that violence leaves behind, Jasbir Jain observes:

> Violence demands a heavy price: loss of trust and faith and freedom; a permanent inhabitation of fear, a continuity and inflaming of the feeling of hatred and revenge bringing about a temporariness in relationships as the areas of refuge go on shrinking. (2009: 25)

The last century witnessed the creation of a zone of comfort and modes of creative expression reaching pinnacles of excellence, but these times have also witnessed possibilities for new kind of rivalry and violence. With the rise of fundamentalism, new and serious challenges confronted the ideas of reason, democracy, freedom and secularism. If bigotry and political creed were the sources of violence in the first half of the twentieth century, sectarian nationalism and fundamentalism emerged as the new bases for contesting ideologies and the resultant violence in recent times. Taslima Nasreen in one of her lectures elaborates on the theatre of violence the present day world is and attributes it chiefly to the conflict between the ideologies of secularism and fundamentalism. She says: 'It is a conflict between the future and the past, between innovation and tradition, between those who value freedom and those who do not' (1996: 289).

The strange co-existence of creative and destructive possibilities in man, the contradictions within, have engaged the attention of many writers. Here are two instances, one of a creative writer, and another, of a critic: K. Siva Reddy, a Sahitya Akademi award-winning Telugu poet, in one of his poems, 'At the Same time' captures the inner dynamics of human psyche:

> How is it possible to respond sensitively
> And become immune to the same at the same time?
> Here it is possible–
> Enormous contradictions appear any moment ....
> Climbing up and sliding down take place simultaneously
> I love someone, repulsion manifests at the very instant
> I nourish my body-tree providing water daily
> And cut it bit by bit until I uproot it completely. (2003: 4)

Jasbir Jain is the critic who dwells on the question:

> The human ability to hold opposites together is amazing just as the ability to hang on to hope in the face of disaster, to erase cultural pasts in order to preserve what one begins to believe is true and important for identity formation. Is this resilience, transformation or submission to the powers of others? Is it survival or myopia? (2009: 23)

Violence of the religious or communal variety has become so much a common feature in the history of India that at regular intervals the riots erupted causing large-scale destruction and untold suffering, thus playing havoc with the lives of innocent individuals. Amitav Ghosh, in one of his interviews observes: '... this particular kind of upheaval, the communal riot, is something that really is quite distinctive of South Asia. I don't know of any other place where it is such an endemic form of social violence' (Silva and Tickell 2003: 218). This paper focuses on how Ghosh diligently portrays the face of fear in the wake of devastation by war and terrorism, mob frenzy, mayhem and massacre, as one is confronted with faceless violence especially of the communal variety that is unique to the subcontinent.

It is true that in terms of identity and nationalism, India's vastness, with its contradictions, defies comprehension. Ashis Nandy mentions that anyone who attempts to interpret it ends up projecting one's deepest fantasies and what ultimately emerges is a projection of 'the interpreter rather than the interpreted' (1983: 79–80). But, despite the surface differences and distinctions of community, language, creed, and region, it is the collective consciousness more than anything else that concretises the notion of a nation. As K.C. Baral affirms, 'the affiliative relationship between a nation and its citizens is mediated at different levels under different conditions in which the nation does not exist simply as an impersonal representation, but variously moulds and shapes our personality' (2000: 73).

For one who is brought up in the Bengali milieu, it is natural that Tagore exerts a sure influence on Amitav Ghosh. In fact, in one of his interviews he reveals that Tagore was an obvious literary and intellectual influence on him along with Satyajit Ray who has shaped his 'way of looking at things' (Silva and Tickell 2003: 216). It is important to note that Tagore, despite his modernity, opposed nationalism as an import from western culture; he termed it 'a great menace,' and also *'bhougolik apadevata'* or geographical demon (Qtd in Nandy 1994: 7). In his book *Nationalism* Tagore expresses the belief that India 'has never had a real sense of nationalism' (Tagore 1985: 64) and it would do no good to compete with western civilization in its own field. Instead, he looks back to India's past tradition that sustained the society through the ages where one can find co-existence that is not based on 'a conspiracy of fear' that emanates from borders, barricades, the shadow lines that we draw in our minds, but on 'adjustment of races' which implies acknowledging the real differences between them and yet seeking some basis for unity. Such a pluralistic tradition has been in evidence in India at the social level, if not at the political level. Saints like Nanak and bhakti poets like Kabir, Chaitanya and Tukaram upheld this tradition in their writings. K.C. Baral terms this phase as 'pre-integrated phase of Indian nationalism' (2000: 73).

It was with the entry of Gandhi in Indian politics that consolidation of nationalist feelings took shape (the integrated phase) and the non-violent nationalism he introduced was also in tune with the traditional Indian way of pursuing non-imperialist and the non-interventionist policies. More importantly, he perceived his nationalism to be 'intense internationalism' that does not recognize exclusivities. According to Ashis Nandy, Gandhi's unbridled antagonism to the concepts of nationalism and modernism and his defence of Indian traditions carried with it 'intimations of a postmodern consciousness' (1994: 2). It is such a critique of nationalism and the spirit of intense internationalism that permeates through the fictional oeuvre of Ghosh, from *The Circle of Reason* to *River of Smoke,* with *The Shadow Lines* providing a good example of his thematic concerns. The crossing of boundaries comes naturally to Ghosh's characters, which is conveyed though the imagery of flight. In Ghosh's third novel, *In An Antique Land,* the narrator, in a childlike manner, gleefully expresses a sense of marvel at the similarities of ancient civilizations of India and Egypt. Through the characters of Thamma, Robi and Ila in *The Shadow Lines* the narrator shows that nationalism can be a source of terrible psychological violence especially when it is manifested in its more militant and sectarian forms. The novel rather projects the post-integrated phase of nationalism wherein groups and conflicting interests subvert it from within. The novel questions the validity of master-narratives as the nameless narrator is tutored in his childhood by his uncle and mentor, Tridib, of the many uses of precise imaginings, and invention of stories for ourselves—otherwise one would never be free of other people's inventions. The novel, as such, is not merely about questioning but also reconstructing identities and inventing stories as the narrator retrieves the truly authentic story surrounding the death of his uncle, Tridib, amidst other people's versions.

Besides nationalism, the novel attempts to grapple with issues of secularism and communal politics. As is well known, neither secularism nor religious faith sanctions violence. In fact, every religious faith professes principles of tolerance and compassion. Secularism in the western version has certain exclusivities; it does not recognize religion in public life. One could follow religion in one's private life but since public realm is a rational affair it does not allow space for religion. Non-western concept of secularism, with its respect for all religions, provides space for continuous dialogue among religious traditions and between the religious and the secular. In ancient India, Ashoka was a symbol of secular values as he showed tolerance towards other religions though he was a practising Buddhist even in public life. In medieval times, Akbar is considered a symbol of inter-religious amity and yet his secularism was based on Islam. In the twentieth century, Gandhi proclaimed that his religion was his politics and his politics his religion. The sources of his tolerance could be traced to traditional Hinduism. Everyday Hinduism, everyday Islam or Christianity have always propagated peaceful co-existence of religious communities, and India's traditional life provides a good model in this respect. While commenting on this notion in a similar vein, Amartya Sen observes that the long history of heterodoxy and the tolerance of religious diversity helped not only in the development and survival of democracy in India, it has also contributed to the emergence of India-specific secularism. He says:

> Secularism in contemporary India, which received legislative formulation in the post-independence constitution of the Indian Republic, contains strong influences of Indian intellectual history, including the championing of intellectual pluralism .... Indeed, there are two principal approaches to secularism, focussing respectively on (1) *neutrality* between different religions, and (2) *prohibition* of religious associations in state activities. Indian secularism has tended to emphasize neutrality in particular, rather than prohibition in general. (2005: 19–20)

Ashis Nandy, in his perceptive analysis of the role of religion in South Asia in the last century, observes that it manifested in two forms: as faith and as ideology. Faith, he contends, is a way of life and is plural and catholic operationally whereas religion-as-ideology implies an identifying factor, both at national and cross-national levels, 'contesting for or projecting non-religious, usually political or socio-economic, interests' (2001: 62). When religion is used for purposes other than faith and way of life, it can be a source of terrifying violence. Elaborating on the idea of a single identity Amartya Sen observes that it could be a source of multiple forms of violence:

> Indeed, many of the conflicts and barbarities in the world are sustained through the illusion of a unique and choiceless identity. The art of constructing hatred takes the form of invoking the magical power of some allegedly predominant identity that drowns other affiliations, and in a conveniently bellicose form can also overpower any human sympathy or natural kindness that we may normally have. The result can be homespun elemental violence, or globally artful violence and terrorism. (2006: xv)

He affirms that acceptance of plurality of identities as opposed to a single, hardened, impenetrable closed category, holds promise of hope of harmony in violence-ridden contemporary world.

While maintaining that the concerns of violence remain the same everywhere, be it a conflict of religion or language or ethnicity, Amitav Ghosh draws parallels between the discourses of Hindu extremism in India and those of Khmer Rouge in Cambodia. He terms this ideology as 'supermacism': '... extremist religious movements whether in India or Israel or Egypt or the United states, are often supremacist movements, whatever their rhetoric' (2002: 276). Ghosh observes that for the fundamentalists, religion is only a pretext and that they do not exactly proceed from 'a positive content of faith' but rather from 'acts of negation.' Religion-as-ideology believes in supermacism and polarities and hence it sanctions violence. The rise of fundamentalism in the subcontinent, both in its Hindu and Muslim varieties, could be viewed in the light of ideology taking over faith in the realm of religion. The communal riots that punctuated the course of the history in the subcontinent have left an orgy of violence, a trail of sorrow, suffering and psychic wounds since Partition. These riots, of late, have been associated less with religion and faith and increasingly came to be identified with questions of ideology and political interests and when it is so there is little to differentiate between its brand of violence and violence unleashed by other ideologies, political creeds, and linguistic and ethnic bigotry. Ghosh says: '... the majority of the followers of a religion now profess ideas that are ... essentially political or sociological, then we must be prepared to accept that this is in fact what religion signifies in our time' (2002: 285). The narrator of *The Shadow Lines* tries to come to terms with this tragedy, both personal and communal, and tries to find words to capture the suffering and trauma and then resigns himself to silence, in vain again.

While commenting on the question of connection between literary aestheticism and violence, Ghosh stresses the need to 'recognise the urgency of remembering the stories we have not written' (2002: 62). The violence that took place after the assassination of Mrs Indira Gandhi, Ghosh says, haunted him for a long time and prompted him to provide a fictional metaphor for the futility and banality of such destructive violence. Ghosh recalls: 'Within a few months, I started my novel, which I eventually called *The Shadow Lines*—a book that led me backward in time to earlier memories of riots, ones witnessed in childhood. It became a book not about any one event but about the meaning of such events and their effects on the individuals who live through them' (2002: 60). What was appalling was that the state machinery in 1984 connived in the pogrom of mass murder. History repeated itself at Godhra in Gujarat in February 2002 when the state was used not to impose order, 'but rather as an instrument for the incitement of violence' (Ghosh 2003).

Nationalism and patriotism are intrinsically related to borders, more so in the case of the Indian subcontinent, post-Partition. Suvir Kaul observes, 'At the origin of India and Pakistan lies the national trauma of partition, a trauma that freezes fear into silence, and for which *The Shadow Lines* seeks to find a language, a process for mourning, and perhaps even a memorial' (1988: 269). Thamma, the grandmother of the narrator who plays a pivotal role in the proceedings of the novel, questions the very importance of Partition when she could not find any physical equivalents of the division. She says, 'But if there aren't any trenches or anything, how are people to know? I mean, where's the difference then? And if there's no difference both sides will be the same; ... what was it all for then—partition and all the killings and everything—if there isn't something in between?' (Ghosh 1988: 151)

Through Thamma, Ghosh depicts certain aspects of militant nationalism. Thamma admired terrorists and always wished to be part of them. She was fascinated by the stories of terrorist heroes like Khudiram Bose and Bagha Jatin who were hunted down on the banks of the Buribalam River. She wanted to gain glory by doing menial works for the terrorists. In answer to her grandson's question whether she could have killed the English officer she says that firstly she would have been frightened but she would have prayed to God for strength and the courage to kill the English magistrate. 'It was for our freedom: I would have done anything to be free' (39).

Robi, the uncle of the narrator, serves the purpose of explaining the nature of freedom and violence. The memory that haunts Robi from his childhood questions the validity of freedom that is inseparable from violence. He stops at London on his way to Harvard to spend some time with the narrator and Ila. He talks of freedom that is never free from violence. Robi says, 'You know, if you look at the pictures on the front pages of the newspaper at home now, all those pictures of dead people—in Assam, the north-east, Punjab, Sri Lanka, Tripura—people shot by terrorists and separatists and the army and the police, you'll find somewhere behind it all, that single word, every one's doing it to be free' (246). He says that if he had been working in those areas he would have ordered the policemen to kill anyone who comes in their way including people because they have to do it for unity and freedom. He further says, 'And then I think to myself why don't they draw thousands of little lines through the whole subcontinent and give every little place a new name? What would it change? It's a mirage; the whole thing is a mirage. How can anyone divide a memory?' (247). He asserts the futility of freedom. He says if freedom is possible he would have attained it after the death of his brother Tridib. The mere mention of the place stirs his memory and shakes him like a leaf. Suvir Kaul says: 'Memory is above all, a restless, energetic, troubling power; the price, and the limitation, of freedom; the author, and the interrogator, of the form and existence of the modern nation-state' (1995: 283).

The narrator struggles with silence while trying to reconstruct the past. He says, 'Every word I write about those events of 1964 is the product of a struggle with silence .... I know nothing of this silence except that it lies outside the reach of my intelligence, beyond words—that is why this silence must win, must inevitably defeat me, because it is not a presence at all; it is simply a gap, a hole, an emptiness in which there are no words' (218). He tries to press his memory and finds silence insurmountable: 'The silence that preceded and followed the revelation was a moving statement on the actualization of internal violence. The search and the revelation together cause a harrowing experience for the narrator' (1999: 269). The narrator realizes the long lasting power of silence that kept him in its grip for such a long time. It took him fifteen years to discover the connection between his nightmare bus ride back from school and the catastrophe that struck Tridib and the others in Dhaka. Suvir Kaul points out, '... *The Shadow Lines* is an archaeology of silences, a slow brushing away of the cobwebs of modern Indian memory, a repeated return to those absences and fissures that mark the sites of personal and national trauma' (1995: 269).

The riots are transient in nature and draw less attention once they are over. But they are always alive in the memories of people who become its victims. The narrator could not remember the exact dates but recollects that a test series was to be held on that day in which the wicket keeper Budhi Kunderan made his maiden century on debut. He proceeds to verify the riot in the paper but to his surprise it happens in Khulna, in East Pakistan. Later, after a careful research in the library he discovers the reasons and connections between the riots in Calcutta and Dhaka that became the cause of the catastrophe in the family. The narrator goes through the papers of the period of the tragic incident and finds the news item in bold print with the title: 'sacred relic reinstalled' (224). Then he looks for the news related to the incident. The disappearance of the sacred relic known as Mu-i-Mubarak which was believed to be the hair of Prophet Mohammad himself from its place in Hazratbal Mosque on 27 December 1963, two hundred years after it was installed in Kashmir, resulted in a great stir and '... life came to a standstill in the valley of Kashmir' (225).

Pakistan's religious authorities declared that the 'theft of the relic was an attack on the identity of Muslims' (226). Pakistan spoke of 'genocide' and described it as an attempt to uproot the hopes of Kashmiris, preventing them from being their own spiritual nation. The Mu-i-Mubarak was 'recovered' by the officials of Central Bureau of Intelligence on 4 January 1964. After reading the same report for a fifth time the narrator suddenly remembers that his grandmother, May, and Tridib left for Dhaka the day before the relic was reinstalled. And this time he finds everything clearly connected. Meenakshi Mukherjee says, '... the narrator's desperate search in the archives to recover lost events has to be seen as an example of insisting upon one's story, a resistance to being swallowed up by narratives made up by others' (1997: 264).

The narrator remembers his school days when riots took place in Calcutta. One day the narrator waits for his overcrowded school bus but to his surprise finds only a dozen boys who sat on a bench at the back. They all stare at his water bottle, which is followed by a rumour that 'they' have mixed poison in Tala Tank from where the water supply is made to entire Calcutta. The word 'they' is neither questioned nor explained, but is understood. The narrator on his way home finds the streets empty 'except for squads of patrolling policemen' (202). Every object creates fear in one's heart when things are not normal and this time it was a rickshaw parked in the middle of the road. The narrator says: 'At that moment we could read the disarrangement of our universe in the perfectly ordinary angle of an abandoned rickshaw' (203). A mob is seen moving towards the bus and soon starts pelting stones on the bus. The narrator says that Tablu, one of the boys, cried 'for all of us .... It would not be enough to say we were afraid: We were stupefied with fear' (204). The novelist makes it clear that violence is inextricably linked with fear:

> It is fear that comes of the knowledge that normalcy is utterly contingent, that the spaces that surround one, the streets one inhabits, can become suddenly and without warning as hostile as a desert in a flash flood ... it is the special quality of fear of the war between oneself and one's image in the mirror. (204)

It was much later that he recognizes the illogical connection between that incident and the riot in Dhaka that killed Tridib.

The communal riots follow their own 'grotesque logic' (229) fed by rumours, devoid of basic streak of humanity as evidenced in the life of the subcontinent. The carnage let loose on such occasions, the manner in which the progrom is executed, the animal instincts that come out into the open in an atmosphere of frenzy and violence convert human life into an accidental freak. Before the riots erupt, there would not be any hint or 'augury' that would suggest the impending carnage. The situation would be 'replete with the fullness of normalcy' (227). And then all mayhem would follow as by design, in a pattern. Unable to measure the 'stirrings of silence' Tridib had fallen a prey to that 'seamless silence (227). The grandmother of the narrator, Robi and May were witnesses to the ghastly scene of Tridib being consumed by a fanatical mob.

There is a symmetrical pattern to the modus operandi of the two communities, perhaps the only similarity in times of mutually exclusive identities. Ghosh writes: 'Ironically it is through self-destructive violence that the people of the subcontinent assert a common inheritance and affiliation; in the near symmetry of their killing of each other they deny that they might be different in the first place' (2002: 62). In Dhaka, Robi accompanies Mayadebi, Thamma, Tridib and May on their visit to his grand uncle. Thamma and Mayadebi with the help of Khalil convince their insane uncle to follow their car in the rickshaw. The trauma of riots and carnage, the texture of fear, although indescribable, leave a lasting impression on the minds of the loved ones who witness the gruesome violence and loss of life. This distressing experience is presented in the novel through Thamma, May and Robi. Thamma attempts to wreak a psychological revenge at the time of the war with Pakistan in 1971 by offering blood to the soldiers in a frantic hurry as if in a fit of madness. May is filled with guilt conscience for the rest of her life as she thinks she was, to some extent, responsible for the thing happened as it was she who wanted to rescue the old man from the fury of the mob and unwittingly let Tridib get down the car only to be caught in the whirlpool of violence. As for Robi, he had many nightmares haunting him through his adolescence and youth.

The search of the narrator comes to an end with May completing the picture of that fateful day. Not only Thamma and Robi who carry the wounds of Tridib's murder but May too is traumatized by the memory of that incident. She lives with the tragedy and never shares it with anyone until the narrator comes to her before leaving London. She finds solace in the narrator who also happened to be a friend of Tridib. She narrates the incident from the point when they started from the old man's house. She gets down from the car and is followed by Tridib who pushes her down and runs towards the mob. The old man is pulled off from the rickshaw by the time Tridib reached it. The mob drags him in when he tries to make his way to the old man. May narrates:

> He vanished. I could only see their backs. It took less than a moment. Then the men began to scatter. I picked myself up and began to run towards them. The men had melted away, into the gullies. When I got there, I saw three bodies. They were all dead. They'd cut Khalif's stomach open. The old man's head had been hacked off. And they'd cut Tridib's throat from ear to ear. (250–51)

All the time she holds herself responsible for the death of Tridib, but now she says, '... I didn't kill him; I couldn't have, if I'd wanted. He gave himself up; it was a sacrifice. I know I can't understand it, I know I mustn't try for any real sacrifice is a mystery' (251–52). The narrator feels grateful to May, as she has given him the glimpse 'of a final redemptive mystery' (252).

The novel is not the story of an individual or a particular family but it is an account of the trauma of individuals who become victims of avoidable violence, even as they try to be free of the shadows that divide them. The governments have no use for 'memories of riots' (230). Their methods follow a fairly predictable pattern. Initially they start with 'rhetorical exchanges' such as mutual, symmetrical accusations for remaining passive in times of 'frenzy of looting, killing and burning.' And when the riots subside, congratulatory notes are exchanged 'over their respective successes in quelling disturbances' (230). When only a few people get killed, governments have no use for them. The irony is the gory incident in which Tridib and others get killed is not of much importance to the government, as such it disappeared from the collective imagination 'into the crater of a volcano of silence' (233). Conversely, individuals struggle and live with the shattering experience, reconstructing and re-living it if they happened to be witnesses. When there is no recorded account available as to what happened, one has to go in search of the causes of, silly as these might appear, and the actual details about the incident as the narrator does in the narrative and retrieves the incidents of violence from recesses of history and comparing the coincidences drawn from memory.

Aesthetics of negation implies foregrounding the negative and the fragmented while upholding, cherishing and even celebrating, albeit in an implicit manner, the positive and the harmonious. Amitav Ghosh portrays violence and its shattering impact on the lives of individuals in the novel in an eloquent fashion by extricating the silences and lending a voice to them. The portrayal of different forms of frenzy and violence does not make the narrative a dark or a cynical one. The brilliance of the novelist's craft provides an axis on which the destructive and constructive, the useful and the harmful, are carefully balanced. Eloquence permeates through silence, sense of oneness breaks the barriers, notion of internationalism blasts the shadow lines while harmony is celebrated vis-à-vis communal discord. Jasbir Jain raises a pertinent question in this regard: 'As a counter argument, one can state that if violence and conflict can travel across groups, communities and countries, why is it not possible for humanistic impulses to travel across barriers of race, caste, religion and politics' (2009: 25)?

Notes

1. But who can live for long
   In an euphoric dream;
   Out of the mirror they stare,
   Imperialism's face
   And the international wrong.

   ('1 September 1939')

   Column by column in a cloud of dust
   They marched away enduring a belief
   Whose logic brought them, somewhere else, to grief.

   ('The Shield of Achilles')

   In the nightmare of the dark
   All the dogs of Europe bark,
   And the living nations wait,
   Each sequestered in its hate;

   ('In Memory of W.B. Yeats')
2. It is a celebratory drama that marked the occasion of Nigerian independence in 1960 but it turned out to be a cautionary tale for mankind as the humans are prone to committing same mistakes, a process which is shown in the stunning similarity between the attitudes of three present day men given to violence marked by jealousy, greed and immorality and of their earlier births that go back by eight centuries in time in the drama: they have not learnt their lessons from history despite the passage of time and the path of progress.

Works Cited

Baral, K.C. 'Imaging India: Nation and Narration.' *Rethinking Indian English Literature.* Eds U.M. Nanavati and Prafulla C. Kar. New Delhi: Pencraft International, 2000. 71–81. Print.

Damodar Rao, K. 'Silence as Possible Mode of Response in Amitav Ghosh's *The Shadow Lines.*' *The Novels of Amitav Ghosh.* Ed. R.K. Dhawan. New Delhi: Prestige Books, 1999. 136–42. Print.

Ghosh, Amitav. *The Shadow Lines.* Delhi: Ravi Dayal, 1988. Print. All page numbers are to this edition.

——. 'The Ghosts of Mrs Gandhi.' *The Imam and the Indian.* New Delhi: Ravi Dayal, 2002. Print.

——. 'The Gujarat Carnage.' (31 January 2003) <http://www.amitavghosh.com/essays.html> Web.

Jain, Jasbir. 'Terrorism at the Feet of Buddha: From Taliban to LTTE and the In-between.' *Crossing Borders: Post 1980 Subcontinental Writing in English.* Ed. Jasbir Jain. Jaipur: Rawat Publications, 2009. 23–37. Print.

Kaul, Suvir. 'Separation Anxiety: Growing Up Inter/National in *The Shadow Lines.*' *The Shadow Lines.* Delhi: Oxford UP, 1995. 268–86. Print.

Mukherjee, Meenakshi. 'Maps and Mirrors: Co-ordinates of Meaning in *The Shadow Lines.*' *The Shadow Lines.* Delhi: Oxford UP, 1997. 255–67. Print.

Nandy, Ashis. *The Intimate Enemy.* New Delhi: Oxford UP, 1983. Print.

——. *The Illegitimacy of Nationalism.* Delhi: Oxford UP, 1994. Print.

——. *Time Warps.* Delhi: Permanent Black, 2001. Print.

Nasreen, Taslima. 'On Islamic Fundamentalism.' *New Quest* 119 (September–October 1996). 289–92. Print.

Sen, Amartya. *The Argumentative Indian: Writings on Indian Culture, History, and Identity.* London and New Delhi: Penguin, 2005. Print.

——. *Identity and Violence: The Illusion of Destiny.* London: Allen Lane, 2006. Print.

Silva, Neluka and Alex Tickell. 'An Interview with Amitav Ghosh.' *Critical Perspectives.* Ed. Brinda Bose. New Delhi: Pencraft International, 2003. 214–21. Print.

Siva Reddy, K. 'At the Same Time.' Trans. K. Damodar Rao. *Kakatiya Journal of English Studies* 23 (2003), 4. Print.

Tagore, Rabindranath. *Nationalism.* Madras: Macmillan, 1985. Print.

17

Novel as History: A Reading of Amitav Ghosh's *The Glass Palace*

P. MALLIKARJUNA RAO AND TENNETI SHYAMA KRISHNA

Amitav Ghosh has emerged as a prominent Indian English novelist on the post-Rushdie Indian literary scene that is known for its experimentation and trend-setting. As Ravi observes, 'The novel of the Eighties has evolved from a new ethos, a transformed sensibility and startlingly original perspective' (2003: 7). Ghosh has eight novels and several diverse non-fictional works to his credit. He has received international attention and appreciation for his works and awards came his way naturally. Ghosh's writing career began in the 1980s which marks a watershed in the annals of Indian English novel.

The Glass Palace is a historical novel written by Ghosh in 2002 and it shares the contemporary trends of the period. Before initiating an appraisal of the novel, it is imperative to trace the emergence of historical novel as a sub-genre in Indian English fiction to place the discussion in context.

Historical fiction made a fairly early appearance in the sub-genre of historical romance in the late nineteenth century. Many novels were about the relations between the English and the natives, the stories of Maharajas, etc. Later, the historical and political events of the freedom struggle attracted the attention of the writers of the day and the theme of the nationalist movement was treated by them in different ways. Subsequently, several events that occurred in the post-Independence period such as the Partition and its terrible aftermath, the accession of princely states to the Indian Union and the two wars on the frontier furnished fresh material to the novelists.

In the novels of the late 1950s deification of Gandhi was on the wane, as he ceased to be an awe-inspiring figure any longer. In these novels, the focus shifted from the historical events and personages to the depiction of nuances in the social and psychological relationships. But in the novels of the 1980s history has made a comeback though in a different format. There is generic blurring of the two disciplines of History and Literature. The postmodern theory challenged the arbitrary division of these disciplines and tried to focus more on 'what the two modes of writing share than on how they differ' (Hutcheon 1988: 105). Saleem Sinai, the protagonist of *Midnight's Children,* is a metaphor for India's history, whose predicament aptly sums up the one for the modern novelist when he says that he is 'handcuffed to history'.

Amitav Ghosh's novels are remarkable for their re-presentation of history which is ubiquitous in his novels. Ghosh is always deeply inclined to the study of events from a historical perspective. Yet, the central focus is more on the individual's predicament in a given historical circumstance rather than on the circumstances themselves. In his interview to Hawley he admits: 'My fundamental interest is in people—in individuals and their specific predicaments. If history is of interest to me it is because it provides instances of unusual and extraordinary predicaments ...' (Hawley 2005: 6). His third novel *In an Antique Land* is a typical example of this view. It is the tale of an Indian slave, Bomma, from the twelfth century, dug out by the author-persona in his expedition to Egypt in 1982. Empirical research in social anthropology prompted Ghosh to write his first history-based fictional venture, *In an Antique Land.* It is an experiment in many ways, especially in its attempt at historiography. Ghosh does not believe in the distinctions people make between fiction and non-fiction. He says '... I distrust also the lines that people draw between fiction and non-fiction. I think these lines are drawn in order to manipulate our ways of thought: that is why they must be disregarded' (Hawley 2005: 9).

Interestingly, historiography and historical fiction are parallel in nature as the elucidation of each would show. Historiography is the writing of history based on scholarly disciplines such as the analysis and evaluation of the source materials. But there is more to it. B.V. Rao, a Professor of History, commenting on historiography in the preface to his popular work, *Concise Book of World History* (1991) says, 'As already mentioned, a historian will have to make use of his talents to present his matter in a creative manner. Unlike a scientist who deals mostly with dead matter, a historian deals with interesting human situations of the past. If he cannot add flesh, blood and soul to the dry bones of facts of history, his narrative of the past appears so unreal. Therefore, he has to use his imagination to make the past real and credible to his readers. This manner of presentation—a process known as historiography—is more likely to come under art than science. Therefore, history can be considered a science in so far as it uses the scientific method and an art for the manner of its treatment and composition ...' (2). This exposition underscores the creative element of historiography. As Linda Hutcheon observes, both are '... linguistic constructs, highly conventionalized in their narrative forms ... they appear to be equally intertextual, deploying the texts of the past within their own complex textuality' (1988: 105). In a similar manner, a writer of historical fiction too assumes the role of a historiographer in thoroughly examining the history represented in the fiction, blending it into his work. While doing so, the artist in him takes precedence over historian in creating the plot and appropriate milieu employing his imagination and acumen where history is obscure or silent. If he deviates from the known historical facts as a consequence and takes liberties with history, the outcome is what is known as historical romance. Nonetheless, Amitav Ghosh's historical novels are a consummation of his creativity and a sense of history without being prejudicial to the essential historical facts.

While the novel *In an Antique Land* is configured out of his academic research work, his novel *The Glass Palace* emerges from his meticulous explorations into the turbulent past of Burma and India of the colonial era, through the World War II and its aftermath, with the main focus on the theme of the individual's crisis during the said times. Speaking about the intense research that went into the writing of the novel, Ghosh says, 'When an American writes a historical novel he or she can generally rely on the historians to have done the research. I didn't have this luxury available to me. I had to do much of the primary research while also telling a story' (Hawley 2005: 12).

Ghosh explains in his author's note appended to the novel how he scrupulously proceeded with his collection of historical facts essential for making of the novel. He had travelled to places, met people of consequence who recounted to him the events of 1941 that form the core of the narrative. He earnestly acknowledges the services of historian Walter A. Desai whose work he consults for his attempt at recovering the traces of 'the erased life of the deposed king Thebaw' (Ghosh 2004: 552).

By his own admission, *The Glass Palace* is a novel, a fictional work with history of the sub-continent as its backdrop, and yet, but for king Thebaw, Queen Supayalat and their daughters none of its principal characters bear any resemblance to real people, living or deceased. However, his near-obsessive urge to render the backgrounds of his characters' lives as closely as he could, made him read hundreds of books, memoirs, travelogues, gazetteers, articles and notebooks, published and unpublished, in the five years it took him to write the novel even as he travelled thousands of miles, visiting and re-visiting, so far as possible, all the settings and locations that figure in the novel (Ghosh 2004: 549).

The story of the founders of the Indian National Army as well as the Indian presence in Burma is unknown to most Indians, since there is very little written about it. Ghosh claims that this has prompted him to probe into these historical episodes to chronicle them in his stupendous work. In the light of these facts the novel may be considered a work of art with history of the times represented through the history of the individuals in its true perspective.

The Glass Palace may be designated as a postmodernist text. *The Britannica Concise Encyclopedia* defines postmodernism as, 'Any of several artistic movements since about the 1960s that have challenged the philosophy and practices of modern arts or literature. In literature, this has amounted to a reaction against an ordered view of the world and therefore against fixed ideas about the form and meaning of texts' (Answers.com).

Temporal distortion is a common technique in modern fiction: fragmentation and non-linear narratives are central features in both modern and postmodern literatures. Temporal distortion in postmodern fiction is used in a variety of ways, often for the sake of irony. Historiographic metafiction, a word coined by Linda Hutcheon, refers to the works that fictionalize actual historical events or figures—a feature relevant to the postmodernist text.

These are the essential features that make Ghosh's novels, including *The Glass Palace,* postmodernist. In *The Glass Palace*, Ghosh, however, follows the linear narration, temporal distortion being in the least. This may be attributed to the voluminous size of the novel encompassing the history and geography of three nations extending over two centuries with several characters introduced. Events are told in retrospect only in a few instances such as the account of the past years of king Thebaw, Dinu's recollection of the closing days of Arjun, the Indian Mutiny and the like.

Ghosh takes a fresh look at the events of the colonial era and the momentous events that shaped the course of history of the subcontinent, and the Southeast Asia in his sizeable text of *The Glass Palace.* With his postcolonial, post modernist outlook, Ghosh explores the past to tell us the story that in many respects reflects the enduring postcolonial history. 'Writing with a post-colonial consciousness, Ghosh is certain of his human and historical insights' (Kadam 2006: 18). The series of events following the British occupation of Burma provides Ghosh with an occasion to shed light on the strange case where the exploited, that is the Indians, becoming the exploiter with the Burmese border being opened up by the British, making it a province of India. Things come to a head with the ensuing rebellion in Burma against the Indian settlers followed by World War II. In what may be called a neo-colonial trend, Indians like Rajkumar set forth to exploit the situation and the novel, therefore, is a translation of this bitter truth of history on to the page. Ghosh being what he is, illuminates the obscure and dark corners of history.

Ghosh turns our attention on how, in an ironic way, the exploited turn exploiters, in the background of Burma being annexed by the British, exemplifying oppression as a universal phenomenon. Rajkumar, the protagonist, Indian by origin, sees an opportunity in the quandary when Burma becomes a province of the British India; smuggles Indians into the country where he had once migrated as a boy. He is castigated by his Burmese wife Dolly, and by Uma, known for her progressive outlook, her Indian roots notwithstanding. Uma, out of her love for Dolly, helps Rajkumar marry her, but later does not hesitate to reprove him for his vicious ways. With the riots against Indians in Burma turning violent, she tells him to his face, '... It's people like you who're responsible for this tragedy. Did you ever think of the consequences when you were transporting people here? What you and your kind have done is far worse than the worst deeds of the Europeans' (Ghosh 2004: 247). But Rajkumar, in his arrogance, thinks he is doing them a favour by offering his services to the Burmese, the way the British used to think of themselves.

The Whiteman's burden theory of the British was believed by many Indians as it was believed by the British. Uma is annoyed to learn that the colonizers found a crooked explanation to back up their 'Whiteman's burden theory'. The British tell their Indian sepoys that they were freeing people from their bad kings or their evil customs or some such thing, and the sepoys believed it because the British had believed it. The soldier Uma had met explained to her, 'It took us a long time to understand that in their eyes freedom exists wherever they rule' (Ghosh 2004: 193).

Rajkumar sees an opportunity even in the prospect of the War. Eventually, he becomes a victim of his own doing losing his young son Neel when the War erupts. Burma struggles on, gripped by the junta that outdoes the British in its rule with an iron hand. Within the periphery of India yet another drama unfolds when people like Arjun, another key character who serves as an officer in the British Indian army, have to face conflicting loyalties. Ghosh effectively depicts Arjun's inner conflict in his shifting allegiance favouring the cause of the Indians' struggle for Independence and his efforts to come to terms with the new found truth of British hegemony. Joining the Indian League army, he trains his gun against his own men in the British army to liberate the country from the empire. He dies a martyr fighting the war.

The other dimension to the novel is the depiction of the forgotten history of king Thebaw; his life in exile in India with his Queen and daughters. The novel is appropriately titled *The Glass Palace*; The Glass Palace is the royal abode of the king of Burma. When King Thebaw was exiled to India, he was put up in Outram House in Ratnagiri which provides a sad and pitiable contrast to the glorious Glass Palace which then crumbles bringing down the monarchic rule in Burma. The graphic details of the warfront, the upheavals of World War II leading to the changes in Asian front and in the individual lives are shown in a poignant way. Ghosh's skill lies in bringing to life the historical figures and the social and political milieu of the times by blending the real with the fictional in his novel. Beginning with the tumultuous year 1885, when the British annexed Burma, the narration encompasses the upheavals caused by the rebellion in the country against the Indian settlers and the British, the outbreak of World War-II, and the eventual culmination in the emergence of powers as evil as imperialism, fascism, etc. on the world scene and the tyrannical rule of the military junta that took over in Burma.

Uma's husband, Beni Prasad, the collector of Ratnagiri, dies a disillusioned man, when he sees through the evil designs of the British. Uma, who had lived in his shadow all the while, keenly participates in the activities of the Indian League. But eventually she takes to the Gandhian path once she realizes that non-violence is the appropriate weapon to face the mighty British. While Gandhi is shown only as a shadowy figure, Aung San Suu Kyi, the leader fighting for the cause of democracy in Burma, is shown as a character. Her public speech from the confines of her house, she being under house arrest, is attended by Dinu, accompanied by Jaya. Dinu, being a left sympathizer, loathed the British colonialism, and thinks it was surpassed only by European Fascism and the Japan's militaris.

II

Another predominant thematic concern of Ghosh is migration. The problem of migration has become so crucial in the modern age that writers conscious of its pervasiveness have made an attempt at making it a central theme of their fiction and Ghosh is no exception to it. Migration always gave rise to fluid identities and cultural transplantations, a recurrent theme in Ghosh's novels.

Due to political suppression or wars or famines, men have been known to moving from one part of the globe to another for a better life as refugees. Hence, Hugh Tinker rightly observes, 'Twentieth century, even more than any age before, is the age of the refugee' (1975: 1). When Burma was under attack by the Axis forces, people, mostly Indians, migrated to India. The exodus is given a vivid description by Ghosh in the episode where Rajkumar the protagonist joins the mass departure, leaving everything behind, his fortunes, his dear ones. Brinda Bose's remarks in this context merit notice:

> As the post-colonial-postmodern writer Ghosh is one who sees history as that trajectory of events that causes dislocations, disjunctions, movements and migrations, eventually replacing solid markers with shadow lines, destabilizing our notions of the past in the reverberations of the present. (2003: 16)

The term diaspora refers to the movement of any population sharing common ethnic identity from their native lands to live and work in lands that are often remote from theirs. On the other hand, refugees are those who have been forced to leave their country because of war or social or political or religious reasons. However, while refugees may or may not ultimately settle in a new geographic location permanently, the diaspora does.

The Glass Palace delineates the remarkable lives of a few individuals who are the victims of the vagaries of history. Their lives are interwoven with the catastrophic public events. Besides power politics, the Indian diasporic experience in Southeast Asia is the focal point and Ghosh records its historical implications and meaning with great depth in the novel. The key characters, both historical and fictional, are shown to be passing through the experience with Ghosh's focus on the predicament of the individuals in the momentous historical circumstance. The question of loyalty to one's 'true' identity presents itself to one character after another in the book. Within the framework of the novel, the cultural share is brought into sharp focus by Ghosh. Rajkumar and Dolly, who come from different ethnic backgrounds, are brought together by their conjugal relationship. Consequently, their offspring, Dinu and Neel confront identity conflicts as they are refused to be accepted by the Burman natives. Dinu, from the second generation, wishes to marry Alison of American origin. When she dies in the enemy attack, he chooses to stay back in Burma, and ends up marrying the Burmese girl Maa Thin Aye. King Thebaw's daughters facing banishment to India along with their parents marry Indians. Ironically, their marrying commoners offends the sense of propriety of the British government, which does not appreciate the mixing of races from high and low breeds.

In the fullness of time, the feeling of belonging to nowhere makes Rajkumar lament, '... My father was from Chittagong and he ended up in the Araka; I ended up in Rangoon; you went from Mandalay to Ratnagiri and now you're here too .... There are people who have the luck to end their lives where they began them ...' (Ghosh 2004: 310). Rajkumar echoes the feelings of the unfortunate lot in this world where migration is the order of the day. Both Rajkumar and Dolly are victims of migration, having to migrate thrice in their lives driven by historical forces, as much by their personal decisions.

Ghosh also reveals the flip side of migration with his depicting the sentiment for the 'motherland' put across by the second generation of diaspora whose parents had migrated as indentured labour. Ironically, they had never seen the country called India. While in Malaya, Arjun and Hardy find Indian migrants working as plantation labourers living in grinding poverty in spite of Malaya's prosperous towns. Strangely, the plantation workers in Malaysia, most of them Tamils, join the Indian National Army when the war came to the doors of their territory. Rajan, one of them, tells Arjun that he was born and brought up in Malaya and as such his knowledge of India came solely from stories told by his parents. The same was true of all plantation recruits. 'They were fighting for a country they had never seen; a country that had extruded their parents and cut them off. This made their fervour all the more remarkable' (Ghosh 2004: 522). For them 'India was the shining mountain beyond the horizon, a sacrament of redemption—a metaphor freedom ...' (Ghosh 2004: 522). Arjun wonders whether these recruits had any idea about the poverty in India, the hunger their parents and grandparents had left behind, the caste discrimination, etc. Thus, he shows how these immigrants live in 'imaginary homelands'.

Ghosh claimed that the writing of the *The Glass Palace* has completely transformed him as a person and as a novelist ... changed his understanding of history (Qtd in Kadam 2006: 20). Ghosh's consecration of his vocation as a novelist and a deep commitment to his preferred thematic concerns is made known when he, controversially though, refuses his novel to be nominated for the Commonwealth Writers' Prize. The reason he put forth for such denial was that, 'the issue of how the past is to be remembered lies at the heart of *The Glass Palace* and I feel that I would be betraying the spirit of my book if I were to allow it to be incorporated within that particular memorialisation of Empire that passes under the rubric of the 'Commonwealth'' (Qtd in Hawley 2005: 114). The statement is significant in that the term postcolonialism refers to writings and cultures that were once colonized by the European powers. Postcolonial theory is an attempt to uncover the colonial ideologies implicit in literary texts. At the same time its major task is to deconstruct nationalism. The term postcolonialism has come to replace the terms Commonwealth Literatures or Third World Literatures. This theory, having originated in the mid-twentieth century, is now known as postcolonial studies. All the same, Ghosh concern is with the individuals and families devastated by the forces of history, their heroic struggles for survival and sometimes their helpless submission. He does not believe that one fantasy can replace another as postcolonialists perceive.

Like a typical open-ended novel, Ghosh ends the novel on an optimistic note. Dinu, Rajkumar's elder son, as though in an act of redemption for what his father does to the Burmans, participates in the enduring freedom struggle in Burma to free the country from the clutches of the oppressive rule and Jaya, his niece from the third generation, supports his cause. The struggle is on and unfortunately for countries like Burma, the end of the colonial rule is not the end of exploitation. But there is always hope in people to further the cause of these states, and it is an ongoing process for freedom in its true sense for which history stands a witness, suggests Ghosh. It reminds us of the words of Allan

Nevins who perceives history not as merely a narrative of the past but as, 'a bridge connecting the past with the present and pointing the road to the future' (Qtd in Jayapalan 2008: 3).

Works Cited

Bose, Brinda (ed.). *Amitav Ghosh: Critical Perspectives.* Delhi: Pencraft International, 2003. Print.

Ghosh, Amitav. *In An Antique Land.* New York: Vintage, 1994. Print.

——. *The Glass Palace.* New York: Harper Collins, 2004. Print.

Hawley, John C. *Amitav Ghosh: An Introduction.* New Delhi: Foundation Books, 2005. Print.

Hutcheon, Linda. *A Poetics of Postmodernism.* New York: Routledge, 1988. Print.

Jayapalan, N. *Historiography.* New Delhi: Atlantic, 2008. Print.

Kadam, Mansing G. 'Amitav Ghosh's *The Glass Palace*: A Post-colonial Novel.' *Indian Writings in English.* Eds Bimal Mishra and Sanjay Kumar. New Delhi: Atlantic, 2006. Print.

'Postmodernism.' Answers.com <http://www.answers.com/topic/postmodernism> Web.

Rao, B.V. *Concise Book of World History.* New Delhi: Sterling, 1991. Print.

Ravi, P.S. *Modern Indian Fiction: History, Politics and Individual in the Novels of Salman Rushdie, Amitav Ghosh and Upamanyu Chatterjee.* New Delhi: Prestige Books, 2003. Print.

Tinker, Hugh. 'A Forgotten Long March: The Indian Exodus from Burma, 1942.' *Journal of Southeast Asian Studies* 6.1 (March 1975), 1–15. Print.

18

Re-viewing Colonial Agenda in Amitav Ghosh's *The Sea of Poppies*

S. LATHA AND K.V. RAMANA

Literary texts are increasingly read as constructs of specific historical conditions and circumstances. New Historicism views history as a narrative construction involving a relationship of past and present concerns. It involves Gadamer's hermeneutic understanding of the past as constructed in relation to a present which is also a development out of that past, Hyden White's view of history as narrative construction or 'stories', and Bakhtin's articulation of all human utterances (including literary texts) as social acts which are multi-accentual and available for divergent uses (Rice and Waugh 1989: 253). The new historicist focuses on the multiple contradictory material practices which embed each historical event or expressive act as contexts of production and reception. White says, '... historiography aspires to the condition of science by presenting a third-person narrative which appears to be the reflection of events as they are inherently structured by the process of history. Historiography gathers its authority by seeming to dispense with authorial voice, by simulating scientific discourse which appears to reflect the way the world simply is' (Rice and Waugh 1989: 255). He observes that 'real' events, however, never tell their own stories and that history is always a process of making the real into an object of desire through manipulations of voice and temporality.

After the empire, a need was felt, as part of decolonization process, to cancel the colonial stereotypes. The writers searched for evidence in the rich and varied pre-colonial existence. The urge to rewrite the past grew, as it offered a base—ideological and narrational—on which the writers attempted to 'see' the past-present sequential in a new order, from a perspective each has to invent for him/herself. *The Sea of Poppies* by Amitav Ghosh is a retelling of the modern present through the eyes of the past. Ghosh emphasizes the enormous importance of history by situating every work in a distinct time and place, dealing with issues confronted by a man in India, situated in the global context. He believes history as central to the art of fiction and interprets history both at a personal and social level. 'Where and when' of a text and 'its connectivity to the world around' becomes very important in his case.

The Sea of Poppies is a book that begins in the nineteenth century, and records history over a period of time. The backdrop reminds one of the forgotten history. Narrativity having to do with 'real' events signals objectivity and seriousness. The discourse brings forth the memories of South Asia as a great nautical region and the shipping that suffered terribly since independence. India flourished through the ages with its thriving coastal trade, and travel was possible all the way on water—which now remains as a mere tourist luxury. Delhi, which has become the pivot of the country in a way, killed the coastal shipping. Ghosh feels sorry for the Indians and their loss. In an interview with the *Star Weekend Magazine*, he says:

> ... because of colonisation we have to, say, Royal Albert Museum or the British Museum to know about ourselves. Our history is, in a way, lost, forgotten .... I think the history of the last 200 years has been defaced largely, because of it we have to reclaim a lot of it from the colonial archive. (web.)

Ghosh's first novel of his planned trilogy, *The Sea of Poppies,* is set in North India and the Bay of Bengal in 1838 on the eve of the British attack on the Chinese ports popularly known as the First Opium War—the most important historical event of the nineteenth century. China's vicious nineteenth century Opium Wars act as a backdrop for the entire setting. The Opium Wars and the free trade strengthened the claws of the British. The novel reflects the enormity of the damage caused by the European trade market with its thrust for wealth on the Indian economy. The novel explores the exposure of Indian people to the capitalist demands, mediated through the accumulative logic of British. It encompasses the great economic themes of the nineteenth century like the cultivation of opium as a cash crop in Bengal and Bihar for the Chinese market, transportation of Indians to work on sugarcane plantations for the British in islands like Mauritius, Fiji and Caribbean islands. The lives of ordinary men and women framed against the grand narratives of history give scope to re-present the past.

The origin of capitalism runs parallel to the colonial history, as Indians were still trying to emerge out of the anxieties of feudalism during that period. Capitalism and opium trade developed roots quickly in the Indian soil. The European appetite for money paralysed the Indian minds. For the British, India could be the only place for opium cultivation with its cheap labour. The British dreaded to think that there would be an end to the flow of opium into China. As they understood, they could sell only opium to China in return for importing tea and silk. They felt that 'to end the trade would be ruinous ... for all of India.' Thus, opium became an unavoidable compulsion in the lives of all strata of people.

The estate of Raskhali during the reign of Raja Neel Rattan Halder, the Zamindar, truly reflects the Indian feudal system and the orthodoxy of the times. Lost in luxury the elder Zamindar's entire concentration was on getting money and enjoying life. He regarded with aristocratic contempt the determination of the White mercantile community, and its private accounting of profit and opportunity. Opium was the monopoly of the British in eastern India and their partnership with the local Zamindars encouraged a number of friends, relatives and creditors of the latter to beg for a share in the investment. Unmanageable inflow of money attracted dependents in large numbers. The old Raja knew nothing about Mr Burnham except that he was a ship owner and played a pivotal role in the trade. Each year 'he got back a much larger sum' referred to as his tribute from the 'Faghfoor of Maha-Chin,' the Emperor of Great China. All that mattered was money-making and profit. 'Little did they know of the perils of the consignment trade and how the risks were borne by those who provided the capital' (Ghosh 2008: 85).

Being dutiful by nature, Raja Neel Rattan, his son, stayed away from the financial dealings. After his father's death, the weight and vacuum in the system disgusted him. The year 1837 is significant since it marked the decline in the value of American bills of exchange. Raja Neel Rattan is startled to note that his debts to Burnham Brothers far exceeded the value of the entire 'Zamindari'. But very late in life he realizes that the very system he was upholding pushed him into the harsh realities of life. Their status-conscious orientation and feudal lifestyle led to their downfall.

Ghosh's re-presentation of the history is intricately interlaced with geographical locations and dialects, economies and politics of the times. Against this backdrop, a multidimensional picture of nineteenth century Indian life emerges, filled with the lifestyle of different classes of people with all their emotions, sentiments, habits including food, medicines, luxuries, marriage practices, funeral rites, male-female relationships, trade, cultivation, etc. Such a representation of history reveals the significance of poppy cultivation, its production, distribution and the resultant alienation. The 'profit-motive' drives the mass cultivation of poppy in the place of staple food like wheat.

Poppy was an item produced not to be consumed but to be sold. It slowly induced a colonial consciousness, transforming the farmer into a worker and subsequently into a slave. Distribution helped not the natives but the colonial rulers to perpetuate the rule of the market. Ultimately, poppy led to the natives' alienation and escape from life. 'Drug abuse' left deep anguish in the lives of masses and the nation at large. Ghosh presents this history through the lives and emotions of his characters. The protagonist of the novel stands as an example. Poppies were a luxury in Deeti's days of childhood. No one thought of producing 'the wet, treacly chandu opium' that was made and packaged in the English factory, to be sent across the sea in the boats. The hard toil needed to grow the crop was not encouraging. They felt that it was a horrid exercise for the sane. But this reality of their lives changed when the English forced them into a 'world of no stability.'

> But what sane person would want to multiply these labours when there were better, more useful crops to grow, like wheat, dal, vegetables? But those toothsome winter crops were steadily shrinking in acreage: now the factory's appetite for opium seemed never to be sated. Come the cold weather, the

> English sahibs would allow little else to be planted; their agents would go from home to home, forcing cash advances on the farmers, making them sign asami contracts. It was impossible to say no to them: if you refused they would leave their silver hidden in your home, or throw it through a window ... and, at the end of it, your earnings would come to no more than three-and-a-half sicca rupees, just to pay off your advance. (29)

Deeti, an illiterate, innocent village woman finds it difficult to grasp the swift changes that engulf the villagers' lives. Their alienation becomes unavoidable with the destruction of relationships and the strands of livelihood that had shaped their lives. The idea of not cultivating what one needs was beyond her comprehension. Initially, she could not understand how 'money is no longer treated as money.' But later she understands that money has become capital to earn more money. The same concept of using money to earn more money is outside the experience of the feudal lords like Raja Neel Rattan because:

> As a family, their experience lay in the managing of Kings and Courts ... and the property they disdained to handle themselves, preferring to entrust it to a legion of agents, gomustas and poor elatives ... with new properties there came a great number of dependents ... the Raja would not suffer them to be rented. (Ghosh 85–86)

The horrid place and the entire process of extraction of opium at Ghaziapur factory terrifies Deeti's village eyes. As she rushes in terror through the factory in search of her dying husband, she slowly understands the potency of opium and what the English were doing. She realizes the importance of the trade and its secret strength. For a moment she feels liberated.

> The factory in Ghazipur was so diligently patrolled by the sahibs and their sepoys—for if a little bit of this gum could give her such power over the life, the character, the very soul of this elderly woman, then with more of it at her disposal, why should she not be able to seize kingdoms and control multitudes? (Ghosh 38)

Meanwhile, Raja Neel's arrest comes as a thunderbolt. He understands that his sinking has already started and the inconceivable sure to happen. As he is put in prison he feels that he would be acquitted but bemoans that his family's reputation would never be what it was. When all his people come to see him, he only wishes to turn back to see and 'make sure that his wife, Malati was not among the women: even in the confusion of that moment, it was a great relief to know that she had not stepped out of the zenana—he was spared at least, the humiliation of having the veil of her seclusion torn away' (173).

In places like India and Indonesia, Europeans ruled indirectly through their domination of the local aristocracy. Ideologies of moral, cultural and racial supremacy backed its various ventures. Neel's mode of addressing the sergeant in English makes him furious. It was considered an act of intolerable insolence on the part of an Indian convict and a defilement of the English language. Similarly, Zachary could not permit Paulette, a White woman to travel on board.

For he feels that *Ibis* will be sailing with all lascars which implies that the only European will be its 'officer'. The behaviour of the Captain on the ship reflects the way the English ruled indirectly. As he dictates the 'Laws of the sea' he conveys a menacing colonial note in a veiled fashion:

> There is no better keeper of the law than submission and obedience. In that respect this ship is no different from your own homes and villages. While you are on it, you must obey Subedar Bhyro Singh as you would your own zamindars, and as he obeys me. (Ghosh 404)

Nineteenth century era was enveloped by the empire. European nation-states became powerful as their organizational efficiency led to territorial expansion and symbolic investment in the colonies on a massive scale. The business of colonization gambled and experimented not only with funds but also lives. The destruction of Raja Neel Rattan, who lost his Zamindari estate, power and status or an illiterate village woman like Deeti whose ambition was to cultivate grains are very much a part of history. The pervasive historicity is the impressive feature of the book. It reflects not only the political history but also an understanding of culture, religion, diversity, trade and much more.

Works Cited

Ghosh, Amitav. *The Sea of Poppies*. New Delhi: Penguin Books, 2008. Print.

Rice, Philip and Patricia Waugh. (eds). *Modern Literary Theory*. New York: OUP, 1989. Print.

Star Weekend Magazine <www.thedailystar.net.> Web.

19

The Personal and the Historical in Dina Mehta's Resistance Narrative, *And Some Take A Lover*

K. DAMODAR RAO

The focus on the underprivileged sections in the pre and post-Independence Indian literatures has been a significant phenomenon. Prem Chand, Tagore, Mulk Raj Anand, Ismat Chugtai, Mahasweta Devi have offered sympathetic portrayals of dalits, tribals, the rural poor, and other suppressed sections of the society in their fiction. Since Independence the new voices and standpoints not only demanded attention but also became assertive making the concept of nationhood fragmented into several versions. In the last quarter of the twentieth century, different minorities, ethnic and religious sub-cultures posed a challenge to the concept of national identity. Constructing nationhood becomes a difficult exercise because 'many new voices, perceptions and locations begin to contest a mono-ethnic, monolithic concept of elitist, upper class, patriarchal hegemony' (Gupta 2000: 10). Parsee, Muslim and women writers and many submerged voices have asked for greater acceptance intervening in the consolidation of a simple dominant state ideology. The increasing space that these forces created for themselves within the existing power structure, in the process, questioned the validity of political meta-narratives and the assertion of Third World Fiction as national allegories. The present paper examines how Dina Mehta's *And Some Take A Lover* deals with some of the important issues such as nationhood and individual identity (male/female), concepts that have been much contested, rejected and reconstructed in the field of literature.

History forms the backdrop of many new Indian English novels. A closer look at what has happened, a re-casting of received notions and values has been part of the novelists' agenda in recent times. In his perceptive analysis of the postcolonial situation, Santosh Gupta observes: 'A stronger resistance to ideas received from west, or others, gives rise to the new forms of relationships between tradition and modernity, the self and other, the native, national and outsider, immigrant, exile and diasporic, located within or outside the national borders' (2000: 10). Dina Mehta's novel belongs to this category of resistance writing as it examines 'the new forms of relationships between tradition and modernity,' the native and the outsider, the Self and the Other. Set in colonial India, the novel examines the equation between the colonizer and the colonized, in the backdrop of nationalist movement, Gandhi's sway over the lives of people, and other historical events. The novel also offers vignettes of Parsi sensibility as it focuses on the Parsi way of life, their attitudes, their affinities with the English culture, and their ambivalent role in the freedom movement. These historical and sub-cultural aspects are revealed through the consciousness of a woman-protagonist foregrounding feminine sensibility. Thus, the novel attempts to offer a colonized perspective in terms of political situation, a minority standpoint in the cultural realm, and a woman's point of view in gender relations. As Nilufer Bharucha remarks, 'there is triple marginalization at work here—that of the colonized, women and a minority community' and the novel becomes a good example of the subaltern discourse aimed at the 'empowerment of the decolonized' (Bharucha 137).

The Parsis numbering about 80,000 form 0.015 per cent of the total population of India. They are a close-knit community and are largely concentrated in the metropolis of Bombay. Of all the communities in India they are the most westernized. In fact, even by the end of the nineteenth century they had become urbanised and industrialized. Commenting on the major influences that shaped the destiny of this miniscule community, Piloo Nanavutty says:

> The development of science and technology, which followed in the wake of the Industrial Revolution, also made a strong impact upon the Parsis. They seized every opportunity to study scientific techniques in all walks of life—medicine, engineering, architecture, sociology, and the pure and applied sciences. As this knowledge came from the West, particularly from the paramount power ruling the country at the time, namely, England, it was inevitable that the Parsis became Anglicized in the extreme. Not only was every effort made to master the English language, but English manners and customs were adopted into Parsi family life. (1976: 171)

During the Indian struggle for Independence, the majority of Parsis, with a few exceptions, kept aloof from the political scene. Although they have this weakness for western values and customs, the Parsis' contribution towards making a modern India cannot be set aside. The Parsi novelists attempted to capture the ethos of the community, their problems and preferences, in their novels. While projecting a community that 'takes pride in living together, sharing collective memories and perpetuating the value of its heritage,' the novelists have been objective in depicting the Parsis' 'unquestioning acceptance of the western way of life, their attitude towards the Indian Freedom Struggle and the Partition, the confusion faced by them resulting into alienation and even cultural amnesia in some cases, their multiplex of loyalties and social and cultural distancing and so on ...' (Pathak 1999: 211).

Most Parsis in Dina Mehta's novel try to imbibe western values and have a close connection with the English. They do not hesitate to deride their fellow countrymen, their struggle for freedom, and their leaders. Roshini, the main character in the novel, for instance, is convent-educated and western-minded until she falls in love with Sudhir, an obstinate Gandhian: 'She spoke English better than her adopted mother-tongue, Gujarati. She even thought in English ... . She read no Gujarati books or papers. She did not know Persian, the language of her ancestors' (188). Roshni recalls how her aunt, Piroja, had otherwise been a liberal but when it came to the native-colonizer equation she always sided with the latter—'In Pirojbai's home M.K. had been the arch-traitor, the unmentionable, except with abuse, but a large portrait of George VI had adorned the wall over her bed and she felt a burning sense of loyalty towards her king' (38). She considers Gandhi's followers 'wicked' and the title 'Mahatma,' a 'misnomer' (38). Roshni's mother, Shirinbai, was also westernized like the elders of other Parsi families and she does not approve of Roshni's involvement in the nationalist movement and, subsequently, her association with Sudhir. She scorns at Roshni and her newly acquired habit of wearing *khadi*: 'Don't I know you and your new-fangled notions? .... You didn't even hesitate to dress in those hideous *khadi* sarees'—(39). Roshni is equally firm in her views and retorts: 'Why not? *Khadi* is rough and coarse, but not vulgar, ... It's more decent to wear homespun than to deck yourself in cheap, foreign, mass-produced georgettes and silks' (39). Dina Mehta's fictional account clearly points out how the westernized communities, aristocratic and privileged sections of the society connived with the colonial enterprise much against the aspirations of their fellow countrymen and worked against the nationalist interests.

Dina Mehta's achievement lies in the fact that she projects the issues of individual identity and feminine sensibility within the framework of larger socio-political and cultural concerns: 'The novel is primarily presented as a love story but a love story whose dimensions touch and are touched by the turmoil that was going on in the country in the years immediately preceding the Independence' (Pandey 1997: 91). Roshni's love for Sudhir, the focal point of the novel, brings in diverse responses and viewpoints. When her love remains unreciprocated, her own worldview gets transformed. Sudhir is not only a Hindu but also 'Gandhi's henchman' (38) and, therefore, remains doubly unacceptable to her family. Roshni turns down the proposal to marry cousin Framroze, who according to her mother, has 'a brilliant future in law' (37) and who believes in good thoughts, deeds, as enjoined by the scriptures. Roshni cannot imagine herself in the company of Framroze and she only knows there were too many cousin marriages in the community and what damage such marriages had wrought upon them: 'Had her mother stopped to consider what lack of crossbreeding had done to a small community like theirs, which allowed no proselytising and frowned on heterogeneous alliances? Jungo Batliwalla was one such example with his soft, clammy palms, over-fleshed pink lips and the pale pigment of inbreeding' (37).

Under the influence of Sudhir, Roshni becomes an ardent nationalist, takes to wearing *khadi* and subscribes to the nationalist journal, *Hind Namo* against the wishes of her family members. But her love for Sudhir does not run a smooth course right from the beginning. She is, in the first instance, not sure whether Sudhir loves her or she was merely indulging in a fantasy. Even when she thought of announcing to her family members her intention of marrying Sudhir she is caught in self-doubt: 'It was a fantasy she often indulged in, a pitiful game she played, for Sudhir was totally ignorant of her devotion to him, her tenderness and her hurt' (101). She remembers her first meeting with him in Elphinstone College, Bombay, how she had fallen in love with him although at that time he barely nodded to her in the class or when their paths crossed in the college corridors. At a party hosted by Sabrina, she could see that Sudhir and Lajwanti, who was also a Gandhian, indulge in animated conversation that centred around freedom struggle and the image of Gandhi. It also occurred to her that she was a kind of outsider there while Sudhir and Lajwanti presented a picture of soul-companions. She feels miserable when Sudhir and Lajwanti leave the party together after dinner. Earlier, she was a witness to the liaison between Sabrina and Captain Ronald. She feels that she was at the receiving end of an unfolding drama—both at the personal level and the world outside: 'A connection had been welded, as it were, between her domestic existence and the outer world of events; and her confusions were but a quintessential version of the chaos outside' (57).

A ray of hope flashes in Roshni's life, all too briefly, when Sudhir mentions that he could understand her feelings towards him and that he too was in love with her. When she pleads with him to be kind to her and marry her, he responds that he had bigger goals in life, other priorities that need all his attention and energies: 'I have to be single-minded, free for this work ... it's the endless striving with self for—clarity, for detachment and the balanced mind. I must be free, strong, tough, all these things that don't go with—with what I feel for you' (177). Even when Roshni says that she was prepared to go with him to share his responsibilities, not out of blind admiration for him but out of her own concern for the nation ('I don't want to lead a selfish life. I too want to give. I want to serve'—189), he brushes her views aside saying she was not cut out for all the hard work in villages that lies ahead of him: 'You will hate it! Not only the material arrangements of village life, but also the intellectual hemming-in. It is not for you, the neglect, the squalor, the austerity, the—the physical labour, the isolation .... It is not for you' (190). Nilufer Bharucha observes that for Sudhir, the ideal Indian woman was Lajwanti, and not Roshini because for the likes of him who were nurtured on Gandhian ideals, 'female passivity', 'non-threatening ideal woman' and 'womanliness of a mother, and not that of a wife' were acceptable and the nationalists deliberately projected mother-nation image and sought 'to control, domesticate and finally neutralize woman power' (1993–94: 139).

While Sudhir goes to Sevagram in search of his lofty pursuits, Roshni is left dejected. She even writes letters to him saying that she was emancipated and she was ready to join him in his work. But when she does not receive any response from him she feels betrayed. Later, she comes to know of his marriage with Gauribai Mahar, a Harijan girl, through a *Hind Namo* report. Earlier, Roshni was envious of the nationalists like Sudhir and Lajwanti for the ease and familiarity with which they spoke of Gandhi, but now she views the influence of Gandhi as a disturbing factor pillaging the identity and sensitivity of individuals. In the changed context, in the traumatic experience of separation and anxiety, she has no reverence left for Gandhi who has wrought havoc in her life: 'And what manner of man was this Gandhi, who could command such terrible obedience from his people? A despot, a tyrant more implacable than any feudal lord who ever reigned over his serfs. How else to explain Sudhir's action? His betrayal?' (200) Disillusioned, she lets herself be seduced by her friend Mithu's husband, Rustom. While Sudhir rejects her, Rustom treats her only as a sex-object. But for her, the liaison was 'an act of vengeance against the self, to break out of what she had once been; her revenge against the pure-minded virgin, a role Sudhir had thrust on her' (141).

Roshni, eventually, becomes indifferent to what was happening around her. The colonizer-colonized conflict was reaching its final stage and although it mattered little for Roshni that Independence was round the corner, it finds an echo in her personal life when she wriggles herself out of the victim position from the hands of Rustom. She rejects his proposal of marriage in order to free herself from male control ('Such a plain, wholesome decision' – 317) and forges an emotional bonding with her friend, Jer. It was much later that she comes to know of the death of Sudhir in a village in Bengal in his attempts to curb Hindu-Muslim divide. When Sudhir's journal is sent to her, she comes to know of the importance of social work that Sudhir was committed to; his participation in it was wholehearted and devoid of any selfish streak. His death was a testimony to his larger interests. Roshni wishes to lead her life anew, preparing herself for not having anything, 'not even hopes,' to make 'life holy by her actions, to learn how to love' (317).

And Some Take A Lover is not merely a fictional account of Roshni's coming to terms with herself, or of the protagonist achieving self-realization the hard way, but a narrative that invests history with new possibilities of meaning. As Rumina Sethi observes, 'In the last decade or so, historians especially those centred around subaltern studies, have attempted to demythologize the histories of the national movement and highlighted the role of the subalterns in terms of agency, which is diminished in the interests of a homogeneous nationalism' (Sethi 6). There are very few novels in Indian English that dealt with the theme of nationalism in the years preceding Independence and there are still fewer works, to quote Rumina Sethi, 'about the construction of cultural identities in periods of nation-building' (Sethi 6–7). Like Raja Rao's *Kanthapura,* it captures a crucial period in Indian history and presents how the general public, during the freedom movement were guided by the fire of idealism ignited by Gandhi. Sudhir Kumar argues that Kanthapura, the village, is far from being an idyllic (romanticized) one and asserts that what Raja Rao presents in his fictional account is not 'an essentialist approach,' but a nativist approach that is grounded in history. He describes the novel as 'a bold experimental step in 1938' and 'an empire writes back-variety of postcolonialism' (Kumar 1999: 372). Dina Mehta too in her novel deftly presents a nativist approach by portraying personal destinies as entwined with larger social interests and political concerns. And she does this from a minority, and suppressed section's point of view and, as such, the novel remains an important text in subaltern discourse and postcolonial writing.

Works Cited

Bharucha, Nilufer. 'Subaltern Discourse: Strategies of Feminist and Postcolonial Resistance in Dina Mehta's *And Some Take a Lover.*' *The Commonwealth Review* 3.1 (1993–94). Print.

Gupta, Santosh. Introduction. *Contemporary Indian Literature: Positions and Expositions.* Jaipur: Rawat Publications, 2000. Print.

Kumar, Sudhir. 'Is India a Nation? Nation-in-Katha in Raja Rao's *Kanthapura.*' *New Quest* 138 (November–December 1999). 365–73. Print.

Mehta, Dina. *And Some Take a Lover.* New Delhi: Rupa & Co., 1992. Print. All page references indicated in parentheses are to this edition.

Nanavutty, Piloo. *The Parsis.* New Delhi: National Book Trust, 1976. Print.

Pandey, K.M. 'Dina Mehta's *And Some Take a Lover:* A Polyphonic Patterning of Love, Religion and Politics.' Ed. R.S. Pathak. *Indian Fiction of the Nineties.* New Delhi: Creative Books, 1997. 91–99. Print.

Pathak, R.S. *Modern Indian Novel in English.* New Delhi: Creative Books, 1999. Print.

Sethi, Rumina. *Myths of the Nation: National Identity and Literary Representation.* Oxford: Clarendon Press, 1999. Print.

20

From *Purdah* to Politics: A Note on Gita Mehta's *Raj*

J. YELLAIAH AND K.V. RAMANA CHARY

Gita Mehta has been acclaimed as an international cross-cultural critic. Her writing distinguishes itself by freshness as much as by a cosmopolitan outlook. Mehta is not wedded to any 'isms', and that sets her apart from the contemporary women writers of India. To encounter her writing is virtually to make a fresh discovery of India. The present paper makes an attempt to show how Gita Mehta sketches characters by interweaving history and fiction. Gita Mehta's *Raj* is a historiography and it records the Freedom Struggle of India. It is a tale of an individual, Jaya Singh, a born princess in the Royal House of Balmer. Jaya is married to the Sirpur prince and becomes Regent Maharani of Sirpur. Later, she rises to be Maharani and finally enrolls herself as an independent candidate to contest the elections. Thus, Jaya emerges a resolute, politically mature, well-balanced, potential forum for discussion on both cultural and traditional theories. Commenting on the novel, Usha Bande writes:

> It is intricately interwoven with the political events but it has all the tears and romance of a woman's existence in India which saves the work from being a mere record all-too-well-known history of our freedom, or a racy account of the grandeur and frivolity of the exorbitant life-style of the princes. (1991: 239)

Maharaja Jai Singh is a rationalist. He prefers people to power and promotes innovative ideas. He does not hesitate to cross the barriers laid by ancestors. He proves his modernity by asking Maharani to break *purdah* for the sake of the people during the famine that affected the Balmer state. The Maharani acts accordingly and steps out of the Zenana walls and destroys a thousand years of tradition. Though the Maharaja Jai Singh is a modernist, he is loyal to tradition. Inside the fort, the Maharaja appears before the audience in the great Durbar Hall, accepting gifts from the nobles who represent the kings of India. Every day he takes his place on the *gaddi*, the wide cushion covered in crimson brocade that is the traditional throne of Rajput rulers. Behind him stands the *chattri*-bearer holding the royal canopy over his sovereign's head, as in times of war he will hold his sovereign's standard. The Maharaja's head is covered with the red turban of festivity tied with a simplicity that lends dignity but no decoration to the narrow face with the severe eyes. Before him the nobles sit in rows down the expanse of the Durbar Hall, their ceremonial swords laid across their knees, the jewelled hilts tied with gold gauze signifying peace. Relays of dancing girls separate the Maharaja from his guests with their billowing skirts as certain nobles edge closer to the *gaddi* for a private word.

Unlike her father's rationalistic manner, Jaya's mother likes to get her trained in the art of personal decoration, the *solashringar*, the sixteen arts of being a woman. As Jaya is tradition-bound, her mother fears that an educated girl will be an insult to her in-laws. At her mother's behest, Jaya is forced to imbibe not only traditional virtues but also moral values. Consequently, Jaya tosses between tradition and modernity all through her life as Naresh K. Jain observes: 'Jaya's education which is comprehensive is at once traditional and modern' (1998: 209).

Tikka, Jaya's brother, does not like the outdated principles of his father and wants to be educated in England under the guidance of Captain Osborne and his heroic tales. However, he shows his valour and patriotism fighting for the Empress of his country when the British Empire is at war. By March 1915, India raised the army of a million men to defend the British empire, and in the house of Lords, Lord Curzon acknowledged Britain's debt of honour to her proudest colony. When Jaya fears as Tikka is leaving for war to France, he tells her that nothing will happen to him and he can defeat the enemy. But very soon, the Balmer Lancers advance towards Jai Singh; in front of them trot Tikka's riderless horse, a piece of homespun cotton covering its black muscles. At the rear of the procession, Major Vir Singh carries the urn containing Tikka's ashes.

Overcoming grief, the Maharaja slowly gains normalcy. He sends Jaya to Sirpur. In Sirpur, Jaya waits in her wedding finery to greet her husband. Carriage lamps lit the gateways of the City Palace. The Prime Minister tells that Prince Pratap along with some guests is arriving. As it is a custom, the maidservants redden her palms and feet before throwing the veil over her head. As usual with the princes, Prince Pratap too maintains concubines and tells Jaya that theirs is a marriage of convenience. He tells her that he is permitted to travel abroad if he is accompanied by a wife. However, she becomes mother and feels proud of giving an heir to the great throne of Sirpur, but her joy does not stay long as Pratap denies her right as a mother and prevents her from feeding the baby. Commenting on Jaya's desolate condition, Naresh K. Jain opines:

> When she becomes a mother she is forbidden to breastfeed her child, thus depriving her of the 'rights of maternity' just as he had robbed her of the dignity of being a wife. (1998: 210)

In Sirpur, mythology draws its imprint on history. During the Diwali celebrations, the priests hold daily readings from the *Mahabharata* at the

Kamini Temple, and the names of the Sirpur kings are recited to the satisfaction of every citizen present. In January, James Osborne presents his credentials as Ambassador and Plenipotentiary of the British Empire to the Maharaja of Sirpur. Although the ceremony is conducted with every appearance of a diplomatic exchange, Jaya notices with alarm that the Residency officials standing stiffly in their morning coats against the painted frescoes of the Durbar Hall are as numerous as the members of the Sirpur cabinet in their brocade tunics and turbans, facing them across the expanse of carpet over which James Osborne is walking towards the ruler.

All over the country times are hard for the rulers. As the freedom struggle gains momentum, each hour turns the position of the princes precarious. On the other hand, Gandhi has already walked more than two hundred miles away from his ashram towards the seacoast at Dandi where he planned to break the British Empire's laws. Gandhiji enters Sirpur and addresses the people: 'Brothers and sisters, in the name of God I greet you. The high nervous voice immediately silenced the noise around him. We fear the British has no intention of granting us self-government when even the salt a peasant needs for strength to till his fields under the burning sun is taxed and any Indian who dares make his own salt is called a criminal by the Empire' (Mehta 1993: 371). He tells them that a satyagrahi must learn to suffer, to die if need be, to prove the righteousness of his cause.

It is remarkable that Pratap's attitude makes Jaya realize her potentiality. Even though she initially tries to change herself for the sake of her husband, she later pushes herself forward from the Zenana to the people as a ruler. As the nationalist movement is gaining force in British India, she leans for timely advice upon her childhood friend James Osborne who is now the Political Officer to Sirpur and Arun Roy, a nationalist leader and Sir Akbar, the Prime Minister of Sirpur. Dramatically, Jaya needs Arun Roy's help to manage the tribals whom she has nurtured. While travelling through the jungle, Jaya falls a prey to passion with Arun Roy. In this act, she appears to compromise with her values not for individual pleasure but for the protection of her kingdom from the nationalists. Changes in Sirpur strengthen Jaya Devi to reign her kingdom and look after her son Arjun till he becomes a major, but her mother's death deepens Jaya's gloom because she feels that her son's last links to a courageous past have been shattered forever.

Jaya gradually gains responsibility as a leader from her widowhood and invites Arun Roy to Sirpur when the political situation in Sirpur is more critical. But the cunning Arun Roy, even after spending three full nights with her, cheats her arousing nationalistic zeal in the masses. When she understands his betrayal of her trust, Jaya slaps on his smiling face with all the frustration that fumed inside her. She not only suffers the humiliation at the hands of Arun Roy but also the British Raj which gives an ultimatum to remove her from the Regency.

James Osborne helps Jaya with timely news of war and nationalists' progress. Jaya feels the Englishman's presence brings an alien energy in her. After a successful surgery to his broken leg, Arjun returns to Sirpur accompanied by the Prime Minister, Sir Akbar. On the way, a Hindu mob gathers around the car demanding to know why a Hindu king is travelling with a Muslim. Arjun shouts at the mob unaware of the fact that the Hindu Muslim riots were taking place in Sirpur over the Partition, and becomes a victim to the violence of the mob:

> ... Arjun shouted that Sir Akbar was the Prime Minister of Sirpur, but they dragged the old man out of the car and ripped off his clothes to see if he was circumcised. The mob rocked the car to prevent Arjun from getting out. He still managed to open the door. \But it was too late. They had already cut off Sir Akbar's manhood'. (Mehta 446)

Jaya gradually overcomes her grief and gains responsibility with the help of James Osborne. Meantime, the flow of the events is in favour of the nationalists demanding to merge her kingdom in India. Guided by the Raj Guru, Jaya feels she is bound to her people and immerses herself in the motivating lecture of the Guru who reminds her that the first lesson of *Rajniti* is protecting the people. On her return to Sirpur, Jaya holds a meeting in the painted Durbar Hall for the citizens who have travelled from all over the kingdom to inquire about the merger. Traders and Sirpur noble families sit in rows under the chandeliers arguing about the decision. When the tribal chiefs are indifferent, Jaya explains: 'The last Viceroy, Lord Mountbatten, said Sirpur could make its own terms with the new nations of Pakistan and India. He betrayed us. The Indian leaders said we could remain free if we agreed to common policies. They betrayed us. If I had not signed the instrument of Accession, there would have been more bloodshed' (458).

Gaining new strength, Jaya contests the forthcoming elections as an independent candidate. As she writes her name 'Jaya Devi', a sudden smile illuminates the officer's face and he wishes her good luck because the name means victory. Jaya understands how deep was the divergence between the values offered by the social conventions and the real needs of the society. Aruna Devi observes:

> She now understands modifications in the existing social order can cater to such needful demands. It is not only the ruler but also the people themselves who have awakened to the situation. (2005: 120)

Coming out from *purdah*, Jaya, a timid female child, grows to the status of a ruler. She comes out from her shackles of physical repression and brings out a change in the social order. And above it, she becomes a true *Sati-Mata* and learns to endure. She responds to not only her personal crisis but also the crisis of people. Her royal blood always longs to serve the people, each time recalling her teacher, Raj Guru's words that her *dharma* is protection of her people. Jaya feels happy as she does her duty towards her people and country. The novel ends with a note of beginning, the beginning of a new and united India.

Thus, Gita Mehta's *Raj* offers fascinating and vivid insights into an Indian princess' life invariably linked to the history of India during the turbulent period from the end of the nineteenth century to the Independence in 1947. She finely intertwines history and fiction in the novel. It is also a record of the liberation of Indian women as these historical convulsions rocked the social structures of the society.

Works Cited

Bande, Usha. 'Raj: A Thematic Study.' *Indian Women Novelists: Set I.* Vol. 5. Ed. R.K. Dhawan. New Delhi: Prestige Books, 1991. 239–46. Print.

Devi, Aruna P. 'From Zenana to Pavilion: A Critical Analysis of Gita Mehta's Raj.' *Some Perspectives in Indian Writing in English.* Chennai: The Department of English, SDNBV College for Women, 2005. 113–20. Print.

Jain, Naresh K. 'From Purdah to Polo to Politics: A Study of Gita Mehta's *Raj.*' *Women in Indo-Anglian Fiction: Tradition and Modernity.* New Delhi: Manohar Publishers and Distributors, 1998. 208–13. Print.

Mehta, Gita. *Raj.* New Delhi: Penguin Books, 1993. Print.

21

Multiple Temporalities: The Aesthetics and Politics of Time in Arundhati Roy's *The God of Small Things*

JIBU MATHEW GEORGE

'I'd always heard your entire life flashes in front of your eyes the second before you die. First of all, that one second isn't a second at all. It stretches on forever, like an ocean of time,' says Lester Burnham (Kevin Spacey), posthumously, at the end of the 1999 film *American Beauty*. What is time? Is it a mental construct, or in Kantian terms, one of the *a priori* 'ideal' conditions that structure experience? Though time has a realist, objective aspect (according to Newtonian physics), it is also internally heterogeneous. Its true character in lived life has to do with how human beings perceive and represent time to each other and to themselves. As a result, humans wield a certain control over the phenomenon. Such a heterogenization of time is implied in many of our quotidian statements (e.g. time passes quickly), and is vital to historical analyses as well as to narratological studies. Concepts related to time, such as frequency, chronology, and interval have a narratological significance. They are even more significant to the study of historically based fictional narratives such as Arundhati Roy's Booker-Prize-winning novel *The God of Small Things* (1997).

The popular appeal and critical success of *The God of Small Things* is often attributed to factors such as the work fitting the postcolonial cultural codes of what Graham Huggan calls the 'cosmopolitan alterity industry' (2001: 12); its basing itself on pre-novelistic genres such as the fairytale, the popular romance, and the melodrama (Tickell 2007: 5–6); and the fatally enchanting thematic combination of forbidden sex and violent death. However, time and its intricate (re)configurations play an important role in the narrative aesthetics of the novel. The novel self-reflexively reveals its awareness of this temporal flexibility when Roy comments on how a Kathakali performer tells the Great Stories: 'He can fly you across whole worlds in minutes, he can stop for hours to examine a wilting leaf' (1997: 230). While the historical and political implications of its narrative temporality is our main concern, to overlook the aesthetics of the temporal phenomenon is to reduce Arundhati Roy's formally sophisticated narrative merely to a vulnerable object of the critical approaches (Marxist, Feminist, New Historicist, etc.) which Harold Bloom designates the School of Resentment.

Along with the other elements of the narrative, its premeditated temporal flexibility, a typical device of modernist fiction exemplified by writers such as James Joyce and Virginia Woolf, enables Roy to structure her work and achieve her stylistic, cognitive and emotional effects. Through apparently abrupt but carefully engineered transitions and free associations between different points of time, through ominous anticipation and silent recollection, Roy's non-linear, discontinuous narrative achieves an epic, large-canvas dimension, or what is usually called a 'broad historical sweep.' The same practice also lends it a tragic micro-historical intensity. The tragic dimension of the novel rests primarily on the feeling the narrative leaves on the reader that the remnants of the narrative are the hapless twin protagonists, Estha and Rahel, who bore the brunt of vindictive social forces and the catastrophic events unleashed by them. It also arises out of the haunting guilt of not seeing in the present of the novel the direct victims, Velutha and Ammu, a guilt which the narrative compels the society to bear through the reader. The narrative is ordered in such a way that it gives the reader a retrospective trauma born out of the feeling that 'these are the people who went through all this.' The novel ends in the middle of the narrative, in an ironically hopeful way pointing to a '*Naaley*' [Tomorrow] (340), a point of time which has already passed with unimaginable catastrophe. The temporal dimension also adds a tragic sense to the twins' process of growth and maturation (or lack of it), marked by nothing but neglect and deprivation. The temporal reconfigurations recreate the 'enduring resonance of the past in Estha and Rahel's adult lives.' As the protagonists do not grow up psychologically, the novel is often considered an 'anti-*Bildungsroman*' (Tickell 2007: 3). Their story is one of arrested development—inability to progress in time.

The impact of the temporal rearrangement of events is not confined to emotional effects. It is related to the fundamental process of making meaning. The novel is structured by a retrospective hermeneutic. As Émilienne Baneth-Nouailhetas points out in 'The Structures of Memory', *The God of Small Things* is a 'mnemonic narrative' where memory repeatedly traverses the same set of events for clarification (Quoted in Tickell 2007: 145). The relevance of this device lies in the function it serves in discovering what preceding events had meant. The retrospective discovery of meanings, individual and social, is significant in the novel because the child-protagonists through whom the story is told were, when the life-changing events happened, '[a] pair of actors trapped in a recondite play with no hint of plot or narrative' (Roy 1997: 191). For the twins, time is organized around a revealing constellation of life-changing events—the death of Velutha and Sophie Mol, Ammu's departure, and the Return of Estha to their father. As Julie Mullaney rightly notes, while '[t]he elements of the story set in 1969 are primarily narrated through the eyes of seven-year-old twins, Rahel and Estha, ... the tragic repercussions in the present are narrated through the adult Rahel' (2007). The retrospective meaning-making enables the author to explore what Mullaney calls 'the subterranean connections between individual, family and history, local, national, and world histories' (2007: 30).

One has to retain memory for the meaning of all things that have passed. For example, Rahel is able to recognize 'the sweetness' of a certain 'gesture' only in 'hindsight,' twenty-two years later—Velutha introducing the children to his surly hen and showing them his carpentry tools without 'decimat[ing]' the beliefs of the children's world in 'adult carelessness' (190). The whole narrative of *The God of Small Things* is grounded upon the recovery of such small events across time and its 'great events,' connecting and interpreting across conventional temporal boundaries.

Having dealt with the narratological significance of time in the novel, let us explore its politics, an issue which is particularly important in the case of an author who tends to be politically explicit. While traditional views of time consider it an inert phenomenon, a neutral matrix within which events unfold, I contend that representations of time in Roy's novel have ideological implications. My argument here is that *The God of Small Things* has a more complex sense of history and time than implied by the views of the novel as a typical postcolonial phenomenon, and that it may be analysed under alternative historico-temporal frames. The political narrative of the novel is founded upon the implicit tensions among various temporalities—a colonial historical time; a more-entrenched longer temporality which counteracts historical change; a subjective time, which also re-imagines the limits of what are rendered possible by dominant discourses ('what might have been'); and even a mythical time. The multiple historico-temporal frameworks provide a critical alibi for uncovering the larger politics of the novel associated with the unholy trinity of race, class and gender, to which one can legitimately add caste. Each of these temporalities has an internal order. They also interact and overlap. The different characters and groups in the novel wield power in proportion to the degree to which the corresponding temporalities are historically entrenched. In other words, the strength of hegemony depends upon the temporal order on which it is founded.

I base my analysis of Roy's novels on a couple of historico-temporal paradigms which came into vogue in the twentieth century. The catastrophic twentieth century witnessed the emergence of several new schools of historiography. One of the products of this revisionist historical consciousness is the Annales School in France. The attempt of the Annales School has been to reconstruct a history that operates beneath the visible surface of political events and movements. For Fernand Braudel (1902–85), one of the leading members of the School, history operates at various levels and is subject to various temporalities. He calls the first level of time the *longue durée* (longer duration). This is an imperceptibly slow-moving geographical-material time, in which man interacts with his environment for survival (*histoire structurale*). The second level of time comprises social and cultural history (*histoire conjoncturale*), with social groupings, empires, and civilizations. The third level of time is the history of personalities, politics, and exceptional events (*histoire événementielle*). Braudel's focus is on the *longue durée* that characterizes the deep-lying 'structures' of human life. This is the micro-historical temporal substratum that influences and contributes to the history of events but does not entirely yield to it. The longer historical temporality is marked by an 'inertia,' an experiential viscosity which makes it resistant to grand-historical change. This temporality of the everyday is not confined, as Braudel holds, to work routines and material resources, but also includes family constellations, kinship arrangements, peer relations, modes of social interaction, love-making, and reproduction. On account of its relative stability, Braudel grants them the status of structures.

My attempt is to link Braudel's long-temporality to the history of oppression, primarily related to caste and gender, which Roy's novel critiques. Roy herself suggests that one requires a larger temporal frame to understand and give meaning to the tragedies she narrates:

> In a purely practical sense it would probably be correct to say that it all began when Sophie Mol came to Ayemenem. Perhaps it's true that things can change in a day .... Still, to say that it all began when Sophie Mol came to Ayemenem is only one way of looking at it. Equally, it could be argued that it actually began thousands of years ago. Long before the Marxists came. Before the British took Malabar, before the Dutch Ascendency, before Vasco da Gama arrived, before the Zamorin's conquest of Calicut ... . It could be argued that it began long before Christianity arrived in a boat and seeped into Kerala like tea from a teabag.
>
> That it really began in the days when the Love Laws were made. The laws that lay down who should be loved, and how. And how much. (33)

The Love Laws are primarily the laws of caste, made in the mythological past, that govern social interactions, prohibit intermarriage and intermingling, and influence occupational choices, notions of love and desire, of family honour and purity. These laws condition the everyday life of Roy's protagonists the way Braudel's 'structures' do. These laws are the metonymic indicator of a deeply entrenched order of life, a longer historical temporality. It is this order of life, with its own norms, values and prohibitions that Roy refers to by the term History (with a capital 'H'), perhaps the most repeated word in the novel. This involves perpetuation of inherited models of womanhood, familial situations and inter-caste relations. It is this entrenched temporality that enables society to be complacent about the oppressions of caste and gender. This is a temporality which underlies and counteracts that of colonial historical epochs. Its inertia retains old structures in the face of wider social changes and political movements, represented in the novel by Christianity, colonization and communism.

As suggested earlier, another component of this long-temporality is the gendered organization of society, which predates colonial histories. It underlies the restricted lives of Roy's female characters—Mammachi, Baby Kochamma, Ammu, Rahel and the family cook, Kochu Maria, and even the wife of Comrade K.N.M. Pillai, Kalyani. Both Mammachi and Ammu suffer physical abuse at the hands of Pappachi, the imperial entomologist. Kathakali dancers go back home after their performances 'to beat their wives' (Roy 1997: 236). The old order of patriarchy, wherein Ammu has no *locus standi*, is the subtext of the property and inheritance laws which embolden brother Chacko to tell her: 'What is yours is mine, what's mine is also mine' (57). It is this underlying order which makes a mother like Mammachi provide a separate entrance to the house for the fulfillment of 'Men's [sexual] Needs' (295) while punishing Ammu and her twins for her sexual choices. It is an order marked by physical coercion, sexual regulation, disparity of moral norms and unequal distribution of resources.

By counterposing this order of life to the modern political and religious history of Kerala, Roy's political narrative implies that the old structures and systems were so entrenched that historical change, represented by Christianity, colonization, and communism, did not make any substantial difference to the former.[1] Under the British rule, the Anglican Churches converted lower castes, but did so without questioning the inherited order of social life. The new converts, like Vellya Paapen, were called Dalit Christians, and pejoratively, Rice-Christians. Upper-caste Syrian Christianity segregated these Dalit Christians by organizing them under separate churches. In the guise of historical reminiscence Mammachi nostalgically recapitulates the old state of affairs, when Paravans 'were expected to crawl backwards with a broom sweeping away their footprints so that Brahmins or Syrian Christians would not defile themselves by accidentally stepping into a Paravan's footprint' (74). Colonialism too incorporated the caste divides. It is pertinent that the Touchable policemen, originally instruments of the colonial order, spring into action to violently reestablish the older order. Quite appropriately, Roy calls them 'history's henchmen' (1997: 308).

As for the Syrian Christians themselves, they are, or so the legend goes, the descendants of the thirty-two Namboodiri families converted by Apostle St Thomas upon his arrival at Crangannore on the Malabar Coast in AD 52. They represented a native aristocracy that predated colonial rule, and were among the products and beneficiaries of the older social order. This empowered them to utilize the opportunities that colonialism afforded. The rise of this native aristocracy to preeminence during the Raj was made possible by the allocation of power and resources under the pre-colonial order. For example, while colonization, and upper-caste status enabled Syrian Christian women to be better educated, their lower-caste counterparts continued to languish under the same order. This helps us appreciate how colonialism itself has a differential impact on different subaltern groups.

The older order absorbs new traditions. The impact of modern ideologies like communism is, to use Braudel's own metaphor, foam on the surface of water, so much so that Arundhati Roy calls them Kerala's 'flirtations'. Roy is explicit about her view that the Communist Party in Kerala, with its *laissez-faire* social policy, never overtly questioned deeper community structures but accommodated and exploited them:

> The real secret was that communism crept into Kerala insidiously. As a reformist movement that never overtly questioned the traditional values of a caste-ridden, extremely traditional community. The Marxists worked from

> within the communal divides, never challenging them, never appearing not to. They offered a cocktail revolution. A heady mix of Eastern Marxism and orthodox Hinduism, spiked with a shot of democracy. (66–67)

Comrade K.N.M. Pillai bases his manoeuvres against Velutha on the fact that 'all the other Touchable workers in the factory resented Velutha for ancient reasons of their own' (121).[2] The ambiguity of social values suits Chacko to conveniently exploit attractive women workers and at the same time approve of E.M.S. Namboodiripad's political treatise on the peaceful transition to communism. The irony of the situation is captured by Ammu, when she characterizes her brother Chacko as a 'spoiled princeling playing *Comrade! Comrade!*' (65). Comrade Pillai's theory 'Caste is Class' (281) represents an attempt, out of ignorance or convenience, to see one historical order in terms of another. It is a failure to see the different historicities at work while clubbing several struggles together. Class has a certain degree of mobility associated with it, which is unavailable to members of the lower castes in the novel. While under the class-scheme of things, a Paravan like Velutha is able to cross occupational barriers under the influence of modernity in becoming a carpenter, under the more entrenched caste-scheme Vellya Paapen, his father, loyally accepts the questionable world view which retains him as an underdog. It is he who informs the Ipe family, in a duty-bound manner, of the rendezvous between Ammu and Velutha, thus doning the mantle of History's 'deputy' (199). So deep-rooted is even the internalization of world views. Mammachi inadvertently reveals the unnaturalness of this order when she says that 'if only he [Velutha] hadn't been a Paravan, he might have become an engineer' (75).

The enforcers of the *status quo* blur the genesis of the phenomenon of caste into the realm of mythical time, the time of Dharmasastras and Smritis. Religions collude in preserving the order. The eternal law of Karma is invoked in Biblical terms: 'As ye sow, so shall ye reap' (Roy 1997: 31). This is to legitimize the older order as something that transcends historical change itself. Linear historical time warps into a form of the cyclical sacred time. Mythical events are those which are supposed to have happened outside historical time, in, to use the Romanian religious philosopher Mircea Eliade's Latin phrase, *illo tempore* (that time). Roy invokes mythical time, the time of what she calls the Great Stories, in the novel through the classical dance form Kathakali (literally meaning a story-play). The performance of mythical stories enables a mythical transcendence of ordinary time. It becomes possible for the Kathakali artiste to temporarily transcend the present time and the deprived condition it entails, and dwell for a while in the grandeur of mythical time.

When Roy talks about History as underlying oppression and brutality, the objective is not to unfix responsibility, but to critique the superficiality of change and stress the need for a praxis of deeper engagements. She also emphasizes agency in the relationship between Velutha and Ammu, which materializes through 'a chink in History' (214), though consequences can be terrible. It is significant that for this temporal leap, they invoke the primal force of biology, which antedates history: 'Centuries telescoped into one evanescent moment.

History was wrong-footed, caught off guard' (Roy 1997: 176). This is more than figurative language. The invocation of the primal is significant because according to the author, the underlying oppressive order of life too is, in turn, rooted in the primal elements of human nature. She attributes the (state-) violence inflicted on Velutha to 'feelings that were primal,' '[m]an's subliminal urge to destroy what he could neither subdue or deify,' to 'human nature's pursuit of ascendancy' (308–09), something puzzling to contemporary critical trends. This extends the phenomenon not only to the time of clan and tribal warfare, ancient despotisms, and primitive worship, but to fundamental forces within man. Ideologies, be it capitalism, communism, or Christianity, are 'edifice[s] constructed by the human mind, decimated by human nature' (Roy 1997: 287). Paradoxically, it is the primal force of biology which is presented as a counter to historical debilitations. Ammu's reckless challenging of sexual and caste prohibitions is, in the words of Alex Tickell, 'a utopian moment that envisages ... transformation' (2007: 40). Brinda Bose's argument that the erotic serves as the zone of rebellion also reinforces the novels' invocation of this primal principle of life to subvert even an entrenched way of history.[3] While resistance to historical transformation lies in something which is primal, so do the seeds of possible change, however weak these might be.

To return to the larger politics of time, let me discuss another dimension of time, namely subjective time. The idea of subjective time is associated with the French philosopher Henri Bergson (1859–1941). Bergson believed that time was not an external homogeneous medium, but possessed what he referred to as Duration (an inner temporal continuum). Creativity and memory are essential components of reality under an inner temporal perspective. For the individual, time is qualitative and elastic; it could speed up or slow down. What is of importance to inner life has a durational proximity than what is chronologically near. Bergson's ideas of time and consciousness influenced the shape and texture of modernist narratives, whose devices have been adopted by Roy herself. Indeed, we find many Bergsonian characteristics in Roy's novel, such as narrative fluidity; the fading of moments from the past, present, and future into each other; and the dynamic character of consciousness in constituting the inner temporal continuum.

Objective timekeeping is fundamental to keeping order. Homogenized narrative time is an analogue of order, social and political. Relativization of time has a bearing on order in that it can subvert this order. Hence temporal disruption, the freedom utilized in the perception and representation of time, amounts to a symbolic questioning of this order. In the retrospective cause-and-effect chain of events in the fictional world of *The God of Small Things*, it is only this temporal play and reflection that opens up freedom for men and women.

Wherever possible, the characters of *The God of Small Things*, like the arranger of the narrative, resort to a creative chronometry. They purposively manipulate time, memory, and history, their own and those over whom they exercise control. They prolong, freeze, and obliterate time, or connive with various temporalities. If invited to a wedding at Kottayam, Mammachi would whisper 'to whoever she went with' that '[t]he [now well-to-do] bride's maternal grandfather was [her] father's carpenter' and that there was a time when her 'husband's family used to own this whole hill' (168). Baby Kochamma's geronto-politics impotently desires to deny the twins their past, while she herself, as Rahel rightly thinks, is '*living her life backwards* [italics as in the original]' (22). She triumphantly declares that Estha has lost his mind, as though it were a neutral activity of time, and hopes that he might not recognize his sister, when she is to meet him after twenty-two years: '*They might steal their present back* [italics as in the original]' (29). Baby Kochamma is able to make an 'overnight' transition to the age of satellite TV because of the subconscious temporal connections she makes with the past. The theme of 'the growing numbers of desperate and dispossessed people' collates ethnic cleansing, famines, and wars (on the BBC) with all those posing a threat to a conservative order (the lower-caste Velutha, the twins with no locus standi and the millions of the Third World). Women guarding their sexual fiefdoms in soap operas link up with her own half-a-century-old unrequited passion for Father Mulligan. While youth is deprived of romantic consolation, age appropriates time so as to luxuriate in the bygone opportunities of lost love. In a reversal of the age-old theme of mutability, time takes its toll on the young. Thirty-one is 'a viable, die-able age' (3).

But the freedom available with time, this art of time-engineering, is also an enabling strategy for the dominated and the subdued to salvage the relics of the past, (re)order them, imbue them with meaning, and write their own (hi)stories. Rahel's return to Ayemenem is not only to an old place but also to old time, when she and her twin brother had an undivided being. The aspired freezing of time enables the twins to reach out across deterministic boundaries of time, and recover lost links, and lives. In her last days, Ammu also wants time to stand still. The presents which she buys for her eleven-year-old daughter are suitable for a seven-year-old: 'As though sheer willpower was enough to suspend her children's childhoods until she could afford to have them living with her. Then they could take up from where they left off' (159).

What is more important about the subjectivization of time is that it is this inner time sense which retrieves the value of small things, the foremost of the novel's several themes. Many critics have noted the dialectic between public and private histories in the novel (Mullaney 2007: 25), and the endeavour to unearth the latter. But why should private histories and their inconspicuous details count? While the subtext of the novel's narrative is about the connections between the big and the small, it should also be noted that a different time sense is important for small things to matter. Psychological time is an analogue of the small things' struggle for legitimacy against a greater world of overarching structures, insurmountable laws, and forces of conformity. What is of importance to the inner life of little men and women has a durational proximity within the novel than what is chronologically, grand-historically near. As Bergson says in *Time and Free Will*, '... the most common-place events have their importance in a life-story' (1910: 187), a statement which is true of Roy's child-protagonists. So are the tokens of lost time, such as the rosary with a silver crucifix which Rahel had stolen after Estha was 'Returned,' which she retrieves upon her return to Ayemenem (156). The novel is the result of an imperative and obligation not to forget the small things: 'Little events, ordinary things, smashed and reconstituted. Imbued with new meaning. Suddenly they become the bleached bones of a story' (32–33).

Notes

1. It would be interesting to see this form of historicity in the context of Arundhati Roy's activism on contemporary issues. The acceleration of change post-globalization, which Rahel notices upon her return to Ayemenem, and the modern omnipotence in matters of love life (unavailable to Velutha and Ammu) notwithstanding, Roy seems to imply that the order of life ushered in by modern institutions of global capitalism and its ally, the nation-state, is insidiously related to the older social order. Both are sustained by their elite beneficiaries. The effect in both the cases is dispossession. As in the case of the Narmada Dam project, the lives which are affected are of those who are expendable—untouchables and tribals—as in the ancient order of life. The older order and its rules of exclusion persist under new circumstances.
2. Aijaz Ahmad's criticism of Roy's depiction of the Communist Party deserves mention here. Ahmad says: '... it is quite implausible that a Communist trade union leader [Comrade Pillai] would actively conspire in a murderous assault on a well-respected member of his own union so as to uphold caste purity' (1997: 105). It is not that Pillai conspires to uphold caste purity. He does to safeguard his own interests. Pillai's fault is two-fold. As K.K. John puts it, 'Comrade Pillai utilizes his position in the Party to liquidate his Party colleague simply because he considers him his rival' (1999: 121). Further, he is not above prejudices bequeathed by the older social order. He retains them because they suit him. M. Dasan's observation is more nuanced:

   > He not only panders to deep-rooted caste prejudice existing in Kerala society, but also takes pride in his wife Kalyani for not allowing a Paravan—any low caste for that matter—to enter their house. Though he himself claims to have told the workers that their opposition to or hatred of Velutha simply because he is a low caste is wrong, he exonerates himself for his inability to educate them against the feudal hangover. (2001: 29)

   Pillai's second fault, the failure of someone in the vanguard of a progressive political movement and a supposed agent of historical change, consists in his unwillingness to address deeper historical issues.
3. Anna Froula notes in a similar vein:

   > Whereas India's long-standing caste-laws both establish a permanent place for each individual in society and protect the power of the ruling class, Ammu's transgression stresses the exponential threat of dangerous pollution to permeable social barriers. Unchecked, this cultural possibility has the potential to subvert the social order, rendering everyone's place—whether privileged, dispossessed, or in between—as changeable within unstable dominant power structures. (2009: 40)

   Understandably, critics like Aijaz Ahmad disagree. They see the erotic as an inadequate form of political engagement (1997: 113–14).

Works Cited

Ahmad, Aijaz. 'Reading Arundhati Roy Politically.' Review of *The God of Small Things* by Arundhati Roy. *Frontline* 14.15 (8 August 1997), 103–08. Print.

American Beauty. Dir. Sam Mendes. Perf. Kevin Spacey, Annette Bening and Thora Birch. DreamWorks, 1999. Film.

Baneth-Nouailhetas, Émilienne. 'The Structures of Memory.' *Arundhati Roy's The God of Small Things*. Ed. Alex Tickell. London: Routledge, 2007, 142–54. Print.

Bergson, Henri. *Time and Free Will: An Essay on the Immediate Data of Consciousness*. Trans. F.L. Pogson. London: Allen, 1910. Print.

Bloom, Harold. *The Western Canon: The Books and School of the Ages*. New York: Harcourt, 1994. Print.

Bose, Brinda. 'In Desire and Death: Eroticism as Politics in Arundhati Roy's *The God of Small Things*.' *ARIEL: A Review of International Literature* 29.2 (1998), 120–31. Print.

Braudel, Fernand. *The Structures of Everyday Life: The Limits of the Possible*. Trans. Siân Reynolds. Vol. 1 of *Civilization and Capitalism 15th-18th Century*. 3 Vols. London: Collins, 1981. Print.

——. *The Mediterranean and the Mediterranean World in the Age of Philip II*. Trans. Sîan Reynolds. New York: Harper, 1992. Print.

——. *On History*. Trans. Sarah Matthews. Chicago: U of Chicago P, 1980. Print.

Dasan, M. 'Arundhati Hits the Socio-Political Ball.' *The Critical Studies of Arundhati Roy's The God of Small Things.* Eds Jaydipsinh Dodiya and Joya Chakravarty. New Delhi: Atlantic, 2001, 22–36. Print.

Dodiya, Jaydipsinh and Joya Chakravarty (eds). *The Critical Studies of Arundhati Roy's The God of Small Things.* New Delhi: Atlantic, 1999. Print.

Eliade, Mircea. *The Myth of the Eternal Return, or Cosmos and History*. Trans. Willard R. Trask. Princeton, NJ: Princeton UP, 1954. Print.

Froula, Anna. 'In-between and Elsewhere: Liminality in Arundhati Roy's *The God of Small Things*.' *Globalizing Dissent: Essays on Arundhati Roy*. Eds Ranjan Ghosh and Antonia Navarro-Tejero. New York: Routledge, 2009. Print.

Huggan, Graham. *The Postcolonial Exotic: Marketing the Margins*. London: Routledge, 2001. Print.

John, K.K. 'A Band of Masqueraders: A Study of Some Characters in Arundhati Roy's Novel.' *The Critical Studies of Arundhati Roy's The God of Small Things* (eds). Jaydipsinh Dodiya and Joya Chakravatry. New Delhi: Atlantic, 1999, 119–23. Print.

Mullaney, Julie. *The God of Small Things: A Reader's Guide*. New York: Continuum, 2007. Print.

Roy, Arundhati. *The God of Small Things*. New Delhi: India Ink, 1997. Print.

Tickell, Alex. *Arundhati Roy's The God of Small Things*. London: Routledge, 2007. Print.

22

Narrative, Hymen, Laterality: Postmodern Strategies in Mukul Kesavan's *Looking Through Glass*

PRAMOD K. NAYAR

> We are difference ... our reason is the difference of discourses, our history the difference of times, ourselves the difference of masks. That difference, far from being the forgotten and recoverable origin, is this dispersion that we are and make.
>
> —Michel Foucault

Mukul Kesavan's *Looking Through Glass* (1995) is a deft weave of history, theory and fiction and a simultaneous problematizing of these concepts. Drawing effectively from paradigms of these three disciplines, Kesavan presents a beautiful postmodern novel. Like Salman Rushdie's works and Graham Swift's *Waterland* (1983) Kesavan's postmodern work calls into question generic distinctions and blurs boundaries. This paper explores the terrain of Kesavan's first novel as displaying a postmodern topography.

The remarkable feature of *Glass* is the simultaneous existence of multiple registers of discourse—the literary, historical, political and popular cultural. Kesavan provides a documentary-like narration of events. Examples would be the narrator (who is unnamed throughout) detailing the history of the 'Old School' (Kesavan 166–67), Wavell's arrival as Viceroy (211), the Calcutta famine (206) and others. As Roland Barthes has argued in 'The Discourse of History' and 'The Reality Effect', such an 'objective', documentary register is a feature of history writing (1986). The subjective element is *apparently* kept minimal. Hypotyposis triumphs reigns supreme over epideictic narration. And, as Wolfgang Iser argues in 'Representation: A Performative Act', the two worlds in a novel, the world of fiction and the 'real' world, may be bracketed off. In Kesavan, this distinction of historical narrative/fictional narrative merges. The worlds coalesce, and there is the 'simultaneity of the mutually exclusive' (Iser 1987: 220–21).

In *Glass,* the historical narrative is embedded in literary presentation. The historical register is with(in) the subjectivity of the narrator. For instance, the narrator produces officio-legal documents as supports for the Ganjoo family history (21 & 23). Personal idiosyncracies, prejudices and his own chaotic time-transfer have ruinous effects in his engagement with *this* text. Thus, there occurs the implosion of History into Fiction (i.e. the narrator's re-creation). The undermining of this narrative by Kesavan shall be looked at later in the essay.

The use of popular cultural forms is a trait of postmodern texts, as Linda Hutcheon argues (5). Slogans, advertisements, newspaper columns, songs and other such paraliterary discourses are incorporated into the text of *Glass.* The newspaper report provides the narrator the name and residence of his grandmother (246). The slogan painted on the truck 'into' which Masroor disappears (47) becomes a symbol for the military might of British India, and is a subtle comment on those Indians who fought for Britain. Thus, these other paraliterary discourses have crucial roles to play in the narrative. As we shall come to realize, this is yet another mode to decenter any 'master narrative', by providing 'alternative' voices. Such examples may be multiplied in *Glass:* the extracts from *The History and Destiny of the Ganjoos* (the title itself combines the apparently factual 'History' and the sublime imaginary 'Destiny'), letters to the editors of the newspaper *Pioneer* (56), the fictionalised items in Ammi's magazine *Khatoon* (16–18).

The multiple registers, either supplementary or contestatory, are of multiple voices and of an overtly controlling narrator. Most events in *Glass* are filtered through the perception of the anonymous narrator. Other than a few dates and the name of his grandmother, no other identity of this narrator is vouchsafed to us. On numerous occasions, Kesavan takes away the credibility of this narrator. As Linda Hutcheon has argued, we are led to doubt the subject's ability to know the past with any certainty (1995: 10, 117). Many features of Kesavan's narrative make us wary of the narrator's ability to tell us the 'truth'. To begin with there is his amnesia. His retrogressive movement in time disorients him, as when he sees the dateline on the newspaper (13). We are uncertain of the genuineness of his amnesia. Later, we have this narrator's reliance upon Masroor (a fugitive) to tell us the events of 1942 (246–55). This distances us from the first narrator's tale where the apparently omniscient narrator is only a via media for yet another narrator. This is a crucial move in decentering the first narrative level, or the 'master narrative'. The first narrator is reduced to a metadiegetic interlocutor (even interloper). For instance, one of the chapters is titled 'This Truth According to Masroor'. This not only edged the first narrator away from the position of chief speaker but also subtly destabilizes the second narrative level. The use of 'according' suggests the subjectivity, hence the suspectable quality, of 'truth'. The narrator's obsession with illusion such as the movies (169) is another instance where the reality/illusion opposition seems not very sustainable. The narrator also proves his unreliability by being unclear about events. The confusion regarding the details of the Delia seduction scene is a case in point (298–99). The narrator in *Glass,* thus, undermines his own omniscience. Kesavan thus problematizes the notion of narrational authority.

The unreliability of the narrator also introduces the idea of questionable epistemological bases. Uncertainty and fragmentation cloak 'knowledge' in *Glass.* All available knowledge is shadowy, shimmery, and a chiaroscuro (Gibson 1996: 115). The narrator cannot detail the events of 1942. He has to accept first Chaubey's, and later Parwana's versions of the Gyanendra intrigue. Parwana herself, at the narrator's behest, falsifies her 'tragic' story to gain Kaushalya Devi's sympathy (193–203). Masroor has a Machine for 'planting doubt', where the map of India is cut up, joined and shuffled in a jigsaw, thus lending an air of unreality to the concept of a united 'Indian' nation (228–29). Authorities like Jinnah only provide cryptic and obfuscatory comment (aries) on vital issues like the Partition. One notes that Jinnah does not *sign* his comment, thus making it less valuable (177).

Such a fragmentary and shadowy knowledge, the narrator's unreliability, all prevent totalizing. The narrator's prejudices, blindspots, crucial absences and overall yawning ignorance draws a circle of hermeneutic suspicion around his narrative. This postmodern strategy where no unified, totalizing and authoritative narrative is provided, but rather a polyphony or narratives *each* placed under the interrogative. Thus, a story is made of many equally valid, (unreliable) stories, and multiple ways of 'telling' them. Kesavan, thus, subverts our established notions of a conventional novel by undermining the narrative voice, more or less in the manner of Laurence Sterne.

When the narrator is placed under erasure, the possibility of alternative voices emerges. This is the 'excluded third', or the hymenal feature of a postmodern narrative (Gibson 1996: 105–42). The narrator in *Glass* asks certain questions to confirm his own bearings. Masroor, Haasan, Ammi, Intezar, Parwana, to whom these queries are addressed are all alternate contestatory voices. They mire the narrator's terrain by taking knowledge out of his diegetic hands. Thus, the narrator himself turns into the 'excluded third', a border-crosser (the via media mentioned before) himself. This third is always on the threshold of narratives. Thus, hymen-inside and yet outside, and the undecidability of both (ironically, two chapters are, in succession, labelled 'Inside' and 'Outside'). The excluded third here is the other voice (or the other of the voice), which merges, disseminates, contests, supports and floats around. The observer-critic-narrator is sometimes the observed (by Haasan, Masroor or Parwana). He traverses, in his usually unreliable manner, between the roles of narrator and narratee. Of course, it may be argued that it is he who provides us the other narratives.

Here, I return to my previous argument that more than the narrator he is the 'third', the interlocutor. It is this subversive subjectivity that makes me believe in his narratee—which may actually, provide a second level narrative. Thus, as in a 'classic postmodern text', to yoke together unusual terms, the narrative is not homogenized but is the site for the play of differences. The narrator's unreliability, absences, received fragmentary and shadowy knowledge all contribute to *Glass* as a novel premised on differences, thresholds and borders. Any certainty is purely positional, based on local and contingent positions. The strategy of making the narrator the excluded third invites such a reading. We only have limited views of 'reality' such as the narrator's version of Masroor's disappearance, the Chaubey-Parwana fiasco, or the Politicians' role in the Quit India movement. All these 'certain' views are articulated by and within the narrator's position and 'reality'—of a man extremely aware of his interloper and exiled status (due to his retrograde movement into 1942).

This brings us to the next feature of Kesavan's novel. When the narrator rewrites the 1942–47 past for us, he opens it up to the present. This has two-interrelated movements of retrieving the past through textualized remains *and* a refusal to see the past as conclusive or teleological. This is achieved when Kesavan's narrator constantly views the events of 1942–47 with the consciousness of a later date. The narrator does not really gauge the significance of the Movement. 1942 is another date. He ridicules and satirizes it. We note, also, his anger at the movement which has prevented him from returning to his own time. The narrator raves:

> These Quit India heroes had ruined me. Do or Die I remembered Dadi muttering ... well, they had done ... and I wished them dead. They had done me in just as surely as they had done Dadi ... she had been eaten up by remembrance of things past, but these nameless patriots had buggered up my future. (54–55)

This obviously prejudiced view prevents sanctification of the past and the mythicizing of its characters (hence the irreverent reference to 'nameless patriots').

The narrator's own knowledge of history is strictly through narratives, i.e. textualised remains—newspaper reports, photographs, Dadi's oral narratives, and history books. History and historicity become textualized as postmodern theorists believe. The narrator's re-writing or re-presenting the past in/as yet another set of texts (films, photographs, the worded narrative) induces a suspicion of the past. Or rather, it places the past's 'authenticity', and man's ability to 'know' it, under question.

One method of such a destabilizing move (against History) is ridicule (caricaturing, as in the portrait of Jinnah) and irreverence. The other is through an equally irreverent obfuscation and entrammeling of details. For instance, the mystery behind the numerous vanishings is unexplained. Masroor narrates numerous disappearances at the time of Quit India. The magic-realist mode is used effectively here (247–92). Kesavan adds irony and sarcasm to the confusion when he states (through Masroor):

> No one vanished without a trace; the degree of disappearance was in inverse proportion to the victim's commitment to the Congress. Some just become lighter skinned which they didn't mind. Others, more involved with the party, sometimes became transparent. (247–48)

The reference to 'traces' and 'transparency' (both highly favoured deconstructive terms) is not lost upon us, especially since we read the past as 'traces'. This shadowy assimilation becomes a method to prevent concretizing of any knowledge of the past.

Thus, details coexist, run into others and occasionally contest each other. One result of this is narrative laterality. Narrative literality is the contrast to diegetic 'levels' which imply hierarchies (Gibson 1996: 219–24). As with the notion of the narrative hymenal, this flattening ('lalcralising') of spaces becomes a critique of the distinction inside/outside. There occurs an interlacing and redistribution of elements or 'forces' (as Derrida would term them). In Kesavan, we have already noted how the authority of the omniscient narrator is undermined. Other authorities are of equal significance—Masroor, Haasanu Parwana, Chaubev. Even if seen as a second narrative level, to borrow Gerard Genette's formulation, in Kesavan they are not 'parasites'. In *Glass* the novel's signification is produced in the exchange between these narrative levels. The story of the narrator is dependent, for veracity, definition, even constitution, on these other narratives. When he makes the narrator suspect, Kesavan has elevated the 'servant narrative' onto the same plane as the 'master' one. After Michel Serres, the notion of a parasitic subtext has dissolved. For Serres, the parasite is the essence of all relations, the reversible, ambivalent, impure figure which troubles the self-sufficiency, identity of the 'host' (1982: 79). Thus, the other narratives in *Glass* announce the irreducible hybridity of the first narrator's discourse. As in Sterne's *Tristram Shandy,* the 'chief' narrator is first made suspect and then the 'parasite' narrative provides 'stories'. In Kesavan, for instance, narrative laterality occurs when the narrator is unable to 'read' the past effectively. The Quit India Movement's significance is not readily accessible to him (on account of his prejudices, awareness of the future Partition and so on). This reduces the narrator to a hymenal figure who gives the excluded third a voice, such as Masroor's, to attain equal (narrative) stature. Hence, it is Masroor who analyses the situation of 1942. This makes *Glass* a hybridized text where all narratives (we may now drop the term 'levels') coexist in composite relations with each other. The overall motif is, thus, fragmentation, unreliability and the dissolution of boundaries. Kesavan, in a telling comment on history, speaks of an 'emancipation from history, from the habit of seeing time as a series of events, tending to an ending' (192). The narrator does not return to his time, thus leaving this narrative inconclusive. The two times, histories and narratives, therefore, coexist, symbiotically and lateralized and which are to be perceived as purely difference.

From the above arguments we can, thus, list postmodern features of Kesavan's narrative: multiple registers of discourse, the suspect credibility of the narrator, fragmentary epistemology, the anti-totalising narrative, narrative hymenal, the textualising of the past and finally, narrative laterality.

Works Cited

Barthes, Roland. *The Rustle of Language.* Trans. Richard Howard. Oxford: Basil Blackwell, 1986. Print.

Gibson, Andrew. *Towards a Postmodern Theory of Narrative.* Edinburgh: Edinburgh UP, 1996. Print.

Hutcheon, Linda. *A Poetics of Postmodernism: History, Theory, Fiction.* London: Routledge, 1995. Print.

Iser, Wolfgang. 'Representation: A Performative Act.' *The Aims of Representation: Subject/Text/History.* Ed. Murray Krieger. New York: Columbia UP, 1987. Print.

Kesavan, Mukul. *Looking Through Glass.* Delhi: Ravi Dayal, 1995. Print.

Serres, Michel. *The Parasite.* Trans. L.R. Schehr. Baltimore: Johns Hopkins UP, 1982. Print.

23

The (B)Other of Borders: Kavery Nambisan's *The Scent of Pepper*

PRAMOD K. NAYAR

> A boundary is not that at which something stops but, as the Greeks recognised, the boundary is that form which something begins its presence. Martin Heidegger, 'Building, Dwelling, Thinking'.

This paper is concerned with the question of 'Othering' in Kavery Nambisan's *The Scent of Pepper* (1996). Nambisan's novel is a post-Independence, semi-ethnographic narrative of the colonial encounter as it occurs in Kodagu (Coorg) district of Karnataka. The native/outsider issue as embodied in the Baliyanna—Clara relationship forms the core of the tale. However, this is not the only 'Othering' (India as Britain's other and vice versa) in *Pepper.* I detect the process of Othering at three levels in *Pepper,* as a component of the colonial encounter; as a situation resulting from the negotiation between 'nativity' and alterity, its own antinomic equivalent; and as the unspeaking, unspeakable 'Other' of the Self. The paper, thus, throws up finer substrata (sediments?) of the term 'native' where the nomenclature ranges downward from nation, race, tribe to individual. It, thus, locates alterity at the borders of these categories.

I

The most notable feature of *Pepper* is its exploration of the colonial experience. Clara comes out to India to escape England (60). Her life as a staff nurse in England is full of boredom—the word is used five times in a paragraph of fourteen lines (56). She seeks the mysterious and unfamiliar Orient. She acquires an anthropologist's interest in native customs. Clifford Geertz has argued for the ethnographic narrative as the story of a quest. The ethnographer-seeker departs to another, darker world, to study it, and 'have' adventures. 'S/he later returns to the West so that the tales may be told' (Geertz 1997:

45–48). Clara too returns to England, with her storehouse of 'local knowledge' of the Other (192).

In Kodagu, Clara the ethnographer wants to read everything, and 'find out' all about the Kodava race (63). She is drawn by their strangeness. Yet she slowly assimilates (interpellates as another subject) herself into the native race. This conflation of the native/outsider categories occurs precisely because the stranger-outsider is not wholly unfamiliar. To identify someone as stranger, we ought to know a few details about her/him (Bauman 1995: 54). Clara comes out to India already imbricated in the colonial discourse (59–60). Thus, she is not wholly unfamiliar to Kodagu. Likewise the Kodavas' experience of the whites allows them a certain familiarity with Clara. Eventually this results in Clara's 'going native,' by discovering a 'sameness' with her race's (nation's) Other. As Geertz would argue, at this point the other culture appears logical and straightforward, while one's own appears strange (1997: 107). Borders have been transgressed. This assimilation of/into the Other by Clara is captured in a single paragraph. Nambisan writes:

> She (Clara) felt more at home in Coorg. At first when she came, she had been frightened by the gonglike voices of the natives, the curries had ravaged her stomach, ghee and honey overwhelmed her tastebuds .... Now she had grown used to these things and accepted them ... she had even become bold enough to avoid the annual billiards tournament, she began to give the 'at homes' a miss .... Clara couldn't help being different. (1996: 78)

Clara's role as ethnographer is supplemented (I use the term in the Derridean sense) by Baliyanna. Baliyanna frequently articulates the difference between his race/culture/nation and Clara's (54, 86). His comments are, in Gregory Bateson's phrase, schismogenetic: they (re)produce divisions. Baliyanna thus establishes Rupert, Clara's husband and an avowed anti-native, as an outsider, the Other (86). Baliyanna has, thus, framed a nationalist, native discourse. This is achieved by his construction of the 'national Other'. As Donald E. Pease has argued, a patriotic national identity is structured in the imagined relation of absolute difference from this national enemy (1997). However, this narrativizing of the native is not unproblematic, since some identification and reciprocity with the Other occurs in *Pepper* (Zygmunt Bauman argues that this reciprocity builds the bridge between 'us' and 'them': 50–53). Clara's voyeuristic and vicarious pleasure at Baliyanna's companionship (65, 76) is 'reciprocated' when she plays teacher to Baliyanna (81–84) (The Westerner as teacher, protector, provider is a stereotype in colonial discourse. The authority of the English book, appearing at crucial points in the narrative, is also highly significant. Nambisan adopts this strategy of colonial discourse when she brings in the English book (81–85). For a discussion of the authority of the Western text, see Homi K. Bhabha's 'Signs Taken for Wonders'). Once again, the encounter results in the blurring of the native/outsider.

This reciprocity in the process of Othering suggests an inherent ambivalence in colonial discourse. The phobic representation/views of the native is simultaneous with a certain fetishisation. As Homi K. Bhabha has adequately demonstrated in his essay 'The Other Question,' the stereotype functions as phobia and fetish, where identification and alienation, fear and desire co-exist (1995a: 72). A certain recognition of cultural/racial difference and its disavowal occurs when Clara 'takes to' Baliyanna, the Kodava hunt, their food habits and so on. Thus, a part obliteration of the native/other categorisation has occurred in the colonial encounter. The presence of the Other has begun from/at the border of the 'encounter.'

II

If the colonial encounter has problematized 'Otherness' in Nambisan, a closer look at the 'nativism' question reveals more ambiguities. Baliyanna is at war with his brother Appachu for marrying a Westerner. Baliyanna's son, Subbu, however, wishes to continue his education at a Convent school. Chengu Master is deeply in love with the English language. If all these are notations for the East-West (us/them, native/other) encounter, the natives are themselves situated somewhat perilously close to these same borders. Their tribe, so legend has it, descended from the Greeks, i.e. 'outsiders.' Yet, they are the natives in India. This paring down of the identity implies that the culture can never be self-identical. Jacques Derrida in his meditation on the issue of alterity in *The Other Heading* says: 'There is no self relation, no relation to oneself, no identification with oneself, without culture, but a culture *as* a culture *of* the other ... of the difference to oneself' (1992: 9–10, emphasis Derrida's). Hence, Derrida suggests, one must 'welcome foreigners in order not only to integrate them but to recognise and accept their alterity ...' (1992: 77). Thus, the notion of pure nativism, and its pure 'Other' are problematised. Appachu is Westernised, has an English wife, yet remains faithful to a Kodava-Indian faith. Baliyanna's mental miscegenation with Clara (especially in the infantilising dream of sleeping child-like on Clara's stomach, 101), the acknowledgement of an unidentifiable, single origin of their race, all illustrate the argument. The native's otherness to itself, and its integration of an apparent antinomy dislodges the logic of identity, which, as Michel Foucault argued in his classic *The Order of Things,* is a 'history of the same'. The imposition of such a logic—either the native's or the coloniser's—is never total, since the Other cannot be entirely 'outside'. The hegemonic formation of native/national or of coloniser/ruler, embraces what opposes it.

III

Finally, the Self and its Otherness to itself. Rao Bahadur goes insane in a tragic solidarity with his tribe's collective ailment. His son Baliyanna suffers the same illness. The Self is here a part of the racial/social ethos. However, the puzzle is whether the unspeaking, mad Self is at variance with this social (sane?), communally accepted Self? Rao Bahadur's madness is the 'non-being', a 'nothing' and a 'monument of silence' (Foucault 1965). The lethargy and depression is the emptiness of the Self, while also being the projection of the tribe's Self into the body.

Likewise, Baliyanna's Self is at variance, different, an Other, of his social, anti-British self. The desire for carnal fulfilment with the English Clara (itself an orientalist portrayal) breaks his personality. Desire, as Freud had argued redefines the relation of Self and world. What is placed 'outside'—i.e. the inaccessible Englishwoman, since she is anti-native—actually remains on the 'inside', through repression and denial. Thus, in a realm of fantasy (we have already noted Baliyanna's dream) the outside world is brought into the Self. The Other, inadmissible by social convention, is integrated into the Self as fantasy. Baliyanna has, thus, suffered a fracture between his avowed anti-English Self and his desire-filled (unconscious) Self. The Self's Other, I believe, has now been glimpsed. Which then is the 'native' Baliyanna—the nationalist, English-hating one or the deeply sexual one, irrevocably attracted to Clara? When does Baliyanna transgress the border between the Self and its Other? The presence of the Other begins near, or at this 'boundary.'

I argue then, that the problem of drawing borders between native/Other is voiced in Nambisan. Nambisan presents the irreducibility of these apparent 'antinomies' into clear categories. The hyphenated (native-Other) rather than the slash line configuration may have to be preferred. I have demonstrated how, at various levels, the native seems to contain its Other, what is irreducible and undeconstructible is the alterity of Self/culture. This paper marks out a case for reading *The Scent of Pepper* as a text of transgressive boundaries.

Works Cited

Bauman, Zygmunt. *Thinking Sociologically.* Oxford: Blackwell, 1995. Print.

Bhabha, Homi K. 'Signs Taken for Wonders.' *The Location of Culture.* London: Routledge, 1995. Print.

——. 'The Other Question.' *The Location of Culture.* London: Routledge, 1995a. Print.

Derrida, Jacques. *The Other Heading: Reflections on Today's Europe.* Trans. Pascale-Anne Brault and Michael B. Nass. Bloomington, Indianapolis: Indiana UP, 1992. Print.

Foucault, Michel. *Madness and Civilisation: A History of Insanity in the Age of Reason.* Trans. Richard Howard. London: Tavistock, 1965. Print.

——. *The Order of Things: An Archaeology of the Human Sciences.* London: Tavistock, 1970. Print.

Geertz, Clifford. *Works and Lives: The Anthropologist as Author.* Stanford, California: Stanford UP, 1997. Print.

Nambisan, Kavery. *The Scent of Pepper.* New Delhi: Penguin, 1996. Print.

Pease, Donald E. 'National Narratives, Postnational Narration.' *Modern Fiction Studies* 13.1 (Spring 1997), 1–23. Print.

24

The Mango *Sans* Maggots: A Study of David Davidar's *The House of Blue Mangoes*

T. VINODA

David Davidar's debut novel, *The House of Blue Mangoes* (2002), brings this genre back to the epic mode of covering a huge canvas taking in many generations and great many social changes and upheavals. This achievement is unique in Indian English novel especially since few writers have dared attempt it before Davidar. A great deal of meticulous research has also gone into this work with a view to bringing it authenticity. However, Davidar sounds unduly defensive and cautious in the 'Author's Notes' and 'Acknowledgements' appended to the novel. In these two sections, he succeeds in helping us establish parallels between men and events in the novel and the referents to those in real life. He speaks about how he wished to 'recapture memories of an idyllic childhood' and of his grandparents. However, in the same breath he asserts that the novel is 'wholly invented' and that 'it is not autobiographical.' Notwithstanding his ostensibly statutory disclaimers about fictional names, characters, places and incidents of the novel at the beginning of the 'Author's Notes,' David Davidar goes to great lengths giving us information on their historical referents and documented facts of those times. He even gives us a complete list of books on social history, on Raj, the Indian Civil Service, Indian Nationalist Movement, the system of Siddha medicine, etc. that he had consulted to write this novel. His great care and caution reaches its apotheosis when he says: 'I invented three new castes because I did not wish to add fuel to the caste controversies that have raged for centuries now, to the general detriment of the country and the states of Tamil Nadu and Kerala which are my particular interest ...' (418). Such a process of hedging the fictional work is wholly unwarranted in our time when the postmodernist historiographic metafiction has rendered fiction a completely open genre in hitherto unheard of ways. Also, the act of putting on a thinly veiled fictional cover on historical referents is redundant in the wake of the author's obvious anxiety to authenticate his novel with a carefully and assiduously researched sources of social history.

The House of Blue Mangoes, although large in its canvas and coverage, appears to have a unifying vision. The moral centre of the novel is in its vision of family—a vision that is dear to Indian way of thinking. Philosophy, religion, mythology and legend in almost every culture have invariably affirmed the centrality of family and home in man's life. Social practices and codes of behaviour have been built around the idea of preserving these two institutions because it is believed they are the means to man's happiness, transcendence and even redemption. Over the years, conventions, customs and rituals have evolved to fortify these institutions. If man strays, he must return to them, for home and family are held to offer all that man seeks by way of personal happiness and fulfilment. I remember a Jewish story in which a poor destitute old man dreams that a huge treasure chest was buried beneath a bridge about twenty miles and finds that there, indeed, is a bridge but that the soldiers guard it. He goes there the following morning again trudging the whole distance but is disappointed to find that soldiers were still there. He goes there the next day again but the presence of the soldiers renders it impossible to dig beneath the bridge. Not losing hope the old man perseveres going there everyday until the soldiers notice him and ask him why he has been coming there everyday. The meek old man tells them about his dream about the hidden treasure under the bridge. The soldiers laugh with amusement and tell him in turn that they also had a similar dream of a treasure chest but that it was buried under the old man's hearth itself. They ask him to go and get it. The innocent old man takes their story seriously and accordingly goes home to dig under the hearth. Lo and behold, there indeed was the treasure chest!

David Davidar's novel, *The House of Blue Mangoes,* celebrates this age-old ideal of home, family and community. In fact, they constitute the novel's *leitmotif.* Celebration of this ideal, however, is done without simplifying matters. If anything, the novel evidences to an acute awareness of the complexities and problems involved in holding this ideal together, especially in the Indian context. The lives of the three generations traced in this novel assiduously lay bare the complications involved, but nevertheless go on to affirm the ideal of family, community and home.

It does credit to the novel that it locates this ideal in a caste ridden, superstitious, primitive, drought-prone Indian village called Chevathar. A typical Indian village, Chevathar comes to life here in all its colours, flavours and details. Here the village headman ('thalaivar'), Gnanprakasam Solomon Dorai Andavar, desperately tries to avoid caste wars whatever the extremity of the provocation. Nevertheless he was cornered into the fight for other reasons. His own position as thalaivar and the existence of the members of his low-caste was challenged and it finally boiled down to a fight for survival. The upper-caste Muthu Vedhar insults him in public during the Chitra Pournima procession by spitting on him, thus, giving vent to his old hostilities and jealousies. Solomon quietly absorbs this public insult and refuses to retaliate. Yet Muthu Vedhar lunges upon him for a physical assault and it is only now that Solomon acts, manoeuvring to get an upper hand and by telling him:

> You big black buffalo, for all these years I have tolerated you and other jackals that work for you because I have tried to keep the peace. You have insulted me before the village and for that you will pay. I will give you and all those who owe you allegiance a month to leave. If you haven't gone by then I will personally make sure that you'll wish you had never emerged from your prostitute mother's womb. (68)

Once Solomon hurls the challenge at his adversary, Muthu Vedhar, in the heat of the moment, the latter not only turns belligerent but snarls back: 'I said I would reduce you to dust and I will reduce you to dust. I am not leaving this village, it's you and your stinking family who will leave or be destroyed' (68). This was the moment of destiny and subsequently the destructive consequences become an inevitable corollary. It is now a question of personal honour and dignity for both, and however much Solomon wished to reverse the course of events in the interest of peace in the village, he is powerless to do so. Now, for both the sides survival of family and community can only be at the cost of the other. It is essentially an either/or situation rendering co-existence impossible. Attempts to mediate peace by the revered priest, Father Ashworth, or by the district collector have no effect in reversing the situation. In all this it must be observed that it was Solomon who had shown utmost forbearance and that he was reasonable all through. The novel's narrative shows in no uncertain terms that it was the cantankerous and cunning people like Vakeel Perumal who fan out conflagration from the smouldering embers. Solomon Dorai, the village headman, is helplessly caught in the conflagration in spite of his deepest concern for peace. But it must be noted that caste rivalries are responsible in an important way in disturbing the peace of the community especially in a situation where a low-caste village headman is at the helm while the upper-caste landowner is handed in the role of the ruled. The English priest, Father Ashworth, has always been intrigued by the corrosive effect caste has on the affairs of the community:

> When he [Ashworth] had arrived in India twenty-five years ago, he had been appalled above all else by the institution of caste. He tried to understand the viewpoint of those who argued that caste was necessary to give the country's vast and diverse population a sense of identity and belonging, but surely that did not excuse the injustice and barbarity perpetrated in its name! How could any sane and compassionate human being abide the discrimination sanctioned by caste and religion upon his fellows, based entirely on self-serving interpolations in the great religious texts? (30)

Much of the hatred and hostility between the upper-caste Vedhars and low-caste Andavars in Chevathar could be traced to the generations of old caste prejudices. The book even refers to what was known as 'Breast Wars' of 1859 that devastated people belonging to both the castes by subjecting them to arson, looting, stripping of women and other such outrages. It is in this context that Solomon's efforts to maintain peace in the community and at the same time preserve his clan could be termed brave and even heroic, notwithstanding his failure in achieving them. David Davidar is no facile idealist when he pitted the noble dream of the patriarch of the Big House against the mighty forces of caste, superstition and prejudice. Solomon Dorai helplessly goes down fighting for the 'defence of their family home' (127). This was the situation in Chevathar in the closing years of the nineteenth century.

If caste functions from outside as the disruptive force for family and community in the first generation, it is domestic intrigue within the family that is shown to be the divisive factor for the second generation. After Solomon's death, his younger son, Aaron, who has run away from Chevathar for nearly five years, returns to his native village only to be falsely told by his uncle, Abraham (Solomon's brother, who has now taken over as the village headman), that his mother Charity and his brother Daniel had abandoned the place unable to 'live in such reduced circumstances' (127). The effect on Aaron was that 'he was irrevocably confirmed in his hatred of his brother and his mother. 'Faithful to his father's sense of rootedness in family and home, Aaron decides to stay on in Chevathar where his ancestors lived for generations. However, for want of a cohesive family to sustain him, he eventually gets sucked into the vortex of the freedom movement. He becomes a revolutionary fighting for political freedom for the country. However, the priorities in his life are centered round his family and home and in his dying moments he confesses this to his brother Daniel: 'You should go back, anna, take our family back to where we belong .... Don't have the regrets I do. You may not be much like me, but you're the last of us ...' (198). Aaron's sense of family line and of a place where his ancestors belonged is poignantly expressed in these dying moments. It is clear that in Aaron's scheme of things too family and home and the continuation of family branch took precedence over the cause of freedom for which he gave his life. That he admits in his dying moments to regretting his separation from family and home only underscores his sense of loss. Daniel too suffers the same occasionally even when he was doing well in Nagarcoil as a physician and domestic felicity was his in this place what with his mother, wife, sisters and grandfather living with him. For instance, he muses about his childhood in Chevathar when he is living in Nagercoil in the midst of professional success and family togetherness:

> All said and done, he mused, he was of the soil of Chevathar. He felt this most keenly in the early hours of the morning and as night approached ...! miss Chevathar, he thought. I can never be truly myself anywhere else .... It was true that things had started working out for him after he had left Chevathar, but the yearning for it would never leave him. (157)

However, these quiet rumblings of nostalgia burst into open in Daniel only after he is reunited with Aaron. His moment of reunion with Aaron was also his moment of awakening and it is only now that he begins to see contours of his dream of a family and home. And he decides to go back to Chevathar to recover the lost glory of Dorai clan and to establish there a colony, Doraipuram, with his clan rallying there, as many of his relatives as was possible for the enormous wealth he made as a physician. In fact, his huge material success as a Siddha physician comes in handy and his wealth is deployed in the experiment of founding Doraipuram. In Chevathar, he buys back most of the land that belonged to his father by paying undreamt of price. Here he brings to live nearly 150 families distantly related to Dorais by offering land and money on extremely attractive terms. He founded this ideal republic on 12 commandments of which 'the most contentious was the one which banned all political activity within the colony. A couple of cousins objected, but Daniel used his chairman's veto,' saying 'I've seen politics up close and find it abhorrent, ... I've already lost a brother to it, and I will not lose any more of my family if I can help it' (214). He also sought to banish from here caste by requesting all the dwellers of Doraipuram to drop caste names. 'But even Daniel had to concede defeat on the proposal he mooted to remove all traces of caste from the family.' But no one, not even his faithful and devoted follower Ramdoss supported his view on the ground that caste gave them identity. Helpless, he left the community alone and finally decided that he and his immediate family would drop its caste suffix, Andavar. And thus 'Doraipuram' was born thanks to Daniel's prodigious efforts and enormous wealth. Here he built a huge mansion, 'The House of Blue Mangoes,' with 58 rooms all of which were filled with relatives all the time. In this house their family kitchen prepared food for nearly a hundred people everyday. And here he had the son he craved for. Also, it was here that Daniel's mother Charity, who remained until now unhinged after the death of her father and daughter Rachel, was restored to normalcy. Such was the restorative and therapeutic power of the family brought together in terms of the ideal. And Daniel's dream of family, community and home has come true.

> Doraipuram continued to grow. New families poured in and by the end of the third year of its founding, the settlement was home to over a hundred and fifty people, some of whose links to the clan could best be described as tenuous. The brother-in-law of the husband of a third cousin, for example. There were retired airmen, geologists, doctors, engineers, accountants, clerks .... (221)

But it is important to note that all these families are held together by Daniel's vast riches. Daniel probably is not unaware of this. But the force of idealism, sustained by his eminence and wealth seemed to work. Davidar's creation of this ideal community cannot be taken to be naive or simplistic because he shows the awareness of innumerable practical problems. For instance, he puts in here 'maggots' like the rumour mongers such as Victoria who could have vitiated things for the 'great experiment' (224) had it not been for the good hearted efforts of Charity to engage 'chivvying aunts and grannies, cousins and nieces into a variety of tasks' (225).

It must, however, be admitted that the novel simply skirts the complications ('maggots in the mangoes') that might otherwise have destroyed the ideal colony Daniel had sought to set up. And the few complications that are actually shown to vitiate the atmosphere in the colony are too simplistic just as the trouble-shooting efforts made to assuage those problems are puerile and tame to be realistic. Wearing the blinkers, then, the novel progresses focusing simply on the pristine quality of the utopian dream to the exclusion of all practical difficulties that lay in the way of preservation of the dream in real time. As if to defend itself against the naive inattention to the practical difficulties, the novel endows Daniel with the awareness in the final moments by creating a will in which Daniel talks of the maggots in the mangoes that lay hidden in the apparently healthy looking Chevathar mangoes. Speaking ruefully, Daniel expresses in his will his regrets a little before his death:

> … . I regretted the things I hadn't done, I thought about quarrels that hadn't been resolved, I thought about matters left incomplete … . And you, my family, whether you like it or not, are one of my regrets. I've often wondered why I slaved for you all my life when I could have lavished more care and attention on myself … . Every family has within it its maggots—greedy, dishonest, ungrateful people, whose worst qualities are magnified when they are gathered together. So, at the end of my life, my picture of Doraipuram is bleak. Outside, to the world at large, we are an example of just how a family should be. Inside, the rot is beginning to spread. (349–50)

Kannan of the third generation strays from the ideal and even marries and lives outside the clan and home, thereby threatening, for a time, the continuation of the family line itself. It is interesting to note that Daniel who wanted to banish the caste factor from his ideal community, ends up opposing his son marrying outside the caste until the end. May be this is consistent with the terms of his dream of his family. For, the Anglo-Indian girl, Helen, whom his son marries does not quite fit in. The novel devotes enough space to show this by pointing to her incompatibility with the loving and admirable mother of her husband, Lily. There are two points to be noted in the incompatibility of the Anglo-Indian girl in the Andavar clan. First, it appears to affirm the clannishness and casteism of the Andavar patriarchs. Second, the incompatibility of Helen appears to rule out the inter-racial fusion as a compromise solution because it does not work, reminding us of Kipling's belief that 'East is East and West is West and never the twain shall meet.' The novel devotes a considerable space to showing British India. It could be argued that David Davidar in these sections of the novel proves Rushdie wrong in the view that 'nobody can teach you British India better than Rudyard Kipling' (1991: 75). Be this as it may, the novel's thrust on the whole appears to be towards a vision of family, home and community which incidentally might affirm casteism, but this appears to be a safe and guaranteed path to human happiness in Indian context. In the end, however, Kannan has to return to his family leaving behind his incompatible wife, although the return of the native changes nothing of the character of the dream that is at the centre of the novel. Daniel now is replaced by the son, Kannan, as the rallying point for the members of the clan, although in considerably reduced circumstances.

However, the idea of a family, home and community are not as simple as they appear to be. For instance, the contours of family in the Indian context are defined not merely by the parents and children but also by the relatives of the family within the caste. We are not talking of a joint family situation here; it is much larger than that so that it included someone like 'brother-in-law of the husband of a third cousin' (221) of Daniel. But all these innumerable members of the family are held together by the force of Daniel's wealth for a time. And

Daniel is successful in materializing his dream of the family with the power of his wealth. However, not unpredictably this dream of the family begins to erode when the binding force of the wealth begins to loosen and the vigour of the dreamer begins to wane. Eventually, as time passes and as new generations come in, the dream gradually whittles away to become a memory that could only be relived occasionally with such family reunion parties as the one we witness at the time of new year eve at the end of the novel. The dream becomes a memory with the third generation because it is merely inherited, not passionately conceived, much less pursued to make it come true. In other words, Daniel's dream is reduced in the third generation to the immediate family, and gone forever are the days when the fifty and odd rooms in the house were always filled with relatives known and unknown and the family kitchen used to feed nearly a hundred people a day. The dreamer is gone, and so the dream as well. But the novel celebrates this idea of the family without losing sight of the pitfalls in the way.

The House of Blue Mangoes brings to life the familiar Indian situations as lived in villages in all its colours and shades. The novel delights in dwelling on the Indianness of life lived here by pointing to the innumerable distinctive ways that characterize it. The folk ways, the rituals, the festivals, the village politics, the mean as well as the noble aspects, the casteism, the squalor, the ancient system of medicine practised, the structures of our beliefs, practices and superstitions, the self-rule in the form of panchayat, the beggars, and the countless other ways in which Indian life is defined is brought out in great detail. But the best part of Davidar's achievement in this novel is that he does not appear to have written this book for the West as many writers have been doing these days. He sets down the historical facts about English rule in India and their interaction with natives with great respect for accuracy even at the risk of being taken as the postcolonial backlash. Occasionally though, his enthusiasm to capture every nuance of our life gets the better of him so that he lapses from fictional narrative into a kind of essay mode explaining things Indian at great length. The elaborate description of the sedate, somnolent villages in Kilanad district, the story about the sage Agasthiar giving the Tamil country its language, grammar, myth, and legend, etc., going into the intricacies of Siddha system of medicine, narrating the story of *Hiranyakasyapa*, providing simultaneous English translation of a native ditty, etc. somehow have the effect of breaking the integrity of the fictive mode. But if we look at these as eager attempts to put across the lived experience to the non-natives, the novel makes for a lasting impact on the readers.

Works Cited

Davidar, David. *The House of Blue Mangoes.* New Delhi: Viking, 2002. Print. All references to the novel are to this edition and are indicated within parentheses in the text.

Rushdie, Salman. *Imaginary Homelands: Essays and Criticism 1981–1991.* London: Granta Books, 1991. Print.

25

A Critique of Fundamentalism in Githa Hariharan's *In Times of Siege*

ANURADHA ROY

The Indian English novel by women has come of age in the last two decades, not merely in terms of global acclaim represented by international awards but in many other, more significant, aspects. Whether it is in the courage to experiment with narrative techniques, or in the courage to deal with thorny issues of women's sexuality, one immediately notices an unmistakable widening of scope and a growing confidence in stepping out of familiar terrain. One of the most interesting aspects of this development is an increasing interest in negotiating the larger concerns of the nation. The concerns of many of these writers go beyond the woman's question in order to examine the issues of caste, class, gender, community, religion, globalization, development and the complex inter-action of these forces. Perhaps recent happenings in our country have made it impossible for any right-thinking individual to ignore the power-politics operating in most areas of our lives. Writers like Arundhati Roy and Githa Hariharan are actively involved in movements which endeavour to create a more humanitarian society by protesting against forms of injustice and oppression. In her essay, 'The Ladies have Feelings, so ...', Roy protests against the label 'writer-activist' (2001: 196) for, according to her, a writer has necessarily to be an activist in the present situation. She believes that we are at the point in our national history when it is imperative to have strong views and to take sides, however unsophisticated that might appear (197). A similar involvement in the public world is seen in Githa Hariharan. In an interview with Antonio Navarro-Tejero, she states, 'Activism has been a part of my life for a long time, most of my adult life in fact' (2004: 207). Starting with her involvement with women's rights during her college days, she later fought for a re-interpretation of the Hindu Minority and Guardianship Act 1956, and in recent years has been actively involved in advocating nuclear disarmament. The concerns of these writers are, expectedly, not limited to the traditional sexual politics of women's writing but take on a much wider range.

Among the concerns of the public world causing the greatest disquiet in the minds of writers and intellectuals of contemporary India, the most prominent is the growth of fundamentalism. It is a development which strikes at the very heart of the vision of an Independent, democratic and secular India which inspired the founding fathers of the nation, and creates an alternative definition of Indianness. In the last two decades, fundamentalism has created, directly and indirectly, some of the most disturbing incidents in our national history—Ayodhya, Babri Masjid, the Bombay riots, the Godhra incident and the ensuing communal violence in Gujarat and countless other smaller incidents testify to the power of the divisive forces. These incidents have sunk into the collective psyche of the people, just as the horrors of the Partition had left their mark on an earlier generation of Indians and Indian novelists. Many contemporary women writers in English, including Shashi Deshpande in *Small Remedies* (2000) and Manju Kapur in *A Married Woman* (2003) have responded in their own ways to these developments.

In Times of Siege marks an important development in Githa Hariharan's oeuvre. Her earlier novels—*The Thousand Faces of Night* (1992), *The Ghosts of Vasu Master* (1994) and *When Dreams Travel* (1999) concern themselves largely with the private world of individuals, particularly of women. With *In Times of Siege* (2003), the scope widens and makes a contemporary public issue the focal centre of the novel. Hariharan has unequivocally declared her concern at recent developments towards fundamentalism in the nation. In her interview with Antonio Navarro-Tejero, she states, 'The context of *In Times of Siege* is the contemporary India I live in. I feel proprietorial about it, and if I can see there is something wrong with it, I am going to shout as loud as I can .... My novel is set in India and I take on Hindu fundamentalism because as a writer engaged in Indian society, this is the prism through which I view the world' (2004: 204). Fundamentalism has become a raging concern with her, in its global manifestation but also particularly in the form it is taking in India. She comments:

> Prejudice against the 'other'-whether Muslim, Christian, women, Dalit or tribal—is congealing, and growing like a huge, festering garbage dump. The climate is ideal for one set of fundamentalist to feed off another. It's astonishing how similar the worldview of Hindu and Muslim fundamentalists is (and elsewhere in the view of Christian fundamentalists). All of them promote a regressive worldview that mistrusts heterogeneity; that wants to hold back the traditionally voiceless, the women, the marginal castes and classes, the 'foreigner', anyone with a different face or religion or ideology. (2004: 208)

Hariharan's concern is shared by many prominent intellectuals and analysts of the contemporary Indian scenario who regard this tendency as a betrayal of the ideals on which the Indian nation-state was founded. As Amartya Sen points out in 'The Indian Identity' that despite differences, the founding fathers of the nation were unanimous in their 'inclusionary reading of an Indian identity that tolerates, protects and, indeed, celebrates diversity within a pluralist India' (2005: 348).

The transformation of political concern into aesthetically satisfying fictional form has always posed a major challenge for writers. Hariharan chooses to express her concern over the disturbing growth of fundamentalism by focusing on one major aspect—the attempt to saffronize the past, to give it the particular form which suits the ideological agenda of Hindu fundamentalists. In the process, history becomes a site of contestation for cultural and religious supremacy. *In Times of Siege* presents the predicament of a professor of history who is victimized by a group calling themselves the Ithihas Suraksha Manch for a lesson he has written on the thirteenth century reformer-poet Basava. Commenting on the genesis of the novel, Hariharan writes: 'I felt a tremendous compulsion to write about what these sort of manches are doing. I wanted to write not just about a specific aspect of the fundamentalism—or conservatism—we are seeing around us, but the insidious ways in which minds are being shrunk. That is why I set the novel in a university' ('New Voices' 6). She refers to her shock when a volume on the freedom movement written by well-known and highly-respected historians Sumit Sarkar and K.M. Pannikar was withdrawn at the instigation of the 'self-appointed culture police' (6). Such irrational partisanship has led to distortions of our history—events, sites and personalities—as part of an attempt to reduce the complex heterogeneity of Indian culture to a singular identity based on religion. Amartya Sen's enlightening analysis of fundamentalism in the preface to *Identity and Violence: The Illusion of Destiny* (2006) is relevant in this context. Sen argues that fundamentalism stems from restricting oneself to 'a choiceless singularity of identity' in terms of religion or culture while ignoring the complex network of identities which actually constitute a human personality (2006: xvii). He calls such an attempt 'a miniaturization of human beings' (185) and warns that 'the artificial diminution of human beings into singular identities can have divisive effects, making the world potentially much more incendiary' (178). *In Times of Siege* is the author's sincere attempt to speak out against such endeavours through the situation in which an unassuming history professor inadvertently finds himself catapulted.

In the novel, Hariharan chooses to reflect the sanitization of the Hindu past through the attempt to impose a distorted image of an eminent historical personality like Basava. The poet-philosopher is regarded as the founder of the powerful Veerashaiva Movement in Karnataka. A.K. Ramanujan in his well-known translations of the vacanas of the Veerashaiva poets comments on the impact of Basava in his times:

> A new community with egalitarian ideas regarding caste, class and sex grew in Kalyana, challenging orthodoxy, rejecting social convention and religious ritual ... . Basavanna's achievement, in addition to the great vacanas he composed, was the establishment of a Virashaivism, with eight distinctive features, based on a rejection of inequality of every kind, of ritualism and taboo, and exalting work in the name of the Lord. (1973: 63–64)

In a lesson for his correspondence students, Professor Murthy had projected Basava on similar lines as a challenger of orthodoxy and inequality in society and religion. In an extended passage in the novel, Shiv Murthy muses on his perception of Basava drawn from a large collection of authentic sources (*In Times of Siege* 60–63). Rising to the prestigious position of treasurer of Kalyan, Basava was never meant to be a government official, for 'he needed to examine and think and criticize everything that was traditional, sanctioned, as much as he needed to breathe' (60). The community he formed was unorthodox in many ways—it disregarded all inequalities of caste, class and gender and believed that work was worship. The movement surged into 'a wave that threatened to swallow social conventions and religious ritual, staple diet of tradition' (61). Obviously, Basava found many enemies among those whose 'monopoly of god and power and the afterlife' (61) he challenged. There was a violent confrontation between the two groups with Basava failing in his attempts to moderate his followers; a disillusioned Basava died under mysterious circumstances. This account of Basava presented in an obscure history lesson throws Professor Shiv Murthy into the vortex of the storm which forms the core of the novel.

Githa Hariharan's decision to use a controversy about Basava to express her disquiet at recent attempts to toy with history is a master-stroke. It is a startling paradox that Basava, the rebel against orthodoxy and dogmatic thinking, is being defended in the narrative by the very kind of people he resisted. This paradox brilliantly exposes the determination of people with vested interests to distort history to suit their agenda. In her essay, 'New Voices, New Challenges: Concerns of the Contemporary Indian Writer', Hariharan comments, 'Icons are meant to remain on pedestals. Any history or literature that attempts to get a closer look at them in the context of their times, or to give their lives meaning for our times, is bound to get into trouble' (2004: 10). In the novel, Shiv Murthy's lesson raises the hackles of the self-appointed guardians of Hinduism, the Ithihas Suraksha Manch, because it suggests that Basava, who they would like to think of only as a mystical saint-poet, was a social revolutionary who challenged Brahmin orthodoxy and hegemony and, thus, presented a critique of orthodox Hinduism. Such an image clearly goes against the Manch's agenda of sanitizing the past; they would prefer Basava to be presented as one of the great stalwarts of the Hindu religion. To historians like Shiv Murthy, Basava was no obsolete historical personality but a vibrant figure whose great value lay in his passionate questioning of orthodoxy, a questioning which would make him relevant more than eight hundred years later. It is this questioning that the present-day defenders attempt to gloss over as part of their attempt to re-create a flawless Indian past and, perhaps, even more importantly, to suppress the possibility of such questioning in the present. As Shiv soon comes to realize, his lesson on Basava has become a pretext:

> Now the case—or the cause—has grown like a spider's web. Its sticky spittle has moved on to new threads. Now it's no longer caste and temple, or even contesting narratives of an enigmatic historical figure. Now the stage is littered with Muslim invaders, Christian missionaries, sons of the soil and foreigners. The stage has grown and grown till it is a battlefield big enough for the new patriots and their wild and warped nationalistic dreams. (94)

Beleaguered from many sides, from the Manch and their like-minded supporters among historians and the general public as well as from his own department authorities, Shiv often feels that he is in a similar position as Basava and wonders what the latter would have done in his place.

Shiv's predicament and the way he chooses to respond to it is of great significance, not only to the narrative but also to the greater concerns of the writer. Most right-thinking individuals today believe that the power to resist or to change does not lie only with the authorities or with state mechanisms but is vested with every citizen. If there is a message that the novel tries to convey, it is of the need to speak up, to resist such attempts by 'looters of the past' (40). A poster put up by Shiv's ward Meena quoting a German pastor who was a victim of the concentration camps, urging loudly ' Speak Up! Before It's Too late' (27) is a rather simplistic device to make the message clear. At a deeper level, the words of Shiv Murthy's late father, a freedom fighter who had failed to come to terms with the disillusioning reality of independence, 'Do you think that an ordinary man cannot be a hero?' (64) resonate meaningfully through the narrative as the protagonist desperately attempts to deal with the sudden crisis in his life. The demands of the Manch that Professor Murthy should immediately tender an apology and the offensive lesson should be recalled is followed by extensive press coverage. There are anonymous letters accusing Shiv of 'disrespect for our glorious temples and their priests' (78) and even suggesting that he should go to Pakistan where he would get the attention he was craving for. The media coverage continues to grow, with both detractors and defenders jumping into the fray with equal vehemence; while the Manch and its supporters give a call to 'revive Hindu courage' (90), academics protest against what they describe as 'blatant intellectual censorship' (93). There are interviews and panel discussions on television and protest marches organized by his ward Meera and her enthusiastic young activist friends who are united in their hatred of 'fundoos', as they irreverently call the fundamentalists. The public attention rises to a crescendo, creating a mass hysteria:

> Fan mail. Hate mail. Quotable and unquotable quotes. Questions, interviews, sweat and powder and flashbulbs ... Vested interests. Hinduisation of the past ... . Conspiracy theories. Rightist conspiracies, leftist conspiracies. Foreign-handed conspiracies ... . Ministers, lefties, righties, bandwagonwallahs, touts, students, student leaders, spokesmen, spokeswomen. Rent-a-quote swamis (and their estranged cousins rent-a-quote imams). Historians, journalists-turned politicians, engineers turned linguists, computer experts turned archaeologists. (133–34)

And through it all, dazed at this sudden crisis in his peaceful academic life, communing with the spirit of Basava and of his dead father, stands Professor Shiv Murthy, tempted at times to give up the battle and yet realizing that this is his personal tryst with destiny. As the narrative draws to a conclusion, Shiv goes for a long walk before going in for a final departmental meeting on the issue; nothing is stated clearly but one senses that Shiv will refuse to surrender to the call for his resignation. Shiv Murthy is no heroic figure; with 'a gently swelling herbivorous paunch' and his daily bout of uncertainty about whether he should belt his trousers above or below the bulge (64), he is almost Prufrockian. But in the terms set up by the author, he represents the moral courage of the common man with his 'raggedy bit of heroism' (194)—the courage to speak up in times of siege when the free-thinking individual is beleaguered from all sides.

In Times of Siege is obviously a novel written with a purpose and with an unequivocal message. The age-old debate whether the polemical intention of a literary work is detrimental to its literary quality comes into question. It is true that the transformation of political concern into an aesthetically satisfying form is not always successful in the novel and that the seamless integration of fact and fiction is at times missing. As in other recent novels by Indian women writers in English which attempt fictional negotiations of contemporary situations—Meena Alexander's *Nampally Road* (1991), Manju Kapur's *A Married Woman* (2002), Kiran Desai's *The Inheritance of Loss* (2006) and Githa Hariharan's next novel *Fugitive Histories* (2009) among others—fiction at times remains too close to fact without being processed fully through the imagination. There are extended passages where the writer seems to have taken over from the narrator, determined to drive the message home. This can be considered as the major drawback of this otherwise accomplished novel. However, there are many appreciable features. The brilliance of the concept of using the medieval saint Basava to illustrate the narrow-mindedness of contemporary fundamentalists needs to be acknowledged. The character of Shiv is an authentic depiction of an ordinary man suddenly thrown into the vortex of a controversy—confused, sometimes tempted to run away from the situation and yet quietly courageous. Moreover, the sincerity of the message, the writer's conviction that in these times of siege, it is imperative that all right-thinking citizens make their voices heard, is itself a source of strength. The writer is writing about deeply disturbing developments that she and her fellow-countrymen are living through and perhaps this explains the near-desperation of her determination to be heard. Novels such as *In Times of Siege* are significant indications that contemporary Indian English women novelists are showing an increasing interest in treading new terrain, extending beyond aspects of gender to negotiate with larger elements of discord in the nation state.

In a review of the novel, Martina Ghosh-Schellhorn calls the novel 'an ivory tower rarefaction' of the burning issue of fundamentalism. But a complex issue such as fundamentalism does require to be examined in its various manifestations, its tentacles shown to be reaching out in many directions. The sense of urgency conveyed in *In Times of Siege* takes on even greater significance in the context of recent attempts at cultural policing by those who consider themselves guardians of the true Hindu culture. This includes the recent decision by Bombay University to ban the study of Rohinton Mistry's novel *Such a Long Journey*. Such disturbing incidents make us appreciate the relevance of Githa Hariharan's concern regarding attempts to stifle the quality of debate essential for any healthy academic and artistic environment. In his essay, 'The Indian Identity', Amartya Sen argues that India has had a long tradition of critical reasoning and public deliberation in all areas of thought. He warns, 'It is necessary to avoid being imprisoned to formulaic interpretations that are constantly, but often uncritically, repeated in intellectual as well as political discussions on historical traditions—and in so far as traditions are important, these mischaracterizations tend to have a seriously distorting effect on the analysis of contemporary India as well as of its complex history' (2005: 31). It is one such dangerous attempt at 'mischaracterization' that the narrative attempts to deal with. *In Times of Siege* is a timely commentary on a society in which even the world of academics is under siege by forces which attempt to curb intellectual autonomy.

Works Cited

Ghosh-Schellhorn, Martina. 'Fundoos with Zero Tolerance.' Review of *In Times of Siege* by Githa Hariharan. *Biblio: A Review of Books* 8.3 (March–April 2003), 31. Print.

Hariharan, Githa. *In Times of Siege*. New Delhi: Penguin, 2003. Print.

——. 'New Voices, New Challenges: Concerns of the Contemporary Indian Writer.' *Littcrit* 30.1 (2004), 5–12. Print.

Navarro-Tejero, Antonio. 'On Fundamentalism and Nationality: An Interview with Githa Hariharan.' *South Asian Review* 25.2 (2004), 200–21. Print.

Ramanujan, A.K. *Speaking of Shiva*. New Delhi: Penguin, 1973. Print.

Roy, Arundhati. 'The Ladies have Feelings, so ... .' *The Algebra of Infinite Justice*. New Delhi: Penguin, 2001. Print.

Sen, Amartya. 'The Indian Identity.' *The Argumentative Indian: Writings on Indian Culture, History and Identity*. London: Penguin, 2005. Print.

——. *Identity and Violence: The Illusion of Destiny*. London: Allen Lane, 2006. Print.

26

Imaging Naxalism and Familial Implication in Jhumpa Lahiri's *The Lowland*

N. ANIL KRISHNA

A number of revolutions have swept the Indian society with common man in the vanguard sacrificing his own life for shaping the nation's destiny. *'Vasudhaika Kutumbam'*—considering the whole world as a single family—is what an Indian desires to attain. Standing on the native soil, fighting all battles to establish an egalitarian society sans luxurious offshore temptations is the essence of 'Indianness.' Udayan Mitra, the protagonist in Jhumpa Lahiri's *The Lowland* has the volcanic zeal to chastise the social ills and takes part in the Naxalite movement.

Jhumpa Lahiri, a recipient of the Pulitzer Prize for Fiction and the author of 'Interpreter of Maladies,' 'The Namesake,' 'Unaccustomed Earth,' has set her novel *The Lowland* (2013) against the backdrop of Naxalite movement. The novel delineates a story 'steeped in history that seamlessly spans generations and geographies' (blurb of the novel). The Naxalite movement of 1960s is a reckoning moment in history and the novelist re-presents its impact on the greater society. Jhumpa Lahiri recounts the incidents at Naxalbari, a village in the Darjeeling District of West Bengal where the seeds were sown for the movement:

> For generations they'd (tribal peasants) lived under a feudal system that hadn't substantially changed. They were manipulated by wealthy landowners. They were pushed off fields they'd cultivated, denied revenue from crops they'd grown. They were preyed upon by moneylenders. Deprived of subsistence wages, some died from lack of food .... When a sharecropper in Naxalbari tried to plough land from which he'd been illegally evicted, his landlord sent thugs to beat him. They took away his plough and bullock. The police had refused to intervene. After this, groups of sharecroppers began retaliating. They started burning deeds and records that cheated them. Forcibly occupying

> land. Armed with primitive weapons, carrying red flags, shouting Long Live Mao Tse-tung. (2013: 20)

A lengthy exposition explaining the emergence of Naxalism is provided by the novelist running into the first quarter of *The Lowland.* All prominent personalities connected with the movement—Charu Majumdar, Kanu Sanyal—and the radical movements of Vietnam and Cuba have been referred to creating a gripping realistic setting. In an interview, Jhumpa Lahiri says:

> The novel was inspired by an execution that took place in Calcutta in the early 1970s, in the neighborhood where my father was raised. Some students who lived in that neighborhood were involved in the Naxalite movement—a failed attempt at Maoist revolution in India, which brought about a period of violent turmoil for the city. One evening during the repression of this movement two brothers were shot dead by the police in front of their parents and some other family members. It was a fairly common occurrence in Calcutta at the time. (Kalotav 2014)

The cataclysmic impact of the revolutions—agrarian, industrial, political and social—has taken its toll affecting the fortunes of the common people and youth in particular. Right from the Russian Revolution of 1917 to the Telangana Movement, the lower class and emotional strata of the society reacted sharply and spontaneously identifying with the ensuing events. Maxim Gorky's *Mother,* published in 1906, reflects the fight of the proletariat against the Czar rule and in this struggle the mother and the son participate with zeal unmindful of the challenges. Gorky re-presents history from the view point of the proletariat. Howard Fast's novel *Spartacus* published in 1951 is another offshoot of this genre, re-interpreting history from the contemporary perspective. Spartacus (109–71 BC) was a slave leader against Roman Republic who stands as an eternal symbol of how man fights against political systems that oppress human values. Howard Fast deviates from and extends known historical facts, thus, generating interest in the reader. In the recent Indian English novels, fictional stories have been weaved against the backdrop of historical dynamics. Meena Alexander's *Nampally Road* (1991), Kiran Nagarkar's *Cuckold* (1997) and *Ravan and Eddie* (1994), Boman Desai's *The Memory of Elephants,* (2000), Ranga Rao's *Fowl Filtcher* (1987), Rohinton Mistry's *Fine Balance* (1995), are some of the post-1990 additions to this very popular genre. Men of Letters are quick to re-present history interspersing with the fictional events, thus imparting credibility.

The setting of *The Lowland* is portrayed in an evocative style since Jhumpa Lahiri was born of Bengali parents and grew up in Rhode Island, USA. The scene of action in *The Lowland* oscillates between Bengal and Rhode Island coinciding with and reflecting Lahiri's elemental blood-bond. Amy Tan aptly remarks that 'Jhumpa Lahiri is a dazzling storyteller with a distinctive voice, an eye for nuance, an ear for irony' (the blurb of *The Interpreter of Maladies*). *The Lowland* was nominated for the National Book Award and shortlisted for one of Britain's top literary honours, the Man Booker Prize 2013. In her *New York Times Review,* Michiko Kakutani praises Lahiri's 'ability to conjure the daily texture of people's lives, her understanding of how their personal and cultural expectations have shaped their choices, her talent for mapping moods and inchoate emotions with pointillist precision' (2013).

The Lowland is a saga of Udayan's family vis-à-vis left-wing peasants' uprising in 1967. Subhash is the older brother of Udayan. Udayan's family lived in Tollygunge in Calcutta. Udayan was influenced by the lectures of Kanu Sanyal and Charu Majumdar. However, his father tries to wean him away from the Communistic ideology. When Udayan started bringing Chinese Communist magazines home, his father argues with the son and the dialogue between them, mentioned under, betrays their divergent outlook.

> This rhetoric is nothing new .... Our generation read Marx, too. Your generation didn't solve anything, Udayan said.
>
> We built a nation. We're independent. The country is ours. It's not enough. Where did it get us? Who has it helped? These things take time. (37)

Udayan's father dismissed Naxalbari Movement. He said young people were getting excited over nothing.

> ... No, Baba. The United Front thinks it's won, but it's failed. Look at what's happening. What is happening? People are reacting. Naxalbari is an inspiration. It's an impetus for change. (23)

Udayan evinced profound faith in Maoism and was optimistic that as Mao changed China, the same would happen in India. Under his mattress Udayan stored some pamphlets written by Charu Majumdar. Most of them were written when Charu Majumdar was in prison. These essays were brief and bombastic and Majumdar said that India had turned into a nation of beggars and foreigners. He said that the 'reactionary government of India has adopted the tactics of killing the masses; they are killing them through starvation, with bullets' (24).

Jhumpa Lahiri purposefully christens the protagonist as Udayan. Udayan in Sanskrit means eternal sun rise. In *The Lowland,* Udayan is always on the move in search of ways and means to liberate masses from 'all kinds of exploitation of man by man.' He joins hands with the people who intend to 'make a new sun and a new moon shine in the sky of our great motherland' (33). When both Udayan and Subhash successfully completed their High School Education, their father asked them what gift they expect from him. Subhash suggested a marble chess and Udayan wanted a shortwave radio. Udayan wanted more news of the world than what is printed in the daily Bengali paper. Unlike Udayan, Subhash longs for Higher Education and goes to a University in Rhode Island to study Marine Chemistry. Meanwhile, Udayan falls in love with Gauri and involves her in the revolutionary activities:

> They sat along the portico, draped with banners the Students' Union put up. When speeches were delivered on the quadrangle, about the continuing rise in food prices, about the growing population, about the shortage of jobs, they listened to them together. When marches sprouted along College Street, he brought her along. He started giving her things to read. From the bookstalls he bought her Marx's Manifesto and Rousseau's Confessions, Felix Greene's book

on Vietnam .... He mentioned certain friends who had already left Calcutta, to live among the peasants. (59)

Udayan told Gauri that:

> He wanted to see more of India, the way Che had travelled through South America. He wanted to understand the circumstances of its people. He wanted to see China one day. (59)

But that was not to be. Udayan married Gauri and later he was exterminated by the Police for his active participation in the Naxalite movement. Udayan was arrested and taken outside the city:

> Now he stood at the edge of a lowland, in the enclave where he'd lived all his life .... They asked him nothing. They untied his hands, then pointed indicating that he was to walk in a certain direction now, again with his hands raised over his head. Slowly, he heard them say. Make sure to pause after every step. He did as he was told. Step by step he walked away from them. Go back to your family, they said. But he knows that they were only waiting for him to fall into the ideal range. One step, then another. He'd known from the beginning the risk of what he was doing. But only the policeman's blood had prepared him. That blood had not belonged only to the police officer, it had become a part of Udayan also. So that he'd felt his own life begin to ebb, irrevocably, as the policeman lay dying in the alley. Since then he'd waited for his own blood to spill. For a fraction of a second he heard the explosion tearing through his lungs. A sound like gushing water or a torrent of wind. A sound that belonged to the fixed forces of the world, that then took him out of the world. The silence was pure now. (339)

That was the time when Subhash began his third autumn in Rhode Island. He gets the telegram and the message consisted of two sentences:

> Udayan killed. Come back if you can. (83)

Subhash returns to Tollygunge. His parents were disoriented and Gauri was pregnant. After lunch he went out to notice a 'small marker that had not been there before.' He walks towards it. The author writes:

> On it was Udayan's name. Beneath that, the years of his birth and death: 1945–1971. It was a memorial tablet, erected for political martyrs. Here where the water came and went, where it collected and vanished, was where his brother's party comrades had chosen to put it. (93)

Subhash tries to interact with his parents and Gauri. They avoid looking Subhash in the eye. He expects that his parents would ask him to remain in Calcutta, to abandon his life in Rhode Island. But they did not say so. He gives Gauri the book 'One-Dimensional Man' written by Herbert Marcuse which he brought from abroad at the behest of Udayan. Subhash makes all out efforts to heal their wounds and decides to marry Gauri, well prepared to take the responsibility of Udayan's child. He takes Gauri to Rhode Island. Gauri gives birth to a girl child and she was named Bela. He takes care of Bela as a loving father. Gauri pursues her studies and starts teaching philosophy in a college at Southern California. When Bela was 12, he takes her to Calcutta to meet his parents. The years passed. Bela grows up, becoming an environmentalist. As she settles in life, Subhash reveals to Bela that his brother was her real father. Bela gets perplexed and finds fault with her mother for deserting the place where her father died. Subhash too suffers from the loveless marriage and the guilt for pretending to be Bela's father.

Jhumpa Lahiri has complete understanding of people's revolutions and their repercussions. Hundreds of people laid down their lives in pursuit of realizing their dreams of freedom, equality and liberty. There is a spurt of such movements in India. Naxalbari movement is one such revolutionary movement that interspersed with the contemporary Indian history. Obviously, Jhumpa Lahiri's sympathies are with the underprivileged sections waging war against the feudal establishment. She blends fact and fiction brilliantly and *The Lowland* echoes her firm conviction that the fate of an individual is regrettably sealed by the regimented society. Sadly, history repeats.

Works Cited

Kakutani, Michiko. 'A Brother, Long Gone, is Painfully Present.' *New York Times* (19 September 2013). <www.nytimes.com/2013/09/2/ books.> Web.

Kalotav, Daphne. 'Jhumpa Lahiri Revisits Boston University.' 2014. <www.bu.edu/today/2014> Web.

Lahiri, Jhumpa. *Interpreter of Maladies.* India: Harper & Collins Publishers, 2010. Print.

——. *The Lowland.* India: Random House, 2013. Print.

Author Index

Subject Index